Outsourcing Student Success

Outsourcing Student Success:

The History of Institutional Research and the Future of Higher Education

Joseph H. Wycoff

Historia | Research Press

Published by Historia | Research Press
Chicago, IL
Copyright © 2017 Joseph H. Wycoff

Cover image courtesy of Library of Congress Prints and Photographs Division
Washington, D.C. Reproduction number: HAER MASS,9-WALTH,4--31.

ISBN: 0-9996788-1-7
ISBN-13: 978-0-9996788-1-7

For Nell

CONTENTS

List of Figures iii

Prologue: The Cross-Cutting Issues of the Day 1

1 The Scientific Community That Enables Scientific Progress 15

2 A Fact-Finding Agency Directly Responsible to the President 28

3 Essential for Efficient and Economical Educational Procedures 45

4 A Comprehensive and Unified Approach 61

5 The Center of Confluence for Many Social Forces 77

6 Production of Knowledge without Pervasive and Lasting Significance 97

7 In a Pre-Paradigm Stage in Perpetuity 116

8 Great Variance in Assignments and Responsibilities 136

9 ~~A New~~ An Old Vision for Institutional Research 153

Epilogue: From Institutional Research to Data Science 172

Notes 187

Acknowledgments 203

Selected Bibliography 205

Index 217

LIST OF FIGURES

Figure 1 | Portfolios of Institutional Research in Publications from 1938, 1954, and 1962... 40

Figure 2 | Progression of Institutional Research along the Spectrum of Scientific Research Questions.. 42

Figure 3 | Modalities of Institutional Research under Volkswein's Golden Triangle and the Types of Scientific Research Questions.............................. 91

PROLOGUE | THE CROSS-CUTTING ISSUES OF THE DAY

Of Advocates and Entrepreneurs

Michael B. Horn, "a top proponent of higher-ed disruption," stepped down from his position as director at the nonprofit, nonpartisan Clayten Christensen Institute, *The Chronicle of Higher Education* reported in October 2015. In a blog post announcing his decision, Horn indicated his intention to "work on the ground with the entrepreneurs shaping the future of education." Planning "to put his theories into action," *The Chronicle* named one such entrepreneur, Entangled Solutions, a self-described "innovation agency for Higher Education." According to *The Chronicle*, Horn already served on the board of another company offering learning relationship management solutions, described in its literature as an "integrated holistic student success solution."[1]

Horn's decision to enter the private sector reflects a growing trend among public advocates and vendors of education technology to offer entrepreneurial solutions for student success in higher education. While there has never been a shortage of education consultants and technology vendors to higher education during the past fifty years, the new emphasis on student success entails two decidedly different components: outsourcing and data science.

At one end of the spectrum, established education technology vendors seek to leverage their positions in the student information systems and learning management systems markets. For example, Ellucian, the market leader of student information systems under the Banner and Colleague brands, has a section of its website devoted to "Student Success" and the software that "helps keep students on track and supports student success." Likewise Blackboard features its "student success model" as a "cost effective, scalable solution that helps improve student outcomes."[2] For existing vendors of enterprise resource planning or learning management systems, the data science of student success appears to be a natural evolution for their technology.

More notably, at the other end of the funding spectrum, the advent of this new education technology market for the data science of student success has attracted the interests of venture capitalists. In late September 2015, Civitas Learning announced an investment of up to $60 million by Warburg Pincus for its business model. The announcement credited Civitas Learning as having "pioneered the use of data science and design thinking to support higher education institutions as they improve learning and increase degree completion." The article attributed the recent round of investment funds to the growing demand by institutions of higher education. At the time, Civitas Learning promoted its solutions as the "the student success platform for higher education" at the intersection of human commitment and data science. With a clientele of more than 285 institutions and 6.5 million students before the new round of funding, the company then boasted that its "student success science" delivers scalable analytics to transform "static and stale data" into real-time, actionable insights for decision-making. Venture capital funding would enable Civitas Learning to plan for "strategic acquisitions" and expand globally.[3]

In the middle of the spectrum of investments in college student success, IBM entered the new market for student success and data science solutions to advance its business model for the Watson Group. In January 2014, IBM announced its $100 million fund for "venture investments to support an ecosystem of entrepreneurs developing" applications for its newly formed IBM Watson Group, a suite of software and services featuring "cloud-delivered cognitive innovations." In one of the first ventures into higher education, Deakin University in Australia announced in October 2014 its partnership with IBM to become the "first university to implement the Watson Engagement Adviser." Initially, the Watson advisor planned to counsel new students by answering questions on "a range of topics" including admissions, financial assistance, course enrollments, job placement, skills assessment, and academic help. In November 2016, the IBM Watson Group expanded its partnerships to include established vendors in the higher education market to "help students succeed in and outside the classroom."[4]

Lastly, established vendors to higher education have sought to offer student success analytics solutions through acquisition. In January 2016, Hobsons announced the acquisition of the Predictive Analytics Reporting (PAR) Framework, Inc. Hobsons added PAR Framework shortly after acquiring another system capable of collecting, storing, and leveraging student record level data, Starfish Retention Solutions, "a student success and advising platform serving hundreds of colleges and universities." Prior to the acquisition, PAR Framework had been a nonprofit organization that, planning for college access in conjunction with the anticipated enrollment surge originating with the youth generation—later known as the baby boomers. State system heads relied on statewide institutional research studies to measure higher education capacity and productivity in order to envision their policies and campus plans—such as Clark Kerr, who led the adoption of the California Master Plan in 1960. If the offices have now fallen into disrepute among college executives, the era of management fads may also be nearing an end.

For most colleges and universities, however, institutional research offices originated in an accountability movement from outside higher education that encroached on the academic freedom and autonomy of the institution. Rourke and Brooks, representing two such institutions, portrayed institutional research as a peril to academic freedom and institutional autonomy, recommending that institutional research become subject to "an academic orientation…bolstering the point of view of the faculty." Surprisingly, many administrators—including skeptical academics who performed institutional research at their own universities—adopted the recommendation of Rourke and Brooks. To thwart the threat of accountability to external agencies and state directives, the skeptics claimed that each institution manifested particular conditions stemming from their unique missions that made moot any comparisons or the generalized study of higher education administration by institutional research.[11]

In particular, two scholars who worked together at Michigan State University in the 1960s, Paul L. Dressel and Joe L. Saupe, defined the practice of institutional research for higher education scholars and the Association for Institutional Research (AIR) in its early years. Dressel, who edited the first "handbook" of institutional research in 1971, drew sharp distinctions between institutional research and higher education scholarship. Institutional research offices may "probe deeply into the workings" of a single institution, but institutional research could not contribute to academic scholarship for application outside of the specific institution or system of institutions that housed the particular office.[12]

Saupe, the fourth president of the AIR, cowrote with James Montgomery, the second president of the association, a paper in which they further diminished the usefulness of studies conducted by institutional researchers. Endorsed by the Association for Institutional Research in 1970, the two former presidents of the association claimed that the field was "specific and applied" research directed by the needs of each local institution and therefore "institutional research should not be expected to produce knowledge of pervasive and lasting significance."[13] Though representing a membership primarily employed in the institutional research offices of higher education, the official position of the AIR advocated Saupe's concepts on the "nature and role" of institutional research as a function, rather than a discipline or profession, for most of its existence.

Complementing Dressel and Saupe's line of thought, scholars in the field of higher education came to recognize institutional research as a competitor in the production of knowledge about higher education and higher education administration. Early opponents to robust and centralized administrative studies conducted by executive leadership sought to differentiate faculty scholarship from institutional research. In a short time, a consensus paradigm for institutional research took shape in higher education programs and the official publications of the Association for Institutional Research. These scholars advocated that institutional research be regarded as 1) an administrative function, 2) divorced from scholarship on higher education, 3) circumscribed to each particular institution, and 4) most effective when decentralized in an "elaborate profusion" of local units and decision makers. As a consequence, most institutional research professionals subsequently organized their offices to service requests for data by the local officers of their institutions, with no substantive regard for the general accumulation of knowledge about the allocation of institutional resources or effective interventions for student success.

Twenty years later, the flagship journal of the Association for Institutional Research, *Research in Higher Education* (RIHE), published an article summarizing the nature and status of institutional research as constituted in this manner. Noting first that "institutional research is more an art than a science," the article describes a field "in a pre-paradigm stage; no body of scientific theory controls the kinds of questions that can be asked or the kinds of answers sought." The "politics of higher education" directed the research activities and arrested the development of "a cohesive body of knowledge" for institutional planning and effectiveness. Institutional research offices depended "on the perceptions of those within a particular institutional context," hindering the possibility "for a discipline to emerge." In effect, institutional researchers lacked professional autonomy within their institutions. "[O]thers set the agenda for institutional research," the article concluded and advised institutional researchers to resign themselves to the status quo: "There is little incentive for this to change."[14]

The 2014 NASH survey affirmed the prevalence of institutional research offices organized as recommended forty years earlier by Rourke, Brooks, Dressel, Saupe, and the leadership of the Association for Institutional Research. In most respects, the conclusions of the NASH report merely reiterate the conditions of the profession as described decades earlier and demonstrate that little has changed for institutional research professionals since the founding of their association. Unsurprisingly, the American Council on Education (ACE), representing the nation's college presidents, echoed NASH when it further endorsed the need for external vendors and venture capital to provide student success solutions in higher education. In a quick-hit paper on predictive analytics around the same time, ACE observed, "[T]here is a strong sense among pioneers in this space—and on the part of some prominent funders—that pushing into this new territory will pay significant dividends in improved student success."[15]

Remarkably, then, in the past three years, the two associations representing the nation's public system heads and its college presidents became proponents for outsourcing student success solutions as the optimal path for colleges and universities to meet the demands of the future.

Becoming an Institutional Researcher

One is not trained to be an institutional researcher, but rather becomes an institutional researcher. As a section labeled, "Becoming an Institutional Researcher," on the Wikipedia page for Institutional Research suggests at the time of writing, "[t]here is no single academic degree that qualifies one to be an institutional researcher."[16] Like many in institutional research, I came to the profession by an indirect route and from an unrelated academic discipline. My entire academic education is in the discipline of history, initially using quantitative methods to study family labor force participation and economic strategies in the United States utilizing public-use data samples for cost of living studies and census records from the twentieth century.[17]

During an interruption in my graduate education, I worked for approximately six years with market research vendors serving Fortune 500 corporations in the information technology sector in the dot com era during the latter half of the 1990s. At the tail end of the dotcom boom, I joined Educational Outreach at the University of Washington in Seattle, where I had the good fortune to work for two years with an accomplished historian who became a university administrator with a deserved reputation as "a rock star" in the field of educational outreach, as one of his colleagues described him to me. He is widely regarded as an innovator and educational entrepreneur in online learning, self-sustaining degree programs at a public university, and the establishment of community partnerships to extend access to education to underserved students, among many other accomplishments.[18]

I returned to academia for several years to complete a PhD, while transitioning my field interests to the cultural and social history of business associations, institutions, and their leadership in US history. During this period, fortunately as it turned out, I maintained a connection with

7

institutional research by contracting with my former employer at the University of Washington, the local chapter of the American Association of University Professors (AAUP), and other vendors serving academic institutions and policy interests. When I completed my graduate studies in 2008–09, the recession and other circumstances in the job market for US historians resulted in my return to the profession of institutional research. Subsequently, I worked as an institutional research, planning, and effectiveness officer for a community college in Illinois and for a private, nonprofit Catholic institution in New York. From nearly twenty years of research and connections, I have had the opportunity to study the operations and advance the strategic plans of a flagship state university, suburban community college, and regional tuition-dependent private college.

Initially, I was drawn to the field of history because of its apparent complexity. Many may know history as the rote memorization of dates, names, and other trivia. The best academic historians, however, master the theoretical foundations of their own field, their historiography, as well as the theoretical foundations for closely related fields such as linguistics (ancient historians), anthropology (cultural historians), economics (business and labor historians), gender studies (historians of gender and sex), psychology (historical biography), and philosophy (historians of ideas). The study of history is an interdisciplinary branch of knowledge that brings the historian into exchanges and debates with the practitioners of other fields, particularly those who neglect the potential and actualities of change over time.

Not to be confused with institutional reporting to external agencies, institutional research can be as deeply complex and rich as the discipline of history. An adept institutional researcher has use for an academic understanding of institutional theory and organizational change, whether from traditional historical institutionalism, microeconomic theories of the firm, the new institutionalism of sociology, or at the very least the trajectory of organizational efficiency from Taylorism to Six Sigma training. An education, nonetheless, remains the output of colleges and universities, so a well-rounded institutional researcher will also grasp the literature and utilize the findings from national demographics, education science, and developmental psychology on academic preparedness, student learning, freshman resilience, educational ecological systems, and social attitudes about college life. In order to apply the study of institutions and research on learning outcomes locally, an accomplished institutional researcher must then design valid research and perform appropriate statistical analyses to understand how best to improve student success at his or her own institution.

With these theoretical and scientific methodologies, institutional research has the tools to systematically investigate and understand the diverse operations of a higher education institution. In scope, an effective institutional researcher is able to delve into the specialized areas of admissions, student retention, graduate placement, and even alumni giving, among other common areas of institutional operations. In this respect, institutional research is—or could have been—as organically interdisciplinary as history, with the ability to cross over to the operations of the many facets and strategic initiatives of an institution of higher education. Those in the profession often express expectations or hope for greater integration in the strategic and analytical focus of the college.[19] Too often, though, in my experience and from my knowledge of colleagues' presentations at the annual conferences of our profession, the integration of institutional research offices and continuous improvement efforts does not reach such synergy.

How is it, one then may ask, that the work of institutional research offices has not had a greater influence on the performance of US higher education institutions, in such areas as student retention, in the past fifty years?

In a 2014 book on leadership and management in institutional research, published by the Association for Institutional Research, William E. Knight begins his preface by stating his concern "about the unfulfilled potential" of the field of institutional research, noting that "[n]umerous studies have indicated that information is not being used as effectively as it could be by campus leaders."[20] I share the concern advanced by Knight and many others in the institutional effectiveness and research profession that the potentials for these mission-critical offices are too often unrealized in higher education institutions.

Moreover, I have concluded that the all-too-frequent lack of success with strategic planning for organizational efficiency and with continuous improvement initiatives for student outcomes in higher education directly stems from the unfulfilled promise of these offices, or rather the "elaborate profusion" of institutional research functions. In effect, the recent survey by the National Association of System Heads (NASH) serves to illuminate how institutional research squanders the wealth of institutions—both in terms of finances and knowledge. The surprising fact is that forty years passed before chief executives of higher education sponsored an independent investigation into the soundness of scholarship on institutional research and higher education disseminated by peer-reviewed publications and the official position papers of the Association for Institutional Research.

Data Science for Student Success: Fad or Future of Higher Education

The movement to outsource college student success solutions to disruptive innovators in the private sector marks a new era in modern management techniques in American higher education. Nearly every week, higher education news or education technology news features the power of predictive or prescriptive analytics for improvement in student success at higher education institutions. The vended technology and solutions rely on the basic tenets of social science methods applied to student characteristics derived from application forms, enrollment transcripts, sign-in logs, and other unwieldy records routinely collected by higher education institutions. As commonly cited in the marketing literature of the vendors, the key value-added service of data science vendors is the ability to harness "Big Data" from multiple information systems and transform raw information into pearls of wisdom from predictive analytics for data-driven decision-making on student success.

Although the following is not directly a work on data science or its application to student success, the recent advocacy for data science parallels the advocacy for institutional research at its origin in the mid-twentieth century. As the history of institutional research attests, the vendors of data science and educational technologies for student success must work against the label of being or becoming the latest "management fad in higher education." Robert Birnbaum's phrase intends to criticize the ever-changing management paradigms misapplied from the business world. All prior management innovations end as fads precisely because what originates as the promise of managerial innovation and improvement ends in discouragement over irrational exuberance and ambiguous results.

To avoid this fate, data scientists and college executives in higher education will be well served by this history of the institutional research profession, an antecedent of data science in many respects. The American Council on Education recently observed that "higher education is at a transition point, pivoting from harvesting data to learning how to use it strategically" to improve outcomes for students.[21] The assertion reveals a certain naïveté and ignorance regarding the origins and mission of institutional research offices to support strategic decision-making at colleges and universities in the United States. Clearly, both those inside and outside of higher education circles know little about the profession, yet the rise and decline of institutional research over the past one hundred years exemplify with singular conspicuousness the reasons for the ongoing crisis in American higher education policy and administration. In short, the institutional research profession offers an important cautionary tale for those who now vie to be the champions of student success analytics at colleges and universities.

Institutional research predates data science by sixty years as a professional field heralded for its potential to strategically use data to modernize and improve higher education. But while many higher education professionals understand the limitations of institutional research today, very few know extensively the history of the profession and its troubled relationship with efforts to reform higher education administration. No independent and comprehensive history of the field of institutional research exists. The Association for Institutional Research has sponsored a few noncritical publications that summarize the history of the field with a favorable light on its organization.[22] Scholars of higher education mostly ignore the specific administrative professionals and focus on defining the role as a staff function with responsibilities distributed among faculty and staff.

The narrative divides into two halves for the rise and decline of a profession that resulted in the recent momentum to outsource student success solutions to data science vendors. Through the prism of the institutional research profession, data scientists and higher education executives who seek to serve and improve higher education will gain a better grasp of the entrenched culture of non-accountability that exists on American college campuses. Data science for student success, which institutional research originally included in its spectra of subject areas and analytical techniques for the study of higher education, will certainly encounter similar forms of resistance on American college campuses.

The first half presents the social scientific origins of institution research in the mid-twentieth century and explores how institutional research has a similar structure and meets the same criteria as other disciplines that qualify as social sciences. In 2002, the National Research Council (NRC) released a report that offers a framework through which to evaluate and trace the historical development of institutional research as a social science. Through this NRC framework, the historical progression of institutional research from the confinements of self-study to the open-endedness of social science may be discerned through four stages.[23]

First, the research programs at bureaus of institutional research recorded and published by two Midwest universities pioneered the field. These two bureaus became examples to other offices and, collectively, offices of institutional research set the boundaries and defined the major areas of study. By the late 1950s, institutional researchers—like data scientists today—had used predictive models for student success and applied experimental principles to the study of learning outcomes among students.

Second, the Truman Commission spurred the coordination of higher education through state boards and studies. With the example of California ending with the 1960 Master Plan for Higher Education, institutional research extended its scope of study to define standardizable external characteristics for colleges and universities that permitted generalizable knowledge and projections to coordinate state systems of higher education. Through these efforts, institutional research moved in concert with the democratic goals of college access and student success. Concurrently, regional associations began to define the intrinsic qualities of higher education and set the course for quality assurance. In this third trajectory, ending with the endorsement of the American Council on Education, institutional research gained stature and recognition as a linchpin to effective higher education administration under the leadership of college presidents.

As the fourth and final turn, then, the conditions for a social science community dedicated to research on higher education in a manner consistent with other social sciences emerged by the early 1960s. A small community of institutional researchers from across the United States began to define the parameters for the social scientific study of higher education. These professionals met formally to share research methods and findings on an annual basis and to discuss what the community of institutional research portended for the future of higher education. Through forums and publications, the group proposed theories about the nature of higher education in the larger social world and conceptualized apparatus for the measurement of higher education phenomena through collaborative studies. At the moment of its formal organization as a professional association, the momentum to form a scientific community for the study of higher education appeared to be accelerating.

Part two then transitions to the response and successful resistance of key stakeholders in higher education to the promise and professionalization of institutional research. Two political scientists with no prior formal association to the profession, Francis E. Rourke and Glenn E. Brooks, published a work in 1966 on the managerial revolution in higher education. The authors singled out institutional research as a critical instrument in managerial control of institutions: "Institutional research lies at the heart of the trend toward the use of modern management techniques in higher education." Not intended as a compliment, the authors emphasized the many "perils" of institutional research to the institution and to faculty but, especially, to other administrators. In the final analysis, they recommended that institutional research offices of the future be "distinct apart from the business side of operations," effectively breaking with the origins in administrative research and subjecting the work of the offices to "an academic orientation…bolstering the point of view of the faculty."[24]

By the mid-1960s, many faculty and administrators in higher education came to see institutional research as a threat to local autonomy. The second part then provides a lesson for data scientists who wish to avoid the pitfalls of resistance that undermined institutional research on most campuses. The vision for institutional research advocated by Rourke and Brooks was realized in the fifty years following the formation of the Association for Institutional Research (AIR) in 1966. As faculty in the new field of higher education came to recognize institutional research as a competitor in the production of knowledge about higher education and higher education administration, early opponents to institutional research sought to distinguish the practices of institutional research from the practices of faculty scholarship.

A consensus paradigm for institutional research formed among scholars and the leadership of the Association for Institutional Research that effectively arrested further development of the profession for decades. Recently, the AIR compared offices of institutional research to the print shops that desktop computing and printers largely made obsolete on college campuses. The leadership of the association suggested that institutional research officers abandon professional standards, drawing an analogy with former print shop managers: "After attempts to enforce printing standards failed, savvy print shop managers converted to coaching the new army of newsletter producers, and understood that some decline in professionalism was overcome by the quantity of communications that institutions were able to create."[25] Consonant with the consensus paradigm for institutional research for the past fifty years, the AIR envisioned deprofessionalization as the "aspirational" goal for this administrative "function."

The conclusion then considers how the decline and dysfunction of institutional research as a profession connect to recent trends that will fundamentally change the centuries-old mission of higher education and potentially shift the locus of control over higher education administration. Data science for student success entails the aggregation of student record level data from institutions across the nation. These data sets will include basic student records as well as parental information regarding education and income from the federal financial aid form, faculty income and tenure, institutional outcomes, and postgraduate earnings, to name only a few stakeholders in the aggregation of higher education data. Data scientists and college executives will require access to vast quantities of information for the invention of student success journeys that raise questions about privacy, informed consent, and policy making while taking a degree of decision-making out of the hands of college staff, faculty, and students. In short, data science for student success is at the heart of recent trends to reengineer the university.

Vendors of data science, one of the direct beneficiaries of the dissipation of the institutional research profession, must be prepared to rebuff the methods and scholarship used to displace institutional research from the heart of the managerial revolution in higher education. The peculiar conditions and intransigence for reform among higher education administration defines the plight of institutional research during the past half century. For these reasons, college executives and data scientists of student success must anticipate the tested and successful backlash that rendered the profession of institutional research incapable of addressing "the cross-cutting issues of the day—such as the connections between resource use and student success," as the state executives for the systems of higher education in America have concluded.

1 | THE SCIENTIFIC COMMUNITY THAT ENABLES SCIENTIFIC PROGRESS

Institutional Research: More Than Just Data

What makes a system of inquiry an exercise in social science rather than the application of common sense? What, as Ernest Nagel the philosopher of science asked, gives a science that "special excellence" for the acquisition of knowledge above and beyond common sense?

At many higher education institutions today, institutional research may not amount to much more than a mundane college operation to service reporting and compliance requirements set by federal, state, and other external agencies. As a consequence, many chief executives regard the annual national expenditures by higher education on the administration of institutional research as the cost of doing business imposed by government bureaucracies or by marketing opportunities in the various publications targeting college-goers. A college president commented almost forty years ago, "The Office of Institutional Research has three essential objectives: (1) to develop and update routinely institutional profiles, (2) to complete and file 'on a timely basis' (to use the jargon of our time and conditions) required by federal and state reports, and (3) to conduct fundamental research into education itself." Even then, the first and third objectives became increasingly ancillary as the "proliferation of reporting demands," or requests for data, redirected the focus of institutional researchers. The predominance of institutional reporting for compliance and market positioning began to relegate the profession's designation as research, "an evolving misnomer."[1]

In 2008, the editors of *New Directions for Higher Education* published a collection of essays entitled, *Institutional Research: More Than Just Data*, suggesting just how much institutional research had evolved into a misnomer during the ensuing thirty years. Attempting to revalorize the practice of institutional research in higher education, the editor's introductory comments declare, "Offices of institutional research do deal with data, lots of data...However, most offices provide services that go beyond merely counting or reporting." The collection of articles then seeks to inform higher education professionals, presumably, about the many ways in which institutional research differs from "just data."[2]

Indeed, few tasks are more like the torture of Sisyphus than institutional reporting in higher education: its repetitious cycle, the forms annually emptied, the blank cells routinely refilled year after year, submission by submission. The typical office of institutional research completes about a dozen submissions for the federal government, another dozen for its state, and many more to maintain compliance with the requirements of accreditors, credit rating agencies, standardized testing companies, and the myriad of sources for external funding. In addition, the four-year and master's institutions that annually compete for mindshare among the latest cohort of high school graduates respond to two dozen or more requests for data from media sources like the *US News and World Report*, *Peterson's*, *Princeton Review*, and *Wintergreen Orchard House*, to name only a handful.

Institutional reporting is part and parcel of institutional research, no doubt. But the regard for institutional research as a misnomer due to institutional reporting responsibilities amounts to nothing more than a fallacy. In the words of the president above, the entirety of institutional reporting is leveled into a single category such that no clear distinction can be made among an external data submission to support scientific research, government laws, or marketing opportunities. The premise that institutional reporting, or "just data" for that matter, categorically differs from "fundamental research on education itself" does not stand up to examination and scrutiny. In fact, the question of whether institutional reporting is or is not in itself a social scientific enterprise is the prism through which to see the reasons for the rise and decline of institutional research as a profession over the past fifty years.

The general principles provided by the National Research Council (NRC) to define education in general as a social science provide important context for understanding the history of institutional research.[3] Since its inception at a handful of colleges and its introduction more broadly in higher education during the mid-twentieth century, scholars have spilled much ink advocating or denying the scientific value of institutional research and the conditions under which it contributes to generalizable knowledge about higher education. Few, if any, however, explored whether institutional reporting is itself a scientific research activity for the production of generalizable knowledge about higher education.

This history begins, therefore, with the question of what makes a social science and whether institutional reporting—the most basic form of institutional research—already meets the baseline characteristics for a social science of higher education.

Research Conducted in Established or Commonly Accepted Educational Settings

Institutional research perennially stands at the crossroads of social science research and common sense.

In *The Structure of Science*, the philosopher of science Ernest Nagel juxtaposes science and common sense in order to define the "special excellence" and superior contributions "to the acquisition of knowledge" by the former over the latter. Science seeks to understand "why the facts are as alleged" and to shape explanations based on "critical tests of their relevance to the facts" in order to accumulate knowledge systematically. "[T]he organization and classification of knowledge on the basis of explanatory principles…is the distinctive goal of the sciences." The road to social science, as Nagel suggests, is clearly the more difficult, and more rewarding, journey. "The conclusions of science are the fruits of an institutionalized system of inquiry" that refines a body of knowledge, unifies a system of explanation, determines language, produces abstractions, and sustains the critique of its own knowledge and practices.[4]

In contrast, common sense establishes rules that fail to grasp the limits of their reliability or validity and perpetuates knowledge that is "most adequate in situations in which a certain number of [unexplained] factors remain practically unchanged." Common sense entertains "incompatible and even inconsistent beliefs" borne by "an almost exclusive preoccupation with the immediate consequences and qualities of observed events." Common sense relays its beliefs through imprecise language and terminology that muddles "the distinction between confirming and contradicting evidence for such beliefs." Common sense primarily concerns itself with parochial knowledge of "special value" to the particular condition (i.e., institution) that is not subjected to "systematic scrutiny" to assess "the range of [its] validity."[5]

In a manner of speaking, the field of institutional research unwittingly reveals its plight at the crossroads of science and common sense. In June 2015, the Association for Institutional Research (AIR) acknowledged that "the current function of IR [institutional research] is not clearly defined, and the future path of IR is unknown." The AIR established an initiative, "Improving & transforming institutional research in postsecondary education," to address "a concern that current IR practices are not adequate for the challenges that face decision makers today." The preliminary statements on the aspirational practice of institutional research exhibited characteristics of both common sense and science.[6]

In one respect, the initiative reinforces the practice of many institutional researchers who pride themselves on being jacks or jills of all trades, what might be called the myth of the factotum. In the myth of the factotum, the institutional researcher assumes that the needs or natural abilities of decision makers at a local institution provide all of the necessary and sufficient conditions for the practice of institutional research—"data studies."[7] In service to commonsense data studies across the institution and higher education, the institutional researcher champions his or her own ability to "respond to requests for data." He or she knows how to deliver "information to improve [others'] decisions" and to time the release of data for others to make "use of the results…[in] proactive decision-making." Yet the institutional research factotum is not himself or herself a decision maker. Others must bear the burden for decision-making and "expand their unit's [sic] capacity to conduct data studies that align with their own information needs."

In this respect, institutional research also exhibits aspects of—and, already is in name—"an institutionalized system of inquiry" to explain student learning outcomes, bolster strategic planning, and champion continuous improvement in higher education. The institutional researcher always already knows how to respond to requests for data. The institutional researcher further possesses the foresight to deliver data that improves the decision-making capacities of others at the institution or in external agencies. Lastly, the astute institutional researcher times the release of data to maximize the proactivity of decision-making. Each of these capacities imply a refined, unified body of knowledge, critique, and explanation—a social science—that fruitfully services and transforms the commonsense requests of decision makers into more systematic lines of inquiry.

How, then, may institutional research be more fully conceived as a social science distinct from its application by the common sense of decision-makers?

"Sapere aude! 'Dare to know!'" Immanuel Kant's dictum in answer to the question, "What is enlightenment?" stands as one germinal sentiment for any social science. A science requires its practitioners to "'[h]ave courage to use your own reason!'"—to form an understanding independently and to acquire knowledge directly. Moreover, the exercise of one's own reason must take place "as a scholar before the reading public," not as a person may engage reason privately "in a particular civil post or office which is intrusted to him" or her.[8] In short, institutional researchers must claim to be in the best position, unmediated, to design studies that discover the "informational needs" of decision makers in the civil posts of higher education units and to disseminate findings for peer and public review. "Dare to know," while not sufficient, is a necessary and unassailable prerequisite of an institutionalized system of inquiry to be recognized as a social science.

Institutional research is a social scientific enterprise when the practitioner engages in primary research to systematically scrutinize explanations resulting from prior acquisition of knowledge and to enhance the understanding of its education-related phenomena in order to improve practical problem-solving and decision-making. To stand as such, institutional research nonetheless must have a set of phenomena to distinguish its field of inquiry from existing social sciences while also establishing its interrelations with other social sciences.

On the first account, the federal guidelines of the United States for the protection of human research subjects delineate institutional research from the common fields of social scientific research. The "Common Rule for the Protection of Human Subjects" establishes criteria to determine when research is subject to the oversight of a federal department or agency, including research conducted by social and behavioral scientists. To administer its policy and regulations, the National Science Foundation (NSF) provides a document with the rules for the constitution of an Institutional Review Board, typically at the local institution, empowered "to review and have authority to approve, require modifications in (to secure approval), or disapprove all research activities covered by this policy." In American colleges and universities, what constitutes legitimate scientific research with human subjects in the social sciences often is determined by these local boards.

The significant guidelines for institutional research, however, are found in the exemptions to the policy on authority of institutional review boards over certain areas of human subjects research. Specifically, the first exemption distinguishes institutional research from other fields of human subjects research: "Research conducted in established or commonly accepted educational settings, involving normal educational practices." In the definitions that govern many areas of social scientific research on human subjects, the federal policy singles out research and assessment "in established or commonly accepted educational settings" as an area of study that is not subject to the authority and approval of institutional review boards.[9]

Erroneously, the exemption may be construed as an indication that institutional research typically falls short of the scientific designation for "research activities." To the contrary, as other documents show, this is not the intention. Federal definitions for research and human subjects clearly include the group of researchers who systematically collect and report statistics on the educational outcomes of living individuals.

The Human Subjects Regulations Decision Charts from the U.S.

Department of Health and Human Services (DHHS) affirms the designation in its decision tree diagram.[10] Consider, for instance, institutional reporting for educational statistics to the federal government to advance the work of the National Center for Educational Statistics (NCES) at the Institute of Education Sciences. The NCES annually publishes its *Digest of Education Statistics* on educational activities of the United States. These figures include higher education enrollments, retention and graduation rates, average expenditures per student, projections for high school graduates and college enrollees, and other descriptive statistics to support the decision-making of policy makers, higher education institutions, and academic scholarship in general.

The Human Subjects Regulations Decision Charts result in the following tree: Is institutional research "a systematic investigation designed to develop or contribute to generalizable knowledge"? Yes, in that institutional statistics support generalizations for national statistics and projections. Does institutional research "involve obtaining information about living individuals"? Yes, the students, employees, and alumni of colleges and universities. Does institutional research involve "intervention or interaction with the individuals"? Yes, and much of it is collected over an extended period of four, six, or more years. Decision: "Activity is research involving human subjects," or institutional research is human subjects research.

In the illustration of the regulations, the second chart establishes that the DHHS does not explicitly prohibit institutional research and, to the contrary, the US Department of Education requires such research by higher education institutions. The third chart then provides the determination for how institutional research may be distinguished from other disciplines of social science: "Is the research only conducted in established or commonly accepted educational settings, involving normal educational practices?" Yes—as far as institutional reporting goes, the college or university organizes human subjects into a postsecondary educational setting. The designation of institutional research as exempt research clearly follows the initial designation of institutional research as human subjects research. Thus, the DHHS decision tree categorically designates institutional research studies conducted in a college or university for the study of educational outcomes as social scientific human subjects research—the foundation for an institutionalized system of inquiry.

The NSF and DHHS guidance on the exemption to the federal policy and regulations for human subjects research in practice endows institutional research in the United States with unique responsibilities in a distinct setting for its field of study. The officer responsible for institutional research must adhere, without direct oversight, to the "ethical principles and guidelines for the protection of human subjects of research" and conduct research in a manner consistent with all six exemptions to the Common Rule for the Protection of Human Subjects.[11]

By singling out "established or commonly accepted educational settings," the federal guidelines further suggest that colleges and universities that engage in "normal educational practices" represent a discrete area of scientific research activity. At the same time, the key words—"setting," "normal," and "practices"—signify that institutional research shares interests with the fields of study for institutions and social groups (economics, sociology), customs to signify maturation and social class (anthropology, history), and interventions in human behavior and learning (psychology, education). In a formal respect for a social science, institutional research even at its most basic level—institutional reporting of statistics to the federal government—seems to qualify as an institutionalized system of inquiry designed to develop or contribute to generalizable knowledge about humans in society and their social exchanges in educational settings.

The more pertinent question is therefore: how best to institutionalize this type of research on higher education with the "special excellence" of a social science?

Scientific Inquiry Is the Same in All Fields

One indisputable fact for institutional research is that the vast majority of its practitioners are administrators and professional staff employees in higher education who are rarely full-time teaching or research faculty. In the United States, as the first professional file of the Association for Institutional Research indicates, the function has links to the inward-looking exercise of self-study—wherein the particular college or university entrusted to the researchers served as its own private object of study. Likewise, an early professional file on career development emphasizes that the skills of institutional research are "the skills of self-study,"[12] or in the words of Kant, limited to the purview of a "civil post or office."

The institutionalization of institutional research as an administrative function is likely associated with the sheer number, diversity, and dispersion of higher education institutions across the United States. An academic department of institutional research faculty, like English faculty, at each college in the country would have been cost prohibitive and inefficient. Unsurprisingly, two early professional files on career development for institutional researchers note the lack of faculty experience, possession of nontraditional degrees, and an inadequate record of publications among many institutional research professionals.[13] Consequently, the administrative direction of the studies likely obscured how institutional research could take shape as a discipline guided by the significant questions and theories of a social science. The traditional values and attributes of social science as organized in academic departments may have seemed foreign to institutional research offices in administration.

In 2002, the Committee on Scientific Principles for Education Research for the (US) National Research Council (NRC) released a report to clarify "the nature of scientific inquiry in education."[14] Significantly, the introduction suggests that education scholarship in general struggles to overcome its own "skepticism concerning the value and validity of developing a 'science of education.'" Oftentimes, academics split along lines of qualitative versus quantitative methods and basic versus applied research, with schools of education more often favoring qualitative methods and basic research "at the expense of quantitative methods" and applied research.[15] The report arguably suggests that institutional research suffered in the esteem of scholars of higher education due to four relatively peculiar points of emphasis in its practice: administrative, quantitative, applied, and scientific research.

To improve the quality of scientific research in education, however, the NRC report endorses several positions that open the door to understanding institutional research as a social scientific endeavor. Two are most relevant. First, the report acknowledges that education research is "an applied field" and makes clear that applied research is no less scientific than basic research: "What makes research scientific is not the motive for carrying it out, but the manner in which it is carried out." Second, the report states that "the research question drives the design, not vice versa" and specifies three types of interrelated questions: descriptive, causal, and process or mechanism.[16] To emphasize the second point, the inclusion of questions that result in descriptive statistics ostensibly includes institutional reporting.

What this means is that an administrative institutional research office can be institutionalized along social scientific principles 1) by virtue of the manner in which it carries out its work and 2) by the rigor and formalism with which it formulates its questions. The motive and research questions in institutional reporting support the NCES *Digest of Education Statistics* as well as a myriad of derivative scholarship and publications by academics, researchers, and others utilizing the resources of the Integrated Postsecondary Education Data System (IPEDS).[17] Institutional researchers organize and compile the data for each institution annually—the unit of analysis for most studies based on IPEDS data. If the data representing the unit of analysis fails to adhere to basic scientific principles, then the research conducted at the higher levels of analysis, causality, and process/mechanism also suffer from the same deficiencies.

The Organisation for Economic Co-operation and Development

(OECD) reported ten years ago that "the prominence of the business sector has sharpened" in the funding of academic research and development expenditures internationally.[18] University-corporate partnerships in many scientific disciplines have continued to advance in recent years. Administrative institutional research, as a contributor to scientific research in education, fundamentally performs the same role in the higher education industry. Every institution directly funds from its nonacademic support expenditures the research activity that supports the scholarship of academicians in research universities and publications of the federal government. In effect, institutions of higher education in the United States underwrite a substantial portion of the costs for scientific research in education in the United States.

A third conclusion is thus inferred from the NRC's report on scientific research in education: administrative institutional research functions are organized to conduct significant research even if only for institutional reporting. The data definitions and the submissions guidelines accompanying the federal submissions convey the motives, the questions, the manner, and the rigor of institutional research. The descriptive statistics then support the policy research of the federal government and the basic research of academics who have no administrative responsibility within higher education institutions.

While the NRC provides a framework that demarcates institutional reporting as a scientific research activity, the degree to which each institutional research office adheres to these principles is a matter of question. To that end, the NRC also provides guidance on the organization of research agencies that apply to institutional research offices. The NRC report in its final chapter takes the added step to provide "design principles for fostering science in a federal education research agency."[19] A federal agency "to promote and protect the integrity of scientific research in education with the goal of generating knowledge that can inform policy and practice decisions" requires a legion of higher education institutions prepared to practice institutional research with equal integrity and rigor to achieve the same goals. Therefore, the design principles provide the first criterion for the institutionalization of research on higher education as a social scientific enterprise in an educational setting.

The six principles may be paraphrased for the applied research conducted by the administrative offices of colleges and universities:[20]

1. Staff the office with people skilled in science, leadership, and management.

2. Create structures to guide agenda, inform funding decisions, and monitor work.

3. Insulate the office from inappropriate political interference.

4. Develop a focused and balanced portfolio of research that addresses short-, medium-, and long-term issues of importance to institutional policy and practice.

5. Adequately fund the department.

6. Invest in research infrastructure.

The responsibility therein largely falls to higher education executives who must decide whether to staff and fund their institutional research offices to support studies that result in generalizable knowledge for the three tiers of scientific research defined by the National Research Council: descriptives, causes, and processes or mechanisms. At each tier of research activity, the institution gains by the acquisition of generalizable knowledge applicable to higher education administration, planning, and effectiveness.

The immense wealth of phenomena at institutions and the portfolio of studies under the direction of institutional research offices must then be deployed in a manner consistent with the purpose of scientific research in education. Again, the NRC report provides a set of six guiding principles that "underlie all scientific inquiry, including education research" among a healthy community of scholars:[21]

1. Pose significant questions that can be investigated empirically.

2. Link research to relevant theory.

3. Use methods that permit direct investigation of the question.

4. Provide a coherent and explicit chain of reasoning.

5. Replicate and generalize across studies.

6. Disclose research to encourage professional scrutiny and critique.

In substance, the NRC's six guiding principles require a paradigm for institutional research that differs from the reliance on commonsense "requests for data" and informal data studies. As Nagel wrote, an institutionalized system of inquiry must have that "special excellence" to contribute to "knowledge on the basis of explanatory principles" in order to earn the distinction of social science.

The second criterion for a scientific enterprise tacitly requires institutional research to pose significant questions and acknowledge the implicit engagement of theory in the standard administrative practices of institutional research. To this end, the NRC's guiding principles on scientific inquiry elicit more opportunity for institutional researchers to make explicit the theoretical basis of institutional inquiries, methods, and findings. The transparent process of inquiry engages and facilitates honest scrutiny and critique of research agendas, funding, and work by the major stakeholders in higher education.

As an applied field, the study of higher education requires a more nuanced understanding of the practice of basic research than one that idealizes the supposedly indifferent academic pursuit of knowledge for knowledge's sake and the research programs of faculty. To the contrary, to balance the interests of stakeholders from all six "cultures"[22] of colleges and universities, a third criterion of scientific research in higher education favorably considers the responsibility of colleges and universities for the outcomes of their students. Broadly conceived, higher education encompasses much more than the teacher-student dyad and the assessment of student learning in the classroom. As an educational setting, a college or university immerses the whole person in curricular, cocurricular, and extracurricular environments that ineluctably purvey the (sometimes contradictory) mission and values of higher education. In a deeper sense, then, student success is a priority of the paradigm for institutional research through which to formulate significant questions to investigate and define the scientific study of higher education.

As in other social sciences, discipline arises as an important commitment of individuals to the organization of a collective unit of institutionalized research activity. If institutional research as a practice lacks discipline, the quality and effectiveness of higher education in general also lack discipline. As a fourth criterion, scientific research on higher education endorses the primacy of social scientific research principles in the investigation of questions of general and lasting relevance to college leadership and governance. For the institutions of higher education, the fourth criterion requires commitment to the study of higher education and the employment of institutional researchers with appropriate credentials and competencies for scientific research.

Herein, though, we encounter the call to action for institutional researchers to define and map out its future as a discipline. The work must be the work of a community of scholars hungry for debate, tolerant of dissent, open to critique, and in search of the next unknown—for no one scribe or scholar can be regarded or lauded as the final word for an entire discipline. The NRC takes as its subject scientific research on education in general and upholds the general idea that "scientific inquiry is the same in all fields." The NRC promotes the practice of social science for education as a discipline: "Scientific research…is a continual process of rigorous reasoning supported by a dynamic interplay among methods, theories, and findings." More importantly, for this "continual process" of scientific enterprise to be successful, the practitioners must form "a healthy community of researchers…guided by a set of fundamental principles."[23]

The fifth criterion for the structure of institutional research on higher education entails the unmediated inclusion of institutional researchers in the community of scholars who are regarded as directly engaged in the study of higher education for the acquisition of generalizable knowledge. In short, the fifth criterion for scientific research in higher education stops short the concern for who asks the questions (administrators versus academics), the technological complexity of the methods (qualitative versus quantitative), or the utilization of administrative resources to advance generalizable knowledge (applied versus basic research). A healthy community of scholars holds as its paramount concern the maximization of student success in higher education.

A Healthy Community of Researchers Guided by a Set of Fundamental Principles

The degree to which institutional research as a profession meets the five criteria for social science is an open question subject to social and historical conditions. As the future uncertainty for the profession and aspirational statements published by the Association for Institutional Research illustrate, the degree to which the field currently meets the five criteria for social science appears to be ambiguous. As the NRC identifies "a healthy community of researchers...guided by a set of fundamental principles" as the impetus for scientific progress, whether institutional research is or may be a social science largely comes down to the social construction of the community engaged in the activity in a historical place and time.

The National Research Council's report on scientific research in education states unequivocally that an educational setting, a college or university, may be the subject of a scientific study, at the very least an ethnographic study. The criteria merely demand that the study "generate systematic observations about the focal group or site, and patterns in results may be generalizable to other similar groups or sites or for the future." The report also acknowledges that education research is applied research to support decision-making, noting, "[W]e also believe the distinction between basic and applied science has outlived its usefulness...[and] often served to denigrate applied work."[24] This is not to say that each institution may define for itself the program of institutional research that advances scientific research on higher education in isolation. Rather, an initial interest in self-study may lead—significant question by significant question—to a broader interest in the study of higher education in general.

When the institutional research profession enables scientific progress, the evidence is found in the commonality of instruments and practices across the universe of institutions engaged in its practice. The NRC notes, "Embedded in their practice, scientists also engage in the development of objects (e.g., instruments or practices); thus scientific knowledge is a by-product of both technological activities and analytical activities." In the final analysis, then, the NRC locates the driver of scientific progress in the social organization for scholarship on higher education: "[I]t is the scientific community that enables scientific progress."[25] Thus, a healthy community of scholars in higher education will bridge the imagined divide between faculty and administration to form the basis for an academic-industry partnership for the study of higher education.

Given the formal structures of research on higher education described above, the most important question for the study of higher education is: have institutional researchers embraced the discipline of a scientific community that enables scientific progress, or have they eschewed the discipline of social science to organize themselves on other grounds—more specifically, the desultory grounds of common sense?

2 | A FACT-FINDING AGENCY DIRECTLY RESPONSIBLE TO THE PRESIDENT

Long-Term Studies of the Whole Educational Process

The motivation and research questions that gave shape to institutional research in its earliest years remain formative despite subsequent advances, setbacks, and stagnation in the history of the profession. The National Research Council's (NRC) statement on scientific research on education expects no less: the research process itself is "highly contested territory," often producing ambiguous and nondurable results, explored via multiple methodologies, and clarified in periodic "syntheses of research findings."[1] The field of institutional research, to the extent it originated for the advancement of scientific research on higher education, has been subject to fits and starts, reversals, and paradigm shifts like any other scientific enterprise.

Without the guide posts of prior research or the knowledge of similar work by colleagues at other institutions, institutional researchers in the mid-twentieth century first formulated conceptual frameworks for the study of higher education in isolation. Likely for this reason, the consensus history for institutional research closely associated the first offices and bureaus with the practice of self-study. Tethered to the administrative needs of college presidents, the early history appeared to be driven by those who called for the studies rather than why or how researchers conducted the first studies identified under the title "institutional research."

Fortunately, three publications from the mid-twentieth century catalog the advancing program of bureaus and offices of institutional research. These documents capture the origins of the profession in a commitment to scientific principles and practices during its formative era. Moreover, the first publications on institutional research reflect the commitment of the profession to the disclosure of research for professional scrutiny and replication by other institutions across the nation. In this important aspect, institutional research differed in kind from self-study and the provincial needs of a single institution. Unlike self-study, institutional research from its outset invited practitioners to form into a community that transcended the boundaries of any one particular institution.

At the University of Illinois in 1938, the director of the Bureau of Institutional Research published the preliminary steps taken to differentiate its studies from the common sense self-studies of prior eras. Likewise, the Minnesota Bureau published a work in 1954 to recount the formation of its University Committee on Educational Research during the 1920s. Originally designed "to conduct systematic research on the University's admissions practices," by the 1930s, the committee established its first central office and hired specialized staff supported by "an annual budget for committee activities, which encouraged more long-range planning of central office services." Lastly, in 1962, *The Journal of Experimental Education* sponsored an edited collection of articles on the institutional research activity at nearly two dozen institutions across the United States during the previous decade. Recording presentations from one of the first inclusive meetings of institutional researchers from around the nation, the contributors envisioned "long-term studies of the whole educational process."

In the early publications, the editors and authors made explicit their motivations to organize institutional research as a social scientific field. The origins of institutional research in these offices and among these professionals provide a vital link to the praxis of social science. As the NRC noted, "Every scientific inquiry is linked, either implicitly or explicitly, to some overarching theory or conceptual framework that guides the investigation."[2] This assertion provides critical perspective with which to assess the origins of the institutional research profession in social scientific principles with a theoretical basis that oriented action and affected research programs—regardless of whether subsequent scholarship continued to articulate the foundational theory or purpose explicitly.

Sturdy Foundations for a Type of Self-Appraisal

In the white paper commemorating the fiftieth anniversary of the Association for Institutional Research (AIR), William F. Lasher provides a version of the consensus narrative for the origins of institutional research, citing three sources: self-study, survey research in the first half of the twentieth century, and research offices in large public universities. The first origin suggests that institutional research has always been part of higher education and begins with the first study on "organizational structure" performed by the founders of Yale in 1701. In the two centuries following, the presidents of institutions engaged in self-study that "utilized information and statistical analysis...to solve the institutional problems of the day."[3]

The first half of the twentieth-century gave rise to "The Survey Era" as the Carnegie Foundation and regional accreditors such as the North Central Association in the Midwest sponsored a great number of surveys of multiple institutions. By 1937, a review of survey activity in higher education revealed that five hundred studies had been completed in the prior thirty years. Several institutions, most accredited by the North Central Association, organized the first bureaus and offices of institutional research. Like self-study, the bureaus and offices performed research under the direction of "individual faculty members or small groups that were either interested in a particular topic or perhaps were asked by their president to attempt to find solutions to a particular problem facing their institution."[4]

The citations in the consensus history attest to the lack of interest for the history of institutional research among scholars of higher education during the past fifty years. The consensus narrative originates in and still relies on a handful of contributions that have not been further developed or challenged since their publications in 1937, 1960, 1973, and 1979.[5] Invariably, the consensus history emphasizes continuity between the practice of institutional self-study and institutional research as a function. The linkage intimates how the particular interests and needs of individual presidents or institutions defined the scope of activities for institutional research with the first colleges in America. In a point of emphasis, the consensus history suggests that no fundamental change in the study of higher education occurred with the advent of offices of institutional research.

The consensus history then connects the establishment of administrative offices of institutional research to the proliferation of surveys administered on behalf of advocacy groups ancillary to higher education proper. The centralization of institutional research in administrative offices, Donald Reichard reports in the *Handbook of Institutional Research*, resulted from the efforts of the American Council on Education and regional accreditors to instrumentalize and evaluate higher education. Aside from the vague reference to centralization or the establishment of offices, however, the principles and conduct of institutional research otherwise go untold.[6]

The dismally short narratives neglect substantive discussion of the surveys administered during the era and the explicit motivations for formally designating an office responsible for institutional research. As in the historical account of the AIR to mark its fifty-year anniversary, the specific investigations or studies conducted by the first offices of institutional research exist only outside the margins of the text. With these vacuous accounts of the origins of the profession and its impact on higher education, the consensus history dismisses the social and historical agency of the people who organized and directed the newly formed bureaus of institutional research.

Nonetheless, a great deal of evidence indicates that the first bureaus of institutional research from the mid-twentieth century formed during the "survey era" in order to participate in the scientific study of higher education. In a 1933 review of survey research by University of Chicago, Walter Crosby Eells regarded "the increasing number and improved quality of surveys" of higher education as the "application of scientific method to critical appraisals of our institutions." In his subsequent 1937 report for the Carnegie Foundation, *Surveys of American Higher Education*, Eells notes that the proliferation of surveys of higher education institutions reflected a number of factors, including "the development of the scientific spirit in education."[7] Consequently, an era of scientific study of higher education— not simply surveys—may be said to coincide with the formation of the first offices of institutional research.

With this wider lens, the origin of institutional research as an administrative function may be traced more accurately to the scientific spirit that informed higher education research in general during the period. As an anonymous editorial comment in the *Journal of Higher Education* from 1935 states, "Only recently...have [higher education institutions] begun to encourage scientific investigation of the internal problems of the institution itself."[8] The anonymous contributor wrote in favor of bureaus of institutional research as exemplified by the office at the University of Illinois. Accomplished social scientists often led the research activities and brought the rigor of their primary disciplines to bear on the methods used to answer research questions at their institutions. Three of the earliest publications on the studies conducted by institutional research offices offer a window into the first bureaus and offices to lead the original forays into the scientific study of higher education.

In 1938, Coleman R. Griffith provided a firsthand account for the development of the Bureau of Institutional Research at the University of Illinois in the *Journal of Higher Education*. Griffith was a psychologist by training who established one of the first research laboratories for sports psychology in the United States. From 1938 to 1940, he consulted the Chicago Cubs baseball team in what may have been "the first long-term interaction between a psychologist and a professional sport franchise in history." The field of sports psychology regards him as a father of the field, as he predated the formal organization of the discipline by twenty years. Prior to his turn to professional baseball, Griffith worked as the director of the Bureau of Institutional Research, in which capacity he conducted a number of unprecedented studies for the University of Illinois. In 1944, he was promoted to provost at the university before joining the Oregon State

Higher Education System to conclude his illustrious career.[9]

Though regarded as the first centralized bureau of institutional research in the consensus history, Griffith's contributions to institutional research at the University of Illinois are largely neglected by later generations of institutional researchers and scholars.[10] According to Griffith, the University of Illinois had engaged in a wide range of institutional research projects prior to World War II. The university had conducted research on academic program reviews and established benchmarks for the performance of programs, including longitudinal studies on the unit costs and student credit hour productivity of academic programs. The university studied faculty loads by rank and class level as well as the quality of teaching as measured by student learning outcomes. And his Bureau of Institutional Research performed analyses on resource utilization and allocations, including classroom space utilization and enrollment projections.[11] While rudimentary in comparison to the later publications, his original contribution to the study of higher education captures the movement toward more rigorous standards for institutional research at the University of Illinois.

Opening with the suspicion among faculty and administrators for "data," common still today, Griffith considers methods to improve the reliability and validity of institutional studies. The data may come from many different offices in the institution, but required "some special agency to relate these several sets of data in a meaningful way." The data then had to be contextualized with additional insights, "richly clothed with studies of the types of work that are being done in each department." The data also had to be longitudinal in acknowledgment that "[e]ach department has had a history" and requires a "time-wise point of view" to provide a comprehensive picture. Lastly, the history and conditions of the individual departments, Griffith noted, also "are caught up in the history and present practices of the university as a whole."

In each of these facets, Griffith provided important guidelines for compiling institutional data, but he also expounded on the appropriate scope of institutional research activities at a university. His bureau horizontally and vertically integrated the disparate information stores collected by the individual programs and departments of the university. In addition, he is mindful of changes over time and recommends a third dimension for time-series data for the departments. In substance, though, the departments are parts of a larger whole, so institutional research also encompassed the history and mission of the university itself. In this aspect, Griffith suggests how the "special agency" of a centralized administrative bureau for institutional research distinguished itself from the self-studies performed by individual departments.

A key component of the "special agency" of institutional research derived from the university president's demands on the bureau: "From the very first, [the Bureau of Institutional Research] has served as a fact-finding agency directly responsible to the president." Noteworthy, Griffith distinguished between "data" and "facts." His usage of the two terms in the article hints at the responsibilities attached to his bureau. With the former, he emphasized "data…[as] a means to an end, the end being thoroughly educational in intent and outcome." The latter, then, required the provision of some analytical or academic perspective: "some special agency to relate…several sets of data in a meaningful way and to judge the outcomes with the left eye on the cold figures and the right eye on the vital arts of teaching, learning, and research." In this distinction between "data" and "facts," Griffith points out that his Bureau of Institutional Research sought to deliver some level of analysis, contextualized in knowledge of higher education in general, as part of its core responsibilities. In his words, "a bureau can abstract the literature on higher education and clothe the data with comments on the educational principles involved."

Thus, while the Bureau of Institutional Research conducted studies with the university president intended as its primary audience, Griffith's publication after two decades of research aimed to communicate with a much larger audience. In this general assessment of the studies performed for the university, he offered his recollections about the progress of institutional research at the University of Illinois "[as] sturdy foundations for a type of self-appraisal which might well earn the respect of every thoughtful student of university administration." In these terms, Griffith recognized the potential for institutional research as a form of basic research on higher education administration that may produce generalizable knowledge for a community of scholars, or college presidents, engaged in like-minded study.

Finally, in its application to the administration of a university, Griffith carefully positioned the contributions of institutional research to university policy making, while making known its inherent nature to produce more questions for investigation. Near the conclusion, he indicated that the "chief function" of his bureau was "to ask questions" and, when invited, "the recital of the facts." The breadth of facts affirms the scope of research and knowledge anticipated for a single bureau:

> It should know the history of the institution as a whole, of each of the parts, of its student body, of the rapid shifts in the teaching-loads, of its expenses, and of its courses. It should know something about the history of the cultural, agrarian, industrial, and social arena in which the university is placed and to which it must render its services. Within a few days after the beginning of each semester, a bureau can know where sudden changes in any of these items have occurred, and these changes alone, or when they are a part of a trend, ought to excite questions.

These "facts," nonetheless, did not produce unequivocal roadmaps for the direction of policy: "The data collected by a self-appraising agency do not often answer any questions of educational policy." Mindful of the apprehension others had for the quantification of university operations, he modestly reiterated that institutional research was not "legislation by sums, by ratios, or by percentage...[but] one of many resources for a complete picture of what a university is trying to do."

As the first publication to detail the operations and objectives of a centralized bureau of institutional research, Griffith's summary illustrates the connections to university self-study but also testifies to the native impetus of the institutional research process toward new areas of investigation that renders self-study insufficient. After twenty years, Griffith's bureau at the University of Illinois had pressed to the limits of self-study, as his publication in a broadly read journal evinces, and as he states tacitly as his motivations. At a time when only five other bureaus or offices of institutional research may have existed, he submitted a review of the work and organization of his bureau for scrutiny by other "students of higher education administration." Even his cautious description of the influence of institutional research on policy making reflects his encounter with the limits of self-study. "Fact-finding" reads institutional data through the lens of "the literature" on higher education. In order to influence how that data are understood, institutional research must contribute to the literature—as his article did. In the final analysis, the act of publishing his review invited more institutions to erect the "sturdy foundations" of institutional research for themselves and contribute to the literature on higher education administration.

To Encourage Experimentation along New Lines

Sixteen years lapsed following Griffith's publication before another work of similar stature appeared. Indicating nominal interest in bureaus or offices of institutional research, James Doi estimates that only ten administrative bureaus or offices of institutional research existed in the early 1950s.[12] Nonetheless, most of the offices formed before the war continued to perform research for their institutions into the post–World War II era. The fruits of the studies and the accumulated knowledge identified with these offices quietly moved the practice of institutional research away from self-study and closer to social science.

In 1954, the Bureau of Institutional Research at the University of Minnesota released a ten-year review of its program that exhibited more substantive separation from the premises of self-study.[13] Like its counterpart at the University of Illinois, the Minnesota bureau developed from the initiative and "vision" of its president who initially established The University Committee on Educational Research in the 1920s "to conduct systematic research on the University's admissions practices." By the 1930s, the committee established its first central office and hired specialized staff after the subsequent president of university approved "an annual budget for committee activities, which encouraged more long-range planning of central office services." During the late 1940s, the bureau reorganized under a coordinator and two appointees "to share responsibility for directing the program of the central research office." At the time of publication, "with a somewhat enlarged central staff and budget, the research program was broadened," and the Bureau incorporated "experimental studies in the learning situation, the improvement of various types of evaluative instruments, and the general appraisal of outcomes of University instruction." Ruth E. Eckert and Robert J. Keller, directors of the central office at University of Minnesota during the period, led many of the activities for the ten-year period reviewed.

Educated at the University of Buffalo and Harvard University, Eckert published on many subjects directly tied to institutional research during her career. Her studies included issues related to student retention, the value of preparation courses, why faculty serve, PhD students' views of foreign language requirements, and an appraisal of general education outcomes. After leaving her administrative post at the University of Minnesota, as a scholar she contributed to several research studies by Minnesota state committees, the North Central Association, and national organizations for the study of higher education including the American Council on Education and the US Department of Education's first Cooperative Research Committee. Keller, the junior partner in the 1954 review, served as Director of the Bureau for much of the 1950s and later contributed to additional studies of higher education in Minnesota.[14]

By the mid-1950s, the University of Minnesota's Bureau of Institutional Research demonstrated a level of sophistication and a breadth of activity that dwarfs the University of Illinois from the 1930s. Eckert and Keller rightfully congratulated their bureau for having "pioneered...the study of [a university's] own educational programs." After observing that wartime and postwar priorities had resulted in an interregnum in the customary reports on the research performed by the bureau, Eckert and Keller produced a ten-year review of the most significant studies during the decade. More importantly, like Griffith before them, they took the additional step to publish the retrospective in an edited collection for their colleagues at other institutions.

Most impressively, the bureau directors obviously recognized the limitation of self-study at a single institution by the late 1940s. At the behest of the president of the University of Minnesota, the state formed a Committee on Higher Education with representatives "from both the public and private colleges" to study Minnesota's "needs and resources in higher education." Eckert became the chairperson of the work group who conducted the research resulting in the 1950 summary publication, *Higher Education in Minnesota*.[15] Significantly, by 1954, the objects of study at University of Minnesota encompassed "individual courses," "whole departments," "entire schools or colleges," "the University as a whole," and statewide research to support policy making and enrollment projections.[16]

The subject matter under the auspices of the Minnesota Bureau of Institutional Research included many projects mentioned by Griffith in 1938 but also extended beyond the scope he described sixteen years earlier. The institutional researchers at Minnesota thoroughly engaged in research for planning and allocating the use of institutional resources and advanced effectiveness studies to measure differential student learning outcomes based on regional demographics, student characteristics, and mode of instructional delivery (chapters 2, 7, and 10). A few projects studied the shifting educational plans of students in undergraduate programs, the grading practices for undergraduates, and library services to students (chapter 3, 4, and 9). The bureau also attempted to measure former students' outcomes after graduating from the College of Science, Literature, and Arts, curriculum evaluations for the College of Agriculture, Forestry, and Home Economics, and appraisals for PhD graduate studies (chapter 6, 13, and 18).

The editors of the 1954 volume generalized the output from studies conducted over ten years and represented the collection as the result of harnessing "fruitful questions" about the university programs. Each article marked "key developments in program building at Minnesota, illustrating how the University has used this plan of self-study to appraise its practices, and to encourage experimentation along new lines." In the latter respect, the University of Minnesota's Bureau of Institutional Research stepped beyond the excitation of questions and discussion to deliver concrete direction and recommendations for the improvement of university policies, student services, and instruction. Publication of the ten-year review capped an effort to provide a summary of research "to groups on the campus and to persons elsewhere who are especially interested in the problems studied or who may wish to imitate similar studies."

Unlike Griffith, Eckert and Keller had an immediate impact on interest for offices of institutional research. Although Eckert and Keller's publication remained the lone book-length volume to detail the organization and specific studies conducted by a bureau of institutional research prior to 1955, many subsequent publications regarding institutional research in the following decade reference the work of the bureau at the

University of Minnesota. More significantly, a number of presidents organized offices or bureaus of institutional research at the nation's universities. A critical mass of practitioners was reached by the early 1960s, prompting calls for better organization of the new profession.

In 1962, the growing cadre of institutional researchers held their first forums, resulting in an edited collection of articles contributed by institutional researchers from more than twenty different colleges and universities. Published as an issue of the *Journal of Experimental Education*, the collection edited by L. J. Lins, Professor and Coordinator of Institutional Studies at the University of Wisconsin, evidenced the rapid spread of the "special agencies" of institutional research. In addition, the articles recorded the development of standardized research methods and analytical practices across institutional and state boundaries.[17]

Recording a variety of different types of institutional studies, the publication also marks the formal emergence of scholarly reviews for the methods and arguments utilized by institutional research offices. For example, the contributor from Fordham University characterized the research activities first deployed at Illinois and Minnesota as "more or less routine areas [such] as faculty load, class size, [and] space utilization." Noting that Fordham's institutional researchers, like others at the colleges and universities represented in the issue, had moved on to more complex analyses "[o]f greater importance...in such fields as student and faculty images of the University, comparison of senior characteristics with the nation-wide findings...of the career aspirations of college seniors, student retention, and prediction of academic success."[18] As demonstrated by the references to multistate or multi-institutional studies, the scope of institutional research focused more and more on questions affecting institutions as a common group and higher education in general rather than the needs or requests of particular units.

Other institutions improved on the analysis of cost and budget considerations to include inter-institutional faculty salary comparisons (University of Puerto Rico), non-instructional unit cost estimates and budgeting (University of California), and facilities planning (Wisconsin State College System). In addition, the contributors extended the portfolio of institutional research to encompass effectiveness studies for the advancement of continuous improvements locally but also as generalizable knowledge on higher education in the areas of gender equity (University of Wisconsin), independent studies courses (Antioch College), and the use of prediction versus actual grade-point averages to identify inequities in grading by departments and faculty (Saint Louis University). In short, a spectrum of reporting, planning, and effectiveness studies in the portfolio of institutional research emerged in only a few short years following the University of Minnesota disclosure of its studies for wider scrutiny and application.

Although each article did not provide a detailed history of the institution's research functions, several references confirm that presidents formed offices of institutional research locally to supplement less trustworthy results from ad hoc committees or projects. In the opening piece of the Lins volume, Loring M. Thompson of Northeastern University (Boston) indicates that the profession "may be traced back to self-studies of academic programs by faculties and faculty committees," but that the purview broadened to include "enrollments and prospective enrollments" in response to the populous baby boomers who followed "a temporary valley [in enrollments] because of the small number of births during the depression eighteen years earlier."[19]

More specifically, though, Thompson draws a connection for the advancements of institutional research to the partnerships among higher education, government, and the private sector as in other industries such as "automation, space travel, and communications." Considered as a similar class of industry-academic partnerships, Thompson regarded the progress of institutional research as "a movement...for universities to study themselves and to plan consciously for changes within themselves." Offices of institutional research, in this vein, "expected to make studies about the university itself" and "serve university presidents and faculty committees, providing a current, rational basis for leadership in education."

By the early 1960s, the offices had also reached a level of sophistication to consider forming standard methods and replicable approaches to the practice of self-study. The contributors from DePaul University carefully defined institutional research and "its purposes so it may be related to research as it is traditionally understood...just as scientific investigation in the natural and social sciences." In that respect, the authors asserted, institutional research had to deliver more than "empirical evidence and method, but also the primary objective of true research: a contribution to theoretical knowledge." The inquiry may "be pursued on a single institutional level," but the investigators must also design research "that can be replicated and which can, therefore, be broadened to an inter-institutional inquiry."[20] Within this scientific-inspired framework, these early scholars recognized that no one college or university proved capable of providing the answers to the research questions raised by their particular institutions.

Despite producing only three significant publications covering a span of twenty-five years, the first bureaus of institutional research appear to encapsulate the guiding principles identified by the National Research Council for scientific inquiry in education. In the final years of the era, the bureaus and offices posed significant questions linked to theory, investigated empirically, and endeavored to provide explicit reasoning for their findings. The University of Minnesota and the Lins collection disclosed research to encourage scrutiny, critique, replication, and generalization from individual studies. Individually, the institutional research programs of the offices appeared to grow organically as if from the particular problems or interests of the college or university. Collectively, through publication, the researchers began to unfold a conceptual framework for the scientific study of higher education underlying the formation of their new administrative offices.

Always a Fruitful Source of Questions

The original institutional research studies at colleges and universities testified to the critical roles of presidential leadership for the establishment of centralized offices for the accumulation of generalizable knowledge about higher education and the advancement of literature on effective college administration. At the time, no standards or specifications for the collection of statistical information regarding college and universities existed. The administrative officers defined studies according to the research question and the application of findings in terms of their serviceability for the institution and for the president.

Despite these parochial interests, these programs of institutional research began to spiral into investigations on more and more facets of college and university settings. The publications themselves, addressed not to their presidents but to those in higher education generally, signify the moments when the research questions no longer could be answered satisfactorily by self-study alone. Unlike Griffith's 1938 article and Eckert and Keller's 1954 collection, both of which remained anchored to the institutional research of a single institution, the Lins volume from 1962 demonstrated how institutional self-study at twenty different colleges and universities necessarily expanded the scope of inquiry to address questions that coalesced into the framework for an institutionalized system of inquiry into higher education.

Figure 1 presents the original research contributions by the first bureaus and offices of institutional research as recorded in the publications. At the University of Illinois, for which Griffith only provided a synopsis of activities, the various studies mentioned indicate that its portfolio of institutional research already broke ground for a number of projects that individual colleges and universities engage in—and still struggle to engage in—today. For the University of Minnesota, Eckert and Keller provided detailed chapters on each of the studies undertaken. Shared in greater detail, the Minnesota studies step beyond the practical concerns with data and facts to include questions of equity in grading, faculty development, learning outcomes directly correlated with labs, and the prediction of student academic success. Finally, the Lins collection constitutes a dialogue between institutional researchers from almost two dozen colleges and universities. In an endeavor to communicate research findings to each other, the contributors' descriptions of their studies paid greater attention to theory, design principles, phenomena, and mode of argument—replicating the style of writing associated with social scientific articles.

FIGURE 1 | PORTFOLIOS OF INSTITUTIONAL RESEARCH IN PUBLICATIONS FROM 1938, 1954, AND 1962

U. of Illinois (1938)	U. of Minnesota (1954)	Various Univs. (1962)
• Academic Program Benchmarks / Reviews	• Enrollment Trend Projections	• Faculty Salary Benchmarking (Inter-Institutional)
• Longitudinal Studies of Unit Costs and Student Credit Hour Productivity	• Student Geographic Origins	• Mission Review and Development
• Classroom Space Utilization	• Non-Enrollment of Applicants and Student Attrition	• Instructional and Non-Instructional Cost Analysis
• Allocations of Instruction by Class Level	• Grade Practices and Equity	• Curriculum Forecasting
• Faculty Loads by Rank and Class Level	• Curriculum Development's Relationship to Enrollments	• Faculty Satisfaction Surveys
• Quality of Teaching (Student Learning Outcomes)	• Follow-up Studies of Baccalaureates and PhDs	• Facilities Utilization
• Enrollment Projections	• Vocational, Accelerated, and Professional Program Evaluations	• Student Social, Financial, and Parental Backgrounds
• Institutional History	• Faculty Development	• Optimization of Applicant Fees
• Education Policy Research	• Learning Outcomes of Labs and Communication Skills	• Gender Equity in Education
• Budget and Other Resource Allocations	• Predicting Academic Success	• Freshman Motivations for Attending College
	• Student Evaluations	• Automation in Institutional Research

Portfolios of Institutional Research

While the imitation of a formal writing style in itself could not transform self-study into social science, the underlying mutation associated with the centralization of institutional research in administrative offices produced that effect in a few phases. In the first phase, institutional research enlists individual programs and departments in order to convince unit leaders to recognize how their discrete responsibilities fit the institution as a whole. In the second phase, institutional research engages the institution as a whole into the study of statewide or national conditions to plan and coordinate the organization and administration of higher education. In the final phase, institutional research fosters collaboration in multi-institutional investigations that require a degree of autonomous agency for these offices to enable contributions to theoretical and/or generalizable knowledge about higher education.

Ernst Nagel states a general prerequisite for the accumulation of knowledge in his philosophy of science: "[T]he organization and classification of knowledge on the basis of explanatory principles...is the distinctive goal of the sciences." The same principle is evident in the National Research Council's (NRC) monograph on scientific research in education. Invoking "the metaphor of 'accumulating' knowledge," the authors aim to call to mind two features of scientific knowledge: "First, it suggests that scientific understanding coalesces, as it progresses, to make sense of systems, experiences, and phenomena. The imagery also connotes the idea that scientific inquiry builds on the work that has preceded it." In both Nagel's and the NRC's distinct terms, the unprecedented work and publications stemming directly from the studies conducted by centralized administrative offices of institutional research meet the basic tenet for scientific inquiry.[21]

The NRC monograph deploys its premises for scientific knowledge as the foundation for the three types of questions that research on education, in general, pose: "description—What is happening? cause—Is there a systemic effect? and process or mechanism—Why or how is it happening?" Under the first type, education research focuses on measurement of the basic characteristics of students, institutions, theory development, various indicators of performance, and associations or correlations among variables. The second type of research question seeks to discover causal understanding—"Does x cause y?"—to determine whether specified or theorized inputs may change outcomes. The third type of research question, assuming the discovery of causal relationships, then addresses the process or mechanism through which x produces y. The formalization and specificity of research questions stand at the heart of a scientific progress and defines the program of research that stimulates the accumulation of knowledge and calibrates new questions to investigate.[22]

As illustrated in figure 2, the research subjects and questions posed by offices of institutional research between the 1930s and early 1960s fit the typology for scientific research questions in education. The research from the 1920s and 1930s established methods to define, specify, and measure student characteristics and program performance. The efforts initiated a portfolio of research on higher education that inescapably referred back to its prior research and exposed new questions for investigation. By the early 1960s, the basic measures to understand "what is happening" in higher education had become "routine" and offices of institutional research moved forward to investigate "more significant" questions on behalf of administration and faculty (Fordham, 1962). The ability of institutional researchers to provide answers increased proportionally, and, though confused with the interests of particular institutions, the ready availability of tested methodologies and study designs pressed new research questions to the foreground.

FIGURE 2 | PROGRESSION OF INSTITUTIONAL RESEARCH ALONG THE SPECTRUM OF SCIENTIFIC RESEARCH QUESTIONS

Descriptive/Correlates	Systemic/Causal	Mechanism/Process
• FTE Staff	• Enrollment Trend Projections	• Enrollments Forecasting with Variable Parameters
• SCH per FTE Staff	• Inter-rater Reliability and Validity of Grading Practices	• Effect of Relaxing General Requirements on Course-Taking Behaviors
• Faculty Load	• Reasons for Attendance / Choice of College	
• Student Credit Load		
• Unit Cost	• Applicant Behavior based on Application Fee Amount	• Predicted Academic Success
• Student Demographics	• Characteristics and Causes of Retention / Attrition	• Predicting Medical School Success to Plan Admissions
– Gender		• Learning Outcomes by Physics Students by Lab Experiments vs. Lecture Demonstrations with Semi-Randomized Control Group
– Race / Ethnicity	• Level of Occupation by Gender and Degree Status	
– First Generation		
– Geographic Origin	• Pre- and Post-Testing Learning Outcomes in General Education	• Pre- and Post-Testing Learning Outcomes in Independent Studies with Control Groups
• Cost Deviations		
• Classroom Utilization	• Change in Attitudes toward Psychiatry Associated with Program Intervention	• Predicted vs. Actual First-Year GPAs to Determine Inequities in Grading by Academic Departments
• Learning Outcomes by Pace of Curriculum Innovation		
• Curriculum Development Correlation to Enrollments		

Progression of Institutional Research

Questions, not answers, ensure the progress of a social science. As Coleman Griffith modestly noted in 1938, "The data collected by a self-appraising agency do not often answer any questions of education policy, but they are always a fruitful source of questions."[23] By the 1950s, bureaus of institutional research welcomed the responsibility to answer questions of educational policy and reached a level of sophistication in some areas of investigation to pose fruitful questions to direct further investigations. At the conclusion of a review of graduate students in the education program by the bureau at the University of Minnesota, the author concludes, "The findings of this study highlight the need for searching studies of the long-term outcomes of graduate instruction. The study report…represents a first attempt in this direction."[24] By the early 1960s, the offices of institutional research represented in Lin's edited volume devise more rigorous research designs and conduct more studies necessitating specialization and an understanding of prior findings, resulting in the need for (more) full-time, specialized staff in an administrative capacity. The introduction by Loring M. Thompson foresees institutional research "able to make long range studies and come to grips with methods for teaching creativity as well as academic excellence...long-term studies of the whole educational process."[25]

In effect, institutional studies changed over time from the study of an institution to the study of higher education in general, that is, from self-study to social science. The key "organizational device" in this transformation was the administrative office of institutional research: born out of the self-study of institutions but nonetheless borne out by the principles and practices of scientific research about higher education. At its origins, the practice of institutional research was no less entangled in a growing web of external surveys and data requests defined by government agencies, accreditors, policy-makers and institutional stakeholders. Yet in the hopeful and future-oriented perspective of the early practitioners, the demands for a better understanding of effective higher education administration called for the development of institutional research as a social science.

Coordinated and Systematic Conduct of Studies Needed for Institutional Improvement

James I. Doi, then director of institutional research and professor of higher education at New York University, presented a "conceptual framework" for the profession at the Fourth National Institutional Research Forum in 1964. Recognizing the field's links to the nation's largest public and private institutions, he generalized five propositions regarding the origins of the emerging profession:

> 1) the evolution of institutions of higher education from small, relatively simple organizations to large-scale, complex organizations essentially bureaucratic in structure and mode of operation; 2) the emergence of a new style of administration...described as scientific; 3) the evolution of institutional research as a form of organization behavior characterized by sporadic studies and collections of data to that characterized by coordinated and systematic conduct of studies needed for institutional improvement; 4) the emergence of institutional research specialists; and 5) the professionalization of these men [sic].[26]

Doi emphasized the order of the propositions "intended to suggest that each succeeding development is a consequence of the preceding development." The centralized institutional research office emerges in conjunction with "the change in the nature of IR [institutional research] as a form of organization behavior." He acknowledges "institutional research as an organizational function has been and continues to be administration-oriented" while maintaining a commitment to science and generalizable knowledge (proposition 2). He then characterized the main challenge facing institutional research: "[The] total institutional commitment on the part of both faculty and administration to the use of knowledge as the basis for decision-making has yet to evolve."[27]

The first publications on institutional research evidence the accumulation of knowledge about higher education to a point that proved to be no longer manageable in terms of self-study. The first bureaus and offices advanced a portfolio of institutional research that had the potential to form into a scientific study of higher education and its administration. Then, drawing from training in their primary disciplines, the authors who contributed the first articles on institutional research activities adhered to the writing style of social science to convey theoretical premises, explanatory principles, and the accumulation of knowledge. Moving away from implicit engagement with theory to explicit statements of theory and explanatory principles, the articles expose the search for a paradigm of institutional research as social science among its earliest practitioners.

Yet, as Doi noted, the challenge for institutional research was twofold at its origin: institutional research must deliver results to be applied by administrators and faculty while also conforming to the structure of a social science in order to disseminate reliable and valid evidence for generalizable knowledge. On the one hand, the nature of the work pushed the professionals in the direction of an institutionalized system of inquiry to advance theorizing and scientific study of higher education. On the other hand, if the progress of a science depends largely on its community as the NRC suggests, the success of institutional research as a social science in part depended on the ability of its practitioners to engage administrators, staff, and faculty at large to form into a community for the study of higher education. This is to say that it was not the nature, the role, or the function of institutional research that would make possible or limit its progress as social science—that must be determined by which type of community emerged for the scientific study of higher education.

3 | ESSENTIAL FOR EFFICIENT AND ECONOMICAL EDUCATIONAL PROCEDURES

Linkages between Institutional Research Offices and Statewide Coordination

The formal organization of institutional research offices and the initial steps by the practitioners to form a community of professionals coincided with the effort of state, regional, and national organizations to advance the field. Although particular institutions accelerated the practices and program of institutional research prior to 1955, the movement of the field from self-study to social science corresponded to state, system, and national influences on the application of institutional research to coordinate higher education policy-making and long-range planning. Whereas the bureaus and offices initiated organically during the Survey Era with the shared spirit of scientific research on higher education, after 1955, regional and national associations formally advocated for the centralization of institutional research consonant with the precedents set at the Universities of Illinois and Minnesota.

In a brief historical account of the professional development of institutional research up to 1979, James I. Doi noted that the "linkages between institutional research offices and statewide coordination go back to the mid-1950s." Doi served under John Dale Russell, the executive of the state board in New Mexico who first organized meetings between the executive officers of the statewide boards then in existence. In New Mexico, Russell and Doi developed "systematic data collection and analysis" to coordinate policy making for the state board in 1954. The statewide research encompassed analyses refined in the prior decades of the Survey Era, including studies of faculty workloads and unit costs. After Doi left to support the Colorado statewide council, he "replicated many of the same studies with minor modifications." By 1960, he estimated that a dozen states had performed similar studies for their higher education systems.[1]

While Doi's experience and memories feature the influence of Russell and New Mexico on state-board research, other states—California in particular—had already engaged in such studies or did so concurrently. Statewide, regional, and national reports from the era demonstrate the synergy between the formation of institutional research offices and the advancement of research on higher education in general. In some respects, the research agendas directed by statewide boards, professional associations, and accrediting bodies opened institutions to the possibility of centralized offices for inter-institutional studies. The studies on California higher education during the era exemplify the standardization of institutional research and its potential to transcend self-study.

In 1954–55, Thomas R. McConnell led a statewide "restudy" to update "the needs of California in higher education" for the entire system. McConnell, a former dean at the University of Minnesota in the 1930s and 1940s, delivered the 1955 restudy report including comprehensive analyses on enrollment projections to 1970, on institutional types and class levels, class size by program, space utilization, revenue estimates from taxes and fees, and expense projections based on unit costs by class level and institution type. McConnell's report recommended that "a comprehensive review of the entire field should be made in 1960," anticipating the 1960 Master Plan for Higher Education in California. The connections run much deeper, in fact, and the 1960 Master Plan, widely lauded as a model of higher education organization on the state level, to a large degree marks accomplishments resulting from the proliferation of statewide institutional research studies.[2]

The California example demonstrates how the nascent field extended its reach beyond the confines of the discrete, local institutions and joined with statewide communities brought together by the goal of coordinated policy making and long-term planning. In this respect, institutional research as a field of study for higher education did not arise simply due to the size and complexity of individual institutions but in response to the massification of higher education and the perceived priorities of American democracy as advanced by the Truman Commission's Report. The conditions in turn influenced the extent to which institutional research professionals would evolve into a multiplicity of regional policy-making communities or into a professional, scientific community. These two priorities—policy making versus scientific investigation—at times came into conflict, of course, and exerted pressure on the emerging community for research on higher education to choose between two distinct paths forward.

A Careful Review of Administrative Policies in Institutions of Higher Education

In 1947, the Truman Commission released its report, *Higher Education for American Democracy*, calling for more deliberate integration of higher education with the "guiding principles and ultimate goals" of American democracy. Led by George F. Zook, then president of the American Council on Education (ACE), the report proposed a fundamental difference between "the social role" of higher education in an authoritarian or a democratic society. As the principal goal of higher education, the commission declared, "Education for a fuller realization of democracy in every phase of living." Accordingly, institutional, association, state, and federal leaders had a responsibility to "see clearly...the same general ends" of higher education to advance American democracy.[3]

Among the goals, the Truman Commission called for universal access to higher education, with a commitment to personal freedom, adjusted to the needs of the individual, and a social role in the nation. Higher education required a new paradigm in which it was not "merely the instrument for producing an intellectual elite...but the means by which every citizen...is enabled and encouraged to carry his education...as far as his native capacities permit." In order to achieve these goals, the report suggests that classroom teaching and discussions were not sufficient: "Democracy must be lived to be thoroughly understood." To that end, the Truman Commission recommended "a careful review of administrative policies in institutions of higher education."[4]

In the third volume, the Truman Commission called for more effective organization of higher education. Acknowledging that colleges and universities directed their activities "almost totally independent" of each other to that point in American history, "the time has come when more coordinated planning among all of the institutions on a State as well as a national basis, is imperative." In the spirit of its goals, the report recommended more leadership through the adoption of statewide boards to facilitate planning and administration. The statewide boards may address several difficulties in the organization of higher education, such as affording the means "to carry on the necessary continuing studies...[for] a comprehensive and flexible program in higher education." The state programs could then "be coordinated with Federal research programs." As an illustration, the sixth volume of the 1947 report provided a compendium of tables on the data used to support the Truman Commission's recommendations.[5]

Although the Truman Commission did not foster federal legislation or action directly in support of its goals and recommendations, the report influenced the direction of research on higher education within a decade. At the heart of the critique of higher education advanced by the Truman Commission, the individual institutions of higher education proved incapable of advancing the democratic principles and values of the American nation on their own accord. As John Dale Russell wrote in his capacity as the director of the Division of Higher Education, US Office of Education, "To put [the Truman Commission's] recommendations into effect will challenge the best efforts of American educators and statesmen."[6] To that end, the state and federal governments exercised necessary powers when they held public colleges and universities accountable to the citizenry as a whole.

In 1954, after becoming the head of the state board in New Mexico, Russell accepted the challenge put to statewide boards to plan and oversee policies in higher education. In that year, he organized the first meetings of the State Higher Education Executive Officers Association (SHEEO). Paul E. Lingenfeter notes that the origins of state policy leadership for higher education in the 1950s may be traced directly to the Truman Commission. The state boards increasingly faced an important question related to the public and private benefit of higher education in America, as raised by the commission: "what is the proper relationship between accountability to the public interest and the traditional freedoms of the academy?"[7] The challenge increasingly confronted the states that expected the enrollment demands of the young baby boomer generation to tax the physical plant and faculty resources available at the time.

As Doi recalled, state boards conducted institutional research in order to permit comparative studies on public institutions defined in part by the democratic principles invoked by the Truman Commission. In this respect, the encouragement for statewide or national institutional research served to coordinate higher education institutions for "the same general ends." By the early 1960s, large states had committed to "statewide planning and coordination" to some degree. Although Russell and Doi's work in New Mexico proved seminal for the organization of state boards, the state of California perhaps best illustrates how the practice of institutional research intersected with a state policy-making community as envisioned in the Truman Commission's report.

The state of California conducted a follow-up study, or restudy, on the needs of Californians for higher education in 1954–55. The original report from 1948, the Strayer Committee Report, committed California to a three-segment system of public higher education: the University of California, the state colleges, and the junior colleges. The Strayer report, however, predated the increased birth rates following World War II that resulted in the baby boomers and the establishment of several new colleges following its recommendations. The scope of the 1955 restudy focused on updating "certain data found in the 1948 report" and in supplemental documentation, as well as a reconsideration of the recommendations from the Strayer Committee "in the light of present and projected enrollments, economic conditions, needs for trained personnel in the State, and the like."[8]

The opening paragraphs on the origin, plan, and scope of the restudy emphasized that it was not "a completely new one, but a re-examination and extension of the Strayer Committee Report of 1948." The restudy staff nonetheless featured personnel with deep ties to scientific study of higher education administration, institutional research and the Truman Commission. George D. Strayer, who headed the 1948 report, was himself an accomplished scholar who advanced quantitative and scientific studies of education administration during the Progressive Era.[9] The restudy's approach insured continuity with Strayer's approach to higher education administration. Thomas R. McConnell, chief consultant for the 1955 restudy staff, served on the Committee of Institutional Research at the University of Minnesota in his capacity as the dean of the College of Science, Literature, and the Arts during the mid-1940s. McConnell subsequently served on the Truman Commission under Chairman Zook in 1947 and penned an impassioned defense of the commission report.[10]

His restudy team also included the counsel of Floyd W. Reeves, the pioneering researcher of higher education from the University of Chicago during the Survey Era, as well as John Dale Russell, a former student and long-time colleague of Reeves, who as mentioned headed the statewide research efforts for the Board of Educational Finance in New Mexico at the time. McConnell, Reeves, and Russell delivered an uncommon level of experience with institutional studies and interstate collaboration for the measure of higher education activity in California. The 1955 restudy thus paid greater attention to the methods and rigor of the research performed in comparison to the 1948 study, as well as prior uncoordinated higher education studies across the state.

In the discussion of enrollments in the state, the 1955 restudy considered the measurement of enrollments as a class of facts that needed to be defined by a common standard. Noting that different institutions or types of institutions employed "variously defined terms and figures," the restudy staff discovered "three enrollment totals for California's public and private institutions of higher education...for 1951" from government reports: 144,163, 188,068, or 270,639 students. Confronted by the variance in the estimated number of enrollments, the 1955 restudy committee determined that "differences in definitions of 'student' account for almost all discrepancies in the figures." To impose rigor on the statistics collected from institutions around the state and "determine as accurately as possible teaching loads and building utilization," the restudy directors provided a formal definition of full-time and part-time undergraduate students, full-time and part-time graduate students, and the full-time equivalent enrollments.[11]

Similarly, the 1955 report explicitly described the definitions, data, and methods necessary to estimate the physical plants at the state's colleges and universities. Notably, the restudy gave special consideration for the comparison of capacity and utilization, and then provided sufficient detail regarding the research process to make possible replication in the collection of "data required" and "procedures" for calculating "the over-all net square feet of floor space per FTE student" in the various instructional activities. By comparison, the 1948 Strayer Committee Report did not exhibit the same attention to detail regarding the measurement of enrollments or plant utilization in the state's colleges and universities. In this respect, both the enrollment and physical plant chapters from the report move beyond the provision of results and recommendations to include the research parameters and methods adopted by the committee.

Lastly, the restudy introduced a unit-expense data analysis absent from the Strayer report. Citing the guidance provided by Thad L. Hungate in his work on "unit costs and his discussion of their values in *Finance in Educational Management of Colleges and Universities*,"[12] the committee undertook a statewide review of college expenditures in the system. Prior studies used the gross expenditures for an activity without standardization for "the number of persons served or the number of persons providing the service." The unit-cost analysis permitted the restudy team to provide more refined analysis and comparisons "in terms of the number of student-credit-hours taught per full-time-equivalent staff member, which is also a method of measuring teaching load." Across the state system, then, the restudy researchers devised a method to measure the economies of scale for college and university operations.

With this added rigor, the 1955 restudy found "a positive correlation between unit expenditures and size of institution," that also corresponded to their locations near large population centers. The unit-cost analysis provided insight into the efficient growth opportunities for the California state colleges. For instance, the report considered that new institutions would also have to be placed near these population centers in order to enjoy the cost efficiencies. Where real estate values may prove cost prohibitive, the report suggested building multistory structures. Given these conditions, the report noted that that the existing campuses could be upgraded and expanded at lower costs to the system than additional new institutions requiring "a proportionate increase in general operating and administrative costs."

The restudy committee also reported that it found no "conclusive evidence" that the size of institution diminished the quality of instruction or student welfare, as the prior 1947 Strayer Committee's report had presumed. For California students outside the population centers of established colleges and universities, the committee noted its plan for scholarships and dormitories as an equalizer in opportunity for students throughout the state. As a result of the analysis and socioeconomic environment, the restudy committee "therefore recommended that no new state colleges and no new campuses of the University of California be established before 1965 and that the potential enrollment be cared for by expanding the facilities of the present institutions." On the recommendation of the restudy report, the regents of the University of California and the State Board of Education adopted a state-level resolution to expand the existing colleges and universities in California until 1965 rather than establish new institutions.

Notably, the joint staff understood its restudy as a form of "institutional research." Under the recommendations for the organization of administration at the University of California, the restudy team pointed out the need for an Office of Institutional Research "responsible to the President's office." To perform its research, the study group relied on special assistants to the presidents who were "ordinarily concerned with immediate problems and often with emergency matters." While the proposal attached no administrative function to the new office, the description of its activities suggested an ongoing and institutionalized system of inquiry for state coordination of higher education:

> Studies concerned with long-term development of the University and with the co-ordination of its varied and widely dispersed educational programs are crucial to the University's future growth. Furthermore, there is need for continuing collection of statistical data on such matters as class size, teaching loads, and faculty services as a basis for educational planning and budget making. There is no office adequately equipped and staffed for assembling these data. There is now no agency to which faculty committees or educational officers can turn for expert assistance in planning and conducting research on such matters as prediction of success in various curricula, standards and procedures for admission, problems of curriculum and instruction, and methods of evaluating educational achievement. Such studies are essential for efficient and economical educational procedures.[13]

In this respect, the restudy team understood collaborative institutional research as a crucial agency for the continuing enhancement and improvement of state higher education and higher education administration in the spirit of the Truman Commission.

Lastly, then, the most salient recommendation of the restudy committee for the direction of higher education in California can be found in its decision to call for a new study in 1960: "Because of the scope and complexities in the field of higher education in California a comprehensive review of the entire field should be made in 1960." The recommendation encompassed the establishment of new state colleges and university campuses after 1965. Therein, the restudy committee set the table for the California Master Plan of 1960, the most comprehensive plan for a state's higher education system ever undertaken by a US state.

The recommendations and resolutions stemming from the restudy signaled the ability of statewide institutional research to influence policy making at many institutions at once. The research team imposed common standards for reporting by the institutions, described the data collection and methodology in order to facilitate future replications of the research, and stated the assumptions and evidence for the recommendations delivered to the state agencies for higher education. To the extent that the regents and state board endorsed the recommendations made by the restudy, the application of institutional research methods to state-level studies marked a key shift in higher education decision-making from the individual institutions to the state. To this extent, the restudy marked a momentous shift toward accountability to the public interests over the autonomy of colleges and universities by making individual institutions assume the role of parts in the whole of state higher education.

Whether to Rely on a Plan, or on "Guidance," or on Atomistic Competition

The restudy recommendations, however, did not fully align with the perceived interests of state constituents and institutional stakeholders. Although the regents and state board adopted the resolution to postpone examination of the need for new institutions of higher education in California until 1960 from the report, state legislators in 1955 approved eight studies regarding the establishment of additional higher education institutions in several regions of California. In this respect, the restudy committee had mistaken the immense public interest in local access to higher education. In January 1956, the Liaison Committee of the State Board of Education and the regents of the University of California acknowledged this shortcoming and charged the joint staff to conduct a new study on the need for new public institutions of higher education in California.

The resulting 1957 report, *A Study of the Need for Additional Centers of Public Higher Education in California*, occurred three years earlier than recommended by the restudy committee.[14] The new study cited five reasons for its break from the proposal submitted only two years earlier: new enrollment forecasts, new data and procedures for estimating the effects of new institutions, legislation calling for studies of eight separate locations, concerns about the ability to expand existing campuses, and unmet student needs in the three-segment system of higher education in California. The legislative actions primarily drove the effort as a comprehensive report on the need for new institutions mitigated the potential inconsistencies and errors stemming from possibly eight separate reports on the needs of the regions of California.

Despite the influence of legislative and political forces that reversed the recommendations from the restudy, the 1957 team largely relied on the statistical work of the previous report while modifying certain assumptions that accommodated the need for additional centers. The 1955 restudy calculations for the expenses per full-time equivalent student in the state colleges established a minimum projected enrollment for new state colleges of "2,000 full-time equivalents of regular...students, after five years of full operation (freshman through graduate classes)." The minimum reflected the judgment of the joint staff that larger student bodies delivered a diminishing return on costs per full-time equivalent student based on the populations reported for eight state colleges in the 1955 restudy (table 53).

With that standard in hand, the committee projected enrollments for thirteen areas in the state of California and identified nine areas that could potentially meet the minimum criteria for a new state college by 1965. Significantly, the projections assumed that "[a]dequate junior college facilities *will precede* additional state college facilities," accounting for enrollments in two of the three segments of California higher education. Per its charge, the report projected the effect of the new state colleges on enrollments at the existing colleges both with and without the additional state colleges. The resulting analysis (table 14, 1957 *Study*) estimated that the state college system would be able to educate approximately 35 percent more students by 1965 if the state established nine additional state colleges in the areas capable of meeting the minimum enrollment standard of two thousand full-time equivalent students.

The joint staff further determined that the University of California should add three additional campuses in order to serve the state population more fully, adopting two thousand as the minimum and ten thousand full-time equivalent students as the target for a "full-scale" university campus. This conclusion, however, reintroduced the assumption that the maximum size of a campus in the University of California system should be near twenty-five thousand students: "it can be assumed that a full-time enrollment on a single existing campus of the University of California that substantially exceeds 25,000 students would tax campus facilities to the point of requiring expansion of a magnitude equal to that of establishing a new campus."[15] As the enrollment projections suggested that both the Berkeley and Los Angeles campuses would likely exceed that maximum by 1965, the 1957 report recommended two new campuses near the population centers, expansion of the existing services near San Diego, and a third potential campus for the San Joaquin Valley.[16]

In its estimate of costs with and without the additional state colleges, the report noted that the difference in full-time equivalent students "represents the number of students who probably would not attend a state college at all if the new institutions are not established." Thus, though the capital outlays and yearly operating expenses for the state increased with the additional state colleges, the large student population signified an "increase in the equality of educational opportunity brought about by placing state college facilities closer to students' homes." The proposed University of California campuses encapsulated the goal of access while also seeking to limit the size of campuses near the largest population centers.

Given this priority, enrollment projections for the entire state served to link the practice and methods of institutional research directly to the goals for coordinating higher education administration in the interest of American democracy as outlined by the Truman Commission. The prerequisite for a junior college to service an area before breaking ground on a new state college guaranteed local access to higher education throughout the state. The 1957 analysis in support of new state colleges based on a formula to maximize college attendance while reasonably managing costs by setting lower-bound targets for campus enrollments then guaranteed broad regional access to advanced fields and degrees. Lastly, the upper-bound limit on the enrollments at University of California campuses established the argument for additional campuses in new areas rather than unlimited and vertical expansion at the legacy campuses. By 1958, backed by an analysis more in tune with the political realities of a democratic society and an expansive geography, the legislature adopted the recommendations of 1957 *Study,* approving four new state colleges and three new campuses for the University of California.

The Master Plan for Higher Education in California, 1960–1975, then capped the era of coordinated institutional research and policy recommendations for the state's higher education system. The California Master Plan has been called "the blueprint for carrying out the mandate for coherence and cooperation" envisioned by the Truman Commission's report as well as the embodiment of "the California Idea...combin[ing] excellence with access and equality of opportunity in the service of state, society, and economy."[17] In addition, Clark Kerr, then president of the University of California who led the Master Plan Survey Team, has been credited for his masterful political leadership in bringing together the disparate stakeholders in the California higher education system to pursue a common goal.

Kerr himself popularized the political challenges in later years, defining "five central issues" addressed by the Master Plan: "(1) How to satisfy the egalitarian imperative, (2) how to satisfy the meritocratic imperative, (3) which institutions should be used to satisfy those imperatives, (4) whether to rely on a plan, or on 'guidance,' or on atomistic competition, and (5) how much should be controlled by higher education itself and how much by the state."[18] Kerr's emphasis, like other scholars', directs attention to the numerous claims and compromises made by stakeholders in California higher education that brought the California Idea to fruition. From these two vantages, cultural values and political savvy appeared to converge to produce the 1960 California Master Plan.

The statewide institutional research studies from the years immediately preceding the 1960 Master Plan, however, have been less well-regarded for their formative contributions. By 1959, when the California legislature authorized the State Board of Education and the regents of the University of California to produce a report on the future of higher education in the state, the joint staff to the Liaison Committee had been in continuous study of higher education in the state for almost five years.[19] The statewide institutional research activities had produced institutional data and resources to provide ample direction for the development of a master plan, as proposed by the restudy in 1955. The opening paragraph on the organization and plan of the 1960 survey acknowledges that "many of the recommendations contained in this report are either direct outgrowths of earlier studies or extensions of recommendations found in such studies." For instance, the Master Plan simply endorsed the authorizations of the new campuses arising from the previous studies while calling for more centers of higher education based on the analysis or analytical methods developed by previous studies.

The influence of the prior reports and recommendations of the board and regents also afforded valuable insights on the political reaction of the various stakeholders associated with the future of higher education in California. For this reason, the Master Plan marks the culmination of efforts to integrate institutional research with statewide higher education policy and planning. The priority of political compromise in the 1960 plan reflects, on the one hand, the extent to which prior institutional research had settled questions about the nature and class of facts relevant to higher education in California. On the other hand, the number of policy and planning questions regarding the state's higher education system seemed to multiply with each new report. In other words, the state had moved from questions of how to conduct the research to questions of how to apply the research for the coordination and improvement of its higher education system.

As the Master Plan explained, the California legislature introduced "23 bills in 1959, three resolutions and two constitutional amendments designed (a) either to establish or to study the need for new institutions, (b) change the functions of the existing institutions, and (c) change the present structure for the organization, control, and administration of publicly supported higher education in the state." Given the mounting legislative activity for particular higher education interests, the California legislature resolved to have prepared a master plan for higher education in the state. Given little more than six months to complete a master plan, the Survey Team relied on prior institutional research where possible or adopted less rigorous research protocols when necessary in order to complete its work. In either case, these shortcuts for the preparation of the 1960 Master Plan would not have been possible without the experience and evidence provided by prior statewide institutional studies.

In general, rather than technical questions of measurement and comparability, the Master Plan then was able to emphasize the extrinsic relationships between the three segments of higher education in California, the autonomy of individual institutions, and "the diverse higher educational services needed by the state." To this end, its proposals for "the structure, function, and coordination" concentrated on the deduplication or "unwarranted expansion" of higher education programming on a statewide basis to achieve "maximum quality at minimum costs." The third chapter, the first to offer substantial new analysis and recommendations, attempted to delimit the "machinery for governing state-supported higher education," including the appropriate types of governing boards, the responsibilities centralized in statewide offices, the educational functions of the three segments, and acceptable terms for state coordination.

While the full details of the Master Plan fall beyond the scope of this work, the proposal provided a basis for understanding the nature of higher education in California, from two-year technical training to multiyear professional education. The report also defined distinct responsibilities for the three segments—the University of California, state colleges, and junior colleges—in the delivery of higher education to the state population. The remainder of the Master Plan then presents the statewide institutional research conducted to support the concrete recommendations to meet the diverse higher education needs of the state. Essentially, then, the bulk of the report updated higher education measures established in prior studies: enrollment projections, student quality, institutional capacity and utilization, faculty supply and demand, unit costs and expenditures, and anticipated revenue from state resources.

Chapters IV and V of the Master Plan consider students in terms of "the problem of numbers" and "the problem of quality." Whereas the 1957 *Study* resolved, to a degree, the need for additional centers in order to maximize access and the equality of opportunity, the Master Plan examined enrollment projections largely in terms of adequate distribution of students across the three segments of higher education. The status quo projections, assuming no new state colleges or campuses then already approved by 1957, painted a dire picture for several institutions: "unless present enrollment trends are modified in some way, there will result within a few years grave overcrowding of site capacity on certain state college and University of California campuses." To manage growth at the flagship university campuses and state colleges, the Master Plan proposed redirecting fifty thousand "lower division students" from the state colleges and university to the junior college system by 1975 in order to allow these two segments "to concentrate more of their resources on the upper division, and graduate students."

Closely related to the redistribution of lower division students to junior colleges, the chapter on student quality examined the "validity" of student admission standards, academic performance, and retention—as stated, "selection and retention loomed large" for the Survey Team. To its disappointment, "the data made available to the Survey Team by the three public segments fall far short of the completeness desired for judging the validity of admissions requirements." As a result, the Master Plan called for all three segments to conduct studies and report statistics for the validity of their entrance requirements "judged by (a) scholastic success, (b) persistence, (c) rate of dismissal, and (d) scores on standard tests."

The Survey Team, nonetheless, oversaw an examination of college transcripts to inform the Master Plan. The evaluation suggested that the current standards for admissions to the University of California and the state colleges yielded questionable results as many students failed to achieve a B average in their first year. As a key component of the Master Plan called for the establishment of junior colleges in every area of the state, the Survey Team recommended that the admissions criteria for four-year institutions become more restrictive. Based on the analysis of grade outcomes in the four-year institutions, the Master Plan recommended that 100 percent of the state's high school graduates be eligible for junior colleges, 33.3 percent eligible for state colleges (down from 50 percent), and 12.5 percent for the University of California (down from 15 percent). The proposed admission requirements supported the redistribution of lower division students from the state colleges and university to the junior colleges, as the adjusted enrollment projections targeted.

With the rationalization of the three-tier system and the enrollment projections settled, the Master Plan could then focus on the resources necessary to deliver on the framework of the plan. The remaining chapters returned to subjects addressed by previous institutional research studies: physical plant capacity and utilization, faculty supply and demand, adult education, and unit costs to estimate the necessary expenditures for higher education. In each of these areas, the Survey Team had the luxury of drawing on or modifying prior methodologies that had supported policies adopted in the past. For instance, the Survey Team adopted the premise from the 1957 report that the University of California campuses enrollments be capped at 27,500 students. It also determined that the question of "the relative economic advantages of developing new campuses or expanding existing campuses does not yield a clear-cut answer regarding which is more economical," reversing in full the recommendation from the 1955 restudy. Given equilibrium of costs, the University enrollment cap and related findings made the establishment of new colleges and campuses an issue for state policy and politics more so than an institutional research question regarding the efficiencies or economies of scale for large institutions.

In sum, the 1960 Master Plan, like prior state reports, focused on the external relationships between institutions and the mechanisms necessary to coordinate higher education in the public interest. The Survey Team's overriding objective, and accomplishment, in the Master Plan was to devise an effective system to allocate students across the three segments of California higher education. The focus on externalities brought to the fore a few general concepts about the intrinsic qualities of lower division, upper division, and graduate education but only to the extent that it served measurements and projections for enrollments. After setting a general framework for state higher education and corresponding enrollment projections, the Survey Team had defined a nature and class of facts about California higher education that made possible policy recommendations for admissions, new campuses, faculty supply, unit costs, and revenue.

On the one hand, the statewide institutional research entailed a shift in emphasis to the study of several basic inputs into higher education institutions, whereas the early bureaus and offices of institutional research conducted a wide range of studies on resources, processes, and outcomes. On the other hand, the statewide studies drew more institutions to the practice of institutional research for higher education administration. The technical and advisory committees supporting the Survey Team represented scores of colleges and universities from across the state. In addition, the Master Plan called for annual reviews of admission, retention, grade, and dismissal statistics. In all of these respects, the 1960 Master Plan established foundations for a state community of institutional researchers engaged in policy studies for California higher education.

How Much Should Be Controlled by Higher Education Itself and How Much by the State

While the political compromises and will behind the 1960 Master Plan for Higher Education in California are irrefutable, the contributions from five years of continuous, statewide institutional research by the joint staff of the Liaison Committee cannot be discounted. The foundations for the 1960 Master Plan had been laid by the groundbreaking research of the 1955 restudy, the 1957 report on the need for additional centers, and subsequent statewide research on higher education in California. The Truman Commission surmised that higher education may be structured to suit authoritarianism or democracy. In California, the priority of the paradigm favored American democracy—anti-elitism, access, and opportunity—and engendered state efforts to project enrollments and expenditures no less than three times during a five-year period between 1955 and 1960.

While the attention to enrollments, enrollment projections, student distributions, admissions eligibility, site capacities, and unit costs may seem unrefined or mundane, the scope of statewide institutional research constituted basic descriptive and causal factors for the study of higher education—apropos the criteria of the National Research Council (NRC). The descriptive statistics common to the state studies formed the outward characteristics of institutions that suggest how each fit into a whole sector of higher education. The repeated analyses of enrollment projections based on demography, college-going propensity, and access belied a relatively simple concept of student demand for higher education as the major causal agency in higher education outcomes. Nonetheless, the inchoate paradigm for research on higher education opened up new possibilities for institutional research to transition from self-study to social science.

Thus, the organization of institutional research on a statewide scale—largely under the direction of executives in the colleges and universities—underscored how the field of institutional research may have organized within a paradigm for the study of higher education in the context of American democracy. The methodologies of institutional research became more standardized by repeated multi-institutional studies, and the importance of the assumptions for the projections in effect became more apparent to the stakeholders in Californian higher education. The emerging priorities of a paradigm for institutional research came to include more than the outward adherence to scientific methods but also the mission of higher education in a society with established values—at least in the most basic terms of authoritarianism versus democracy.

In the final analysis, the state studies made the politics and political compromises for Kerr's "five central issues" appear to be more significant than the institutional research and methodologies that isolated the key assumptions for a comprehensive policy analysis for long-term planning. In this regard, the 1960 Master Plan was as much the culmination of state-coordinated institutional research as it was the mastery of state politics on major policy questions confronting California higher education in the early 1960s. In fact, Kerr's own memory of the importance of the balance of policy-making responsibilities between the state and institutions likely reflects the response to state planning in subsequent years. As more and more state committees took the lead in coordinating higher education, critics increasingly articulated concerns for the "autonomy of public colleges" against the interference by the states.[20]

At the same time, the series of statewide studies on higher education in California demonstrate the trials of the field of institutional research when confronted by strong political forces at both institutional and state levels. The 1955 restudy, the most methodologically rigorous of the studies, presented conclusions regarding the establishment of new colleges and universities that ran contrary to the political interests of state legislators. The political pressure to study the need for new state colleges or University of California campuses in several regions of the state forced the state board and regents to scrap the restudy's recommendation that existing colleges and university campuses be expanded rather than new institutions established before 1965.

In backing away from the restudy's findings, the subsequent reports, including the 1960 Master Plan, reintroduced the premise that large institutions proved detrimental to higher education systems and that the cost to build new campuses roughly equaled the cost to expand existing campuses. Enlisted into a policy-making community, institutional researchers in California discovered the limitations on rigorous studies when confronted by the basic political interests of state constituents and their representatives. Research results that ran contrary to the perceived needs of the state's diverse communities met with a groundswell of pressure for more research favorable to existing political interests. In short, the application of institutional research to state policy making introduced priorities that seemed to run contrary to dispassionate scientific principles.

4 | A COMPREHENSIVE AND UNIFIED APPROACH

To Ask the Right Questions and Then Find the Right Answers

In his historical review of institutional research to 1979, James Doi drew attention to the contribution of the regional accrediting bodies and professional associations for the progress of institutional research. The Western Interstate Commission for Higher Education (WICHE), the Southern Regional Education Board (SREB), the New England Board of Higher Education (NEBHE), and the American Council on Education (ACE) organized workshops, conducted survey research, and presented papers on the organization of institutional research offices. Prior to the formation of the Association for Institutional Research (AIR), these associations defined "what works and what does not...[who are the] effective and ineffective directors, and...the criteria used by many institutions in establishing new institutional research offices." Between 1955 and 1965, the rapid advance of institutional research embodied the mounting interest of college and university administrators stimulated by the white papers of the regional and national associations.[1]

As Doi describes, the regional associations organized workshops on institutional research during the late 1950s and early 1960s to foster the creation of offices at institutions across the nation. Colleges and universities joined in an institutional research movement championed by state, regional, and national organizations that guided the direction of the new field of inquiry. The efforts reached a consummation with the 1960 publication from the American Council on Education (ACE), *Research Designed to Improve Institutions of Higher Education.* The ACE document designated institutional research as the "only" effective approach "for the president and those who work with him to ask the right questions and then find the right answers." ACE further endorsed the centralization of institutional research as one of the basic functions of effective higher education administration under the direction of college presidents.[2]

More so than the studies conducted on behalf of state boards and legislatures, institutional research by the regional accreditors and national association representing college presidents cast their attention to the intrinsic qualities of higher education institutions. The priority of institutional research in this vein sought to define effectiveness, efficiency, and excellence in general terms applicable to every college or university. This is to say that higher education institutions share certain inherent and commensurable characteristics that permitted comparisons between institutions pertaining to the typical quality of higher education as well as insights on processes and mechanisms that determine the quality of operations and the performance of colleges or universities. Integrated with the fundamental question of effectiveness in higher education, institutional research moved increasingly away from the episodic, ad hoc work of surveys and one-time projects toward the application of a continuous, collaborative program of research on higher education.

A Starting Point for Evolving New Systems of Conducting Statistical Studies

The California statewide studies, like those in other states, demonstrated the capability of institutional research to enlarge its scope beyond institutional self-study and contribute to inter-institutional, long-range planning for higher education in the United States. Studies of public higher education such as the 1955 California restudy, however, did not require researchers to consider in-depth the nature or general operations of higher education institutions. Each institution formed part of the whole in higher education related by external factors such as state birth rates, demography, and funding. Nonetheless, the three-tier system of higher education divided into junior colleges, state colleges, and a university explicitly introduced qualitative distinctions for the types of higher education institutions. As institutional research became more pervasive, other studies likewise pushed researchers to refine their understanding for higher education activities in ways that applied to multiple institutions and to develop concepts regarding the intrinsic qualities and operations of higher education institutions.

In this vein, concurrent with the restudy, the University of California (UC) participated in the *California and Western Conference Cost and Statistical Study*.[3] The multi-institutional study included the eight campus of the UC system and several institutions from the North Central region (including

Minnesota and Michigan State) as well as Vanderbilt University and the University of Washington. The resulting interstate cost study report captured the unease researchers had with the inherent comparative aspect of inter-institutional research while also exhibiting progress toward generalizable knowledge about the characteristics and operations of higher education institutions.

The opening chapter on the "conceptual framework" of the cost study states, "it was necessary first to define what a college or university is and what it does." The committee opted for minimalist criterion, suggesting that "a college or university is basically an environment for learning." Given the diversity of higher education institutions in the United States, the committee emphasized that every institution is "unique," rendering the "comparison of actual effectiveness…largely subjective." For this reason, the study eschewed any "attempt to judge or measure the quality of learning environments" and focused its effort "solely with certain of the factors required for the creation of these environments." Further clarifying its assumptions, the choices for the scope of its institutional research and definition for higher education directed the investigation toward "one facet—the 'input'—of a college or university," permitting the study largely to ignore outputs. In this respect, the study avoided the question of which "environment is superior to another" in favor of the question of which "environment may be more or less expensive to create."

Despite its effort to narrow the conceptual framework, the study unavoidably pressed the question of what constitutes the nature and effective administration of higher education. Despite the assumption that "unique" institutions are the vehicles for higher education, the research fostered common definitions and methods to measure the "inputs" for instructional expenditures in higher education. The chapter on "instruction" elicited common understanding for class size, teaching assignment and expenditures, and instructional mode. While the unit costs by subject and institution varied widely—of the order of ten-to-one in several cases—the findings suggested "high correlation" between student-faculty ratios segmented by the subject matter.[4] In the conclusion, the committee report noted, "Although costs vary among institutions, levels of instruction, and subject fields, it is possible to isolate the causes of these variations and explain them in terms of influences which exert themselves regardless of subjects or institutions." In effect, colleges and universities may be unique and their stakeholders may make discrete choices regarding the character of learning environments, but the cost of creating a particular learning environment follows principles subject to generalizable knowledge and prediction.

The monograph proceeded to consider other factors in expenditure inherent to learning environments of higher education before concluding with a "theory of costs" for colleges and universities and the future of unit costs studies. The theoretical reflections on the study, while rudimentary, draw attention to fixed and variable costs per student "at the fundamental level of the individual class." The report draws a distinction between the internal and external uses of institutional research, noting the "'public trust'…of institutions of higher education" in the latter case. Looking to the future of unit costs studies, the report anticipated the usefulness of "modern machine techniques" and "mathematical methods" in determining the optimal allocation for "alternative uses of resources." As a seminal work on the unit cost of instruction in higher education, the committee overseeing the inter-institutional study named "the development and refinement of methodology…[as] the researchers' first concern."

Though cautious in its scope, claims, and exposure to inter-institutional comparisons, the study committee made clear that the report represented an important development for the utilization of institutional research. While mindful of the need for cost study data to serve the discrete missions of colleges and universities, the conclusion emphasized the possibility for more advances in the comparative study of institutions within a state, a consortium, or in the nation: "This study has shown that many meaningful and useful definitions of terms and measures can be developed and used on a uniform basis among institutions…The participating institutions agreed, in substance, upon the definitions used, and applied them consistently in the present work. This, in itself, is a notable accomplishment and the study's major contribution to future institutional research."

Aside from the contribution of generalizable definitions, the authors also emphasized both the replicability and refinement of the study's methodology. Stating its goal for publishing the study in a manner consistent with traditional disciplines, the authors surmised, "[T]he methods may serve as a starting point for evolving new systems of conducting statistical studies." The report therefore made available the "procedures and forms used in the study" to enable "future investigations" consistent with the research design in whole or in part.

In addition, the interstate cost study anticipated the spread of institutional research in defined stages. The report noted that the original goals for institutional research typically arise from the need for administration and faculty to understand the unique aspects of their own institutions and how a particular institution fits into the constellation of colleges and universities within a state or nation. The research process—to the degree it distances itself from skepticism for institutional commensurability—forces study participants to consider the nature and operations of colleges and universities in general. The search for a conceptual framework then suggests ideas about the intrinsic qualities and functions common to higher education institutions. As a college or university works through the typical stages of institutional research, the need and value of collaborative inter-institutional research to produce generalizable knowledge about higher education comes to the fore.

Several years following the *California and Western State Cost and Statistical Study*, the American Association of Land-Grant Colleges and State Universities and the State Universities Association (AALGCSU-SUA) charged their Joint Office of Institutional Research to survey the member colleges and universities regarding the organization and performance of their institutional research functions. Led by W. Hugh Stickler from Florida State University, the study provided a digest of institutional research performed at land-grant and state institutions that documented the breadth of activities by the late 1950s. The 1959 report cataloged local, statewide, regional, and national institutional research studies that 1) included one or more land-grant or state institutions and 2) appeared in publication during the prior five years. Among other criteria for inclusion in the report, the projects had to be based on research produced by persons from the member institutions of the land-grant and state university associations. In addition, all ninety-three institutions in the associations completed a questionnaire regarding the current organization of institutional research in the colleges and universities, showing that institutional research progressed along lines anticipated by the earlier cost study.[5]

The bibliography records over one hundred separate academic publications on institutional research at the land-grant and state institutions in the five years following Eckert and Keller's book on the University of Minnesota. Categorized by subject matter, the list of institutional research studies published between January 1954 and July 1959 encompassed many aspects of higher education. Most frequently, the publications focused on admission policies, curriculum, enrollment, faculty, finance, statewide and/or regional coordination and planning, student personnel services, and students. The volume of publications for land-grant colleges and state universities testify to the avid readership for institutional research studies. The study titles indicated the utilization of predictive models to correlate high school and college grades, enrollment projections to forecast college-going in 1970, retention and withdrawals studies to identify factors in success, and comparative analysis of faculty salaries to enhance quality of instruction.

Underlying the publications, moreover, Stickler's report demonstrates the more voluminous number of local institutional research projects conducted at the member institutions of the associations. As part of the study, the institutions provided a summary for each specific project undertaken between January 1, 1958, and July 1, 1959. Appendix D of the report lists over eight hundred institutional research projects conducted by its ninety-three member institutions—or, eight institutional studies per college or university—frequently in one of six categories of institutional research: "curriculum; faculty; instructional program, methods, and materials; physical plant and facilities; students; and student personnel services." In addition, the report affirmed that institutional research organized by statewide boards often focused on enrollment and finance studies. While lamenting the "meagerness" of investigations under some categories and the "abundance" in other areas, the report captured the variegation of inquiry and the areas of specialization taking shape under the auspices of institutional research.

Through the questionnaire on the organization and administration of research programs, the report on land-grant colleges and state universities reveals an environment favoring the organization of centralized institutional research offices in a very short time. The findings showed that nearly half of the institutions still relied on decentralized processes, but only 10 percent indicated they engaged nominally in institutional research. Despite the lack of formal administrative support, the survey suggests that nine in ten land-grant colleges and state universities identified aspects of their self-study activities as "institutional research" only five years after the publicity engendered by the University of Minnesota report by Eckert and Keller.

More significantly, thirty-nine of the ninety-three member institutions centrally organized institutional research under full-time or part-time coordinators at that time. Among these institutions with centralized institutional research activities, sixteen had designated an institutional research officer to carry out the responsibilities. Other institutions centrally directed institutional studies through a president, provost, or dean, the assistant to a line officer, or via committee. Most had centralized institutional research offices only recently. Stickler reported that thirty-five institutions had established new coordinating responsibilities in the past five years, including nine that "activated institutional research agencies, [while] ten have expanded existing institutional research facilities." Further evidencing the "trend toward centralization," ten more institutions had plans under way to activate an agency and others intended to expand capacities, establish advisory committees, and/or pursue "further centralization" more generally.

In his findings regarding the types of publications and studies, Stickler construed the centralization of institutional research programs as a bureau or office that improved the quality and quantity of studies undertaken at innovative institutional members in the associations. While nine in ten respondents in his study reported having the ability to obtain basic information about their current operations, the decentralized processes fell short of centralized operations:

> The amount of institutional research work which can be accomplished by these ad hoc means is generally limited. It is, however, the belief of the

writer—in fact, to his own satisfaction it is his observation—that those institutions which have recognized institutional research agencies (whether on a part-time or a full-time basis, but particularly the latter) are turning out more and better institutional research information, both that which is 'routine' and that which is particular, both that which is repetitive in nature and that which is discrete.

The report identified two factors that made centralized offices more sophisticated than decentralized procedures. The colleges and universities with no or limited institutional research offices often regarded "institutional research as being for the particular college or university and not for public consumption." This, however, ran contrary to the needs of a profession associated with the study of higher education administration and policy making. The centralized and more established institutional research offices often produced research pertinent to the profession and higher education in general: "findings…of such value that they ought to be shared with the profession…in printed form." The second and related factor pertained to the scope of institutional research. At institutions relatively new to institutional research, the studies too frequently focused "on problems pertaining to the particular institutions." The more sophisticated institutions participated in statewide and national studies "in scope and character."

Even so, colleges with advanced centralized offices clearly fell in the minority: "[T]he great bulk of institutional research to date has been local in character and in the main has pertained to operational problems of the particular institution or, at best, of the state in which the institution is located." Stickler noted that "the quantity and quality of institutional research vary tremendously" among the institutions in the association. "In some institutions," he found that "institutional research information is virtually non-existent; in others, it approaches adequacy insofar as the particular institution is concerned." Consequently, state- and regional-wide studies had gained traction on only a limited scale and the report lamented the absence of studies on the national scale or for land-grant and state universities, specifically: "On the national scene adequate information concerning the real and comprehensive problems of land-grant institutions and state universities is conspicuously lacking."

Thus, Stickler's report endorsed the need for "eight major research studies" to be directed by the Joint Study Committee of the two associations. The study subjects included: origins, economic status, and educational qualifications of students; instructional programming; faculty studies; alumni and former student research; enrollment modeling; and research contributions. Whereas "it could hardly be expected that individual institutions would undertake on a large scale problems of regional and/or national significance," he reasoned, the Joint Study Committee of the AALGCSU-SUA was fully justified in pursuing research collectively beneficial to land-grant institutions and state universities.

Stickler's research on the breadth, quality, and structures of institutional research contributed three fundamental advances for the field. First, Stickler took important steps to conceptualize institutional research as a systematic inquiry into the nature and administration of higher education by cataloging and classifying institutional research projects at land-grant colleges and state universities. Second, his report further moved institutional research away from the constricting notions of self-study at a particular institution and toward the ideals of a discipline or social science by asserting the commonality of mission as an argument for coordinated research on higher education. Third, Stickler drew out the importance of institutional effectiveness for research on higher education when he suggested that the association of land-grant colleges and state universities, an association originating in a common mission, had a distinct priority for directing its own studies. In these three facets, institutional research outstripped the more limited purview of both institutional and state boundaries.

Furthermore, in his vision for a sector of higher education, Stickler showed more than a passing interest for the reliability and validity of institutional studies. Toward this end, he discovered that centralized offices of institutional research improved the rigor and the results of studies. Whereas the prior statewide and interstate cost studies advanced procedures for measuring the quantifiable characteristics of higher education, the reports gave little consideration to how best to support an ongoing program of institutional research. For example, the 1960 California Master Plan called for annual reporting, the report did not use the phrase "institutional research" or recommend centralized offices as the 1955 restudy had recommended. Stickler's report provided evidence and one of the first arguments for the centralization of institutional research in an office to buttress college presidencies and effective higher education administration.

The Advantages of Centralizing in an Officer or a Committee

The implementation of institutional research activities by more and more colleges and universities to meet internal and external study needs, combined with the obvious trend toward centralization to improve the sophistication and comparability of studies, led directly to the 1960 publication by the American Council on Education (ACE), *Research Designed to Improve Institutions of Higher Learning*. A. J. Brumbaugh, a former president of the American College Personnel Association during the late 1930s and then a consultant to the Southern Regional Education Board, one of the regional associations advancing inter-institutional research during the period, wrote the report on behalf of the ACE.[6]

In his various capacities, Brumbaugh exemplified a deep and career-long interest in the rationalization of higher education administration. During his career, he published a few works in conjunction with the ACE, including *American Universities and Colleges* (ACE, 1948) and Student *Personnel Programs in Transition* (ACE, 1952). In addition, he wrote a report on the coordination of state higher education for the Illinois Higher Education Commission in 1956, directly participating in the national trend for greater state control over higher education quality and finances. Lastly, after serving as a college president in the early 1950s, he wrote, *Problems in College Administration* (1956). He candidly stated his own position that "the approach to problems of administration must be objective, logical, and analytical," despite the fact that "strong emotional overtones" tended to be expressed when colleges and universities confronted challenges. These and other writings demonstrate Brumbaugh's career-long commitment to ideals for the scientific study and democratic principles of higher education.[7]

The 1960 ACE publication further elaborated on his efforts to rationalize administration by singling out institutional research as a promising new instrument. The foreword by the ACE president recalls the pioneering bureaus at the University of Illinois and University of Minnesota, and summarizes the contemporary interest: "There has been...an increasing recognition of the fact that institutional research, as well as inter-institutional research, might contribute to a better understanding, and possibly better utilization, of our institutions of higher education." New bureaus or offices had been slow to develop, however, and many leaders remained confused about what institutional research "is and what it does." Given the circumstances, the ACE asked Brumbaugh to "evaluate the activity," not for his expertise in institutional research but as "someone broadly familiar with the many aspects of higher education who could survey and report on this field of endeavor."

A proper interpretation of Brumbaugh's analysis must consider the purpose and design of the 1960 ACE report as crucial factors. Although the title of the report does not include the phrase "institutional research," each chapter addresses the context of institutional research as a solution to the problem of higher education administration: 1) needs, 2) areas, 3) conduct, and 4) effects. Brumbaugh strongly discounted any equivalence between "higher education institutions and business enterprise," counseling colleges and universities "to develop their own methods of evaluating their operations in terms of their goals and functions." His analysis consequently suited his inclinations to rationalize the activities of administration and to define the proper domains for higher education departments. To this end, institutional research served executives' responsibility "to ask the right questions and find the right answers" by providing "relevant, factual data—the kind of data that only institutional research can provide."

Brumbaugh eschewed any pretense to limit the scope, methodology, or paradigm for institutional research. As the generic title of his work indicated, "Institutional research, as discussed here, consists of studies and investigations focused on current problems and issues in institutions of higher education. It also consists of studies and investigations of problems and issues that are basic to long-range planning or that may ultimately have implications for institutional operations." In his explanation, the two forms of studies may be distinguished as applied and basic research in higher education. He added that the agenda of his report to the ACE "gives special consideration to applied institutional research, but it is not intended to minimize the importance of basic research." In short, Brumbaugh's evaluation of institutional research activities addressed his career interest in "objective, logical, and analytical" administration of colleges and universities.

Therefore, Brumbaugh almost entirely focused on the application of institutional research for administrative agendas and the gist of his report positioned institutional research activities as an essential component or function of higher education administration. He offered no concrete ideas or limits on the organization of institutional research as an emerging discipline or field among specialized practitioners. Instead, he delivered a comprehensive and forward-thinking statement on the integration of institutional research into the fundamental—and effective—operations of higher education administration. This is no more apparent than when he claims, "[I]nstitutional research is basic to policy formation, whether the policies pertain to the over-all purposes and functions of the institution or to its effective operation."

Brumbaugh's prior monograph on the problems of administration defined policy making as a significant responsibility of higher education leadership. In *Problems*, he wrote that one basic principle of college administration was that "there should be a clear differentiation between policy making and administrative functions," while later asserting that policy making "is properly a board function." In *Research*, although he opens with policy making as a shared responsibility among "trustees, administration, and faculty," he reiterated that the trustees "make or approve policies" while the administrators and faculty "adopt and apply" them. Cast within this framework of principles for higher education administration, then, Brumbaugh establishes a special role for institutional research in which it guided both policy formation at the board level ("purpose and function") and implementation at the administrative and faculty levels ("effectiveness").[8]

Brumbaugh then outlines the need for institutional research in long-range planning, management, and evaluation throughout the administrative functions of the college. Here, the specific needs for institutional research that he offers as examples are not nearly as important as his general dictum: "The key to effective administration is the ability of the president and those who work with him to ask the right questions and then find the right answers." The point of emphasis on the right questions and answers again harkens back to his principles of administration and the problems confronting presidencies. The "first real problem" in the sphere of the president he named as the ability to "to ask the right questions and to get the full answers…before deciding." This similarity strongly suggests that Brumbaugh conceived the responsibilities of institutional research as adhering closely to the responsibilities of the college president.

In fact, Brumbaugh's *Problems* listed "evaluating regularly the effectiveness of the college or university" as the fifth and final "demands on the president." Although the phrase "institutional research" does not appear in this earlier work, the scope of research activities in both papers align in most respects. In the first, he had considered three options for performing a total evaluation or self-study of an institution: outside consultants, an ad hoc research team, or a permanent staff. Despite the fact that his initial statement on evaluating institutional effectiveness was noncommittal to any of the three options, Brumbaugh's *Research* marked a significant shift in favor of permanent staff in an institutional research office—in two important respects.

In the first respect, Brumbaugh's earlier work characterized the second demand of a college president as the establishment of "an effective administrative organization." The totality of the report on institutional research for the ACE elevated institutional research as a basic function of college administration and presidential leadership on par with other major categories of administrative functions. Given its role in policy formation, then, Brumbaugh's conceptual framework for institutional research as an intrinsic administrative function supported presidents' influence or guidance over decisions by college trustees, administrators, faculty, and staff alike while also facilitating "change without creating revolt"—the third demand on presidencies. In essence, institutional research now factored into the principles of administration as an integral function within the sphere of the president.

In the second respect, Brumbaugh endorsed the need for a centralized team to oversee the responsibilities of institutional research in an effective administrative organization, regardless of the size of the institution: "Responsibility for the over-all coordination and direction of institutional research should be centralized. The lack of central coordination is likely to result in wasteful duplication or costly oversight of needed studies. Even in small institutions it is highly desirable that a person or committee be charged with responsibility for promoting, planning, and conducting essential institutional research." In this respect, he understood the emergence of institutional research offices as intrinsic to the rational administration of every college and university rather than as a consequence of an institution's size.

Citing Stickler's study among land-grant and state institutions, Brumbaugh noted the evident trends toward centralized institutional research. After summarizing the findings from Stickler's report, Brumbaugh then concluded, "There can be little doubt about the advantages of centralizing in an officer or a committee the responsibility for planning, coordinating, directing, and reviewing institutional research." Though not overtly committing to a permanent staff over a standing committee, he tacitly advised college presidents that the most effective manner to conduct or organize institutional research was to establish a "full-time or part-time institutional research officer." Brumbaugh thus counseled college presidents to seriously engage the prospect of a centralized administrative function as a necessity for the effective administration of colleges and universities.

As Brumbaugh reviewed the areas, conduct, and effect of institutional research, the overlapping spheres of college presidencies and institutional research became more apparent. In *Problems*, he previously had named four major categories of administrative functions: "academic, business, student personnel, and public relations." In his enlarged vision of categories determined by research areas, Brumbaugh defines eight areas of policy and administrative effectiveness: "goals, students, faculty, curriculum, facilities, administration, finance, and public relations." In this way, Brumbaugh's report to the ACE both affirmed his earlier effort to address the problems of administration effecting presidencies while also refining and extending the sphere of influence for executive leadership in higher education.

Moreover, his concept of institutional research as basic to policy formation fashioned an administrative instrument for college presidents to guide indirectly the policies and qualities of institutions. Too lengthy to enumerate, the general aim of his list of potential studies sought to improve quality in both the academic and nonacademic spheres of higher education under the responsibilities of college presidents. In *Problems*, he had declared, "In the last analysis the judgment of the quality of an institution means the evaluation of the administration of that institution." Brumbaugh's *Research* reiterated this theme while making evident that the scope of institutional research on the quality of administration also encompassed the performance of faculty: "The quality of an institution seldom rises above the quality of its faculty." Brumbaugh's scope for institutional research clearly encompassed both academic and nonacademic studies on the inherent qualities that make an effective administration and institution of higher education.

In short, Brumbaugh envisioned institutional research in a manner that moved the study of higher education from the analysis of outward characteristics of institutions typified by statewide research—enrollments, space utilization, and costs—to include the inherent qualities of institutions: goals, faculty, and curriculum. His final chapter on the effects of institutional research brings to the fore the question of quality:

> Quality is the key word in higher education today. How to maintain and improve quality under changing conditions and new stresses is a major issue confronting our colleges and universities. Boards of trustees, administrators, and faculties must make important decisions about goals, policies, programs, operations, and outcomes in the institutions for which they are responsible. *To make wise decisions, data that only institutional research can provide are indispensable* (his emphasis).

Ultimately, in the context of his previous work on the problems of administration, Brumbaugh positioned institutional research as the most effective means to influence the quality of higher education policies, long-range planning, and administration.

Ultimately, it is important to reiterate that Brumbaugh did not present his vision for institutional research in order to limit its scope or applications. The "eight areas of institutional research" he intended as "only illustrative" of the scope of institutional research. The larger program of institutional research may be "cut in a variety of ways," and he modestly endeavored "to provide a broad view" of its domain so that its value to colleges and universities may be pursued as a common interest. As he wrote, "It is hoped this outline will result in a comprehensive and unified approach to institutional research." Emphasizing this overall goal with an eye to inspiring college and university presidents, Brumbaugh proposed with the ACE's endorsement that the application of institutional research become recognized as a basic function of higher education administration.

Nor is it likely that Brumbaugh intended for institutional research to be preoccupied with the operations of one particular institution and show little regard for generalizable knowledge about higher education. In *Problems*, Brumbaugh lamented the lack of consistency in definitions and methods to measure the effectiveness of higher education in 1956: "One of our common problems is that the information from one institution is often not directly comparable with that from another. We must move in the direction of finding means of establishing comparable data...It is because we employ such varying procedures that our data are not comparable. One benefit I hope will derive from statewide studies is the development of a body of comparable information." His enthusiasm for statewide research is found in the later ACE paper with respect to finance studies. In this section, he enumerates the potential value of knowledge regarding the sources, trends, allocation, and impact of funds on higher education. As he observed, the reliability and validity of research on higher education expenditures "depends first of all on the use of an acceptable system of classification."

Read through the prism of his earlier work on problems in higher education, Brumbaugh promoted institutional research as a resolution to the challenges introduced to colleges and universities by the Truman Commission's report on the alignment of higher education with American democracy. His report on behalf of the ACE closed the loop first opened by George Zook, former ACE president and chair of the Truman Commission. Linked to unresolved problems in administration facing college presidencies, centralized institutional research indirectly rebuffed the traditional culture of elitism in higher education and advanced the mission of greater access to higher education. Understood through this lens, an office of institutional research served as an intermediary between the particular mission of an institution and "the same general ends" of higher education in American democracy. In essence, centralized institutional research potentially harmonized the spheres of policy making and administration in higher education under the auspices of the college presidency.

A Re-Examination of Concepts, Assumptions, and Strategy

In an important respect, the early history of institutional research offers a testament to presidential leadership to produce generalizable knowledge about college administration in the broader effort to coordinate higher education for "the same general ends" of democracy. The challenge of the Truman Commission called on colleges and universities to evaluate their mission and values with an eye to the societal outcomes: "Democracy must be lived to be thoroughly understood." Responsible leaders in higher education exhibited the willingness and openness to refashion higher educational settings and the administration of higher education into the lifeblood of American democracy. In this endeavor, their leadership combined the principles of scientific research, the mission of effective administration, and the democratic ideals for higher education that resulted in the creation of centralized institutional research offices.

Thus, if education research may be said to be an applied science as the National Research Council suggests, the nature of institutional research in part traces back to its origins and purposes as defined by the collective work of college and university presidents on behalf of state boards, regional associations, and, in the final analysis, the Truman Commission. Yet just as policy making potentially influenced the contours of the institutional research community, college presidents' rapid adoption of institutional research as a centralized administrative function channeled the future direction of the profession.

Many of the first institutional researchers in the bureaus or offices of institutional research came from the faculty who presidents selected for reasons of expertise or interests unrelated to higher education in general—a field of study that acquired its formal designation only later, during the 1970s. Many others assumed the role without the benefits of faculty status or an established expertise in any discipline. When the Association for Institutional Research organized in 1965, fully 40 percent of the membership did not have an academic rank.[9] Whereas many of the original contributions and persons in the emerging field of institutional research had discernible links to the scientific study of higher education or the goals of the Truman Commission, presidential leadership and administrative decision-making more explicitly delineated the professional life of institutional researchers.

In the immediate years following, institutional research nevertheless continued to evolve toward a scientific enterprise requiring specialization and organization in centralized administrative offices under the direction of college and university presidents. After 1960, the momentum to form a professional organization for institutional researchers led to the first organized meetings. The onus then shifted to institutional researchers to form themselves into a community expressly engaged in the scientific study of higher education. Since most practitioners had newly come to the field with no prior experience, the profession rested precariously on the opinions and interests of many other stakeholders in higher education: regional associations, state boards, college presidents, faculty, and state constituents in general.

In his contribution to the 1962 collection of articles on the progress of institutional research at higher education institutions in America, Philip Tyrrell advised his colleagues that institutional research was at a turning point: "Institutional research, throughout American higher education, is now at a point, where a re-examination of concepts, assumptions, and strategy is necessary. Institutional researchers should take this re-examination upon themselves, lest others do it for them."[10] Institutional research as a professional field had developed in parallel with external agencies and inquisitive scholars who pursued the study of higher education in the tradition of the scientific spirit. By the early 1960s, the organic development of the offices on college campuses had pushed the boundaries of research into wider and wider circles of non-academic and academic activities on campuses. The research portfolio of the offices seemed to grow annually as the promise of institutional research on higher education suggested no limits on its contributions or insights regarding day-to-day operations, state planning, and institutional excellence. The time was ripe for a new paradigm for institutional research that transcended the frameworks of both self-study and the Survey Era.

5 | THE CENTER OF CONFLUENCE FOR MANY SOCIAL FORCES

An Avenue for Exchange of Methods and Results of Research

The research conducted by the first bureaus and offices of institutional research established a framework for the scientific study of higher education. As illustrated in figure 2 (chapter 2), the first centralized offices of institutional research engaged in activities that met the three criteria for scientific study: investigations of descriptives, causality, and process/mechanism. One of the first practitioners, Coleman Griffith outlined how to apply scientific methods and research design to institutional research for a single higher education institution. Initially, as Griffith counseled, institutional researchers focused on reporting "facts"— analytical insights derived from the application of higher education literature to institutional "data"—for others to act upon. By the 1950s, institutional researchers like Ruth E. Eckert and Robert J. Keller at the University of Minnesota recognized the need to direct studies on the institution as whole and extended the scope of research to include statewide and multi-institutional studies on the extrinsic characteristics of higher education. Subsequently, state committees initiated comprehensive studies of public colleges and universities to coordinate planning, as exemplified in the California studies, and transform institutional research into an applied field to shape policy making in support of democratic systems of higher education.

Heading into the 1960s, institutional researchers and their like-minded colleagues among accreditors and other professional associations extended the scope of research to cover the intrinsic qualities of higher education. In the late 1950s, Eckert served on the North Central Association Committee on Planning committee with A. J. Brumbaugh, who subsequently wrote the 1960 paper on the potential of institutional research for the American

Council on Education, and Floyd W. Reeves, the University of Chicago scholar who conducted many of the studies associated with the Survey Era. Eckert later described the committee's recommendation to study the intrinsic qualities of higher education institutions in order to affect a program of progressive improvements: "The committee's most useful contribution was the development of systematic means for promoting institutional excellence. Whereas most higher education institutions in its [North Central Association's] nineteen-state area had met its standards for accreditation, the time had clearly come to move beyond sheer acceptability. A follow-up program was therefore initiated, involving periodic self-studies and visits of N.C.A. teams to review evidences of continuing development."[1] Underlying the recommendation for systematic investigations to promote institutional excellence, the committee signaled a shift from systematic investigations of extrinsic causal factors to plan for future outcomes to the systematic investigation of intrinsic mechanisms to refine policies and practices for the continuous improvement of institutional effectiveness.

Moreover, the phrase "institutional excellence" marked the growing use of abstractions and generalities with which to define the portfolio of research on the nature of higher education. The 1962 collection of articles edited by L. J. Lins, Professor and Coordinator of Institutional Studies at the University of Wisconsin, and published as a special issue for *The Journal of Experimental Education* stands out from the previous literature in its frequent reference to abstractions and generalizations. Still relatively unknown, the contributors continued to emphasize the new types of studies open to the emerging field. For example, the contributors from Fordham University, like other universities represented in the publication, branched out to study issues "[o]f greater importance…in such fields as student and faculty images of the University, comparison of senior characteristics with the nation-wide findings…of the career aspirations of college seniors, student retention, and prediction of academic success." A period of seminal innovations, the portfolio of research on higher education undertaken by the first offices of institutional research remains the unacknowledged basis for research on higher education as a social science today.

At the same time, the portfolio of research presented and exchanged at the first forums emboldened institutional researchers to elaborate on the theoretical and policy implications of their studies. As Lins noted in his introduction to the 1962 volume, "In preparing this publication, the editor sought to provide reports…useful to persons in each institution irrespective of its type, size, or goal…[and] providing an avenue for exchange of methods and results of research."[2] Sharing the studies with general applicability to higher education, the contributing authors more deliberately considered abstract concepts to inform institutional research designs and the general application of the results. Several articles from the collection offer theoretical contributions to institutional research that could have ossified into a paradigm for a field of study about higher education. In several respects, the first published forum proceedings mark the capstone to a period in which institutional research progressed stepwise toward the social scientific study of higher education.

Scrupulously, the founders of the field embraced the distinctions between basic research and applied research in order to conceive institutional research as the basis for a social scientific community. The agencies and their directors, dispersed geographically and culturally, proved capable of partnering in collaborative studies with a focused and balanced portfolio of scientific research in higher education. Their balanced approach to basic research for generalizable knowledge and applied research for institutional excellence provided a platform on which to organize the administrative offices into a very large array for coordinated measurements of higher education phenomena. During the first half of the 1960s, they looked to themselves to form a scientific research community to generate studies, accumulate knowledge over time, provide important insights on policies and practices of administration, and plan for a more democratic system of higher education that pushed the boundaries on the limits to institutional excellence.[3]

The Spectra of Institutional Research

In his widely cited work on the structures of science, Thomas Kuhn notes, "Paradigms gain their status because they are more successful than their competitors in solving a few problems that the group of practitioners has come to recognize as acute." Among the problems that paradigms solve, the first is the designation of a "class of facts" that comes to represent the "nature of things." In that respect, the paradigm holds a priority in the practice of science by guiding what passes as fact, what stands as the next problem to solve, how to approach a solution to the problem, and so on. The paradigm itself, however, does not need to be explicitly identified, to be fully interpreted, or to provide "discoverable rules" for the practice of the science. The community of scientists organized within the paradigm nonetheless forms from the process of initiation to the professional discipline or field of study through coursework and training wherein the theoretical applications of the paradigm are presented with ready-made solutions demonstrating the force of the paradigm. "While paradigms remain secure," Kuhn concludes, "they can function without agreement over rationalization or without any attempted rationalization at all."[4]

The new scientific enterprise of institutional research, however, originated from the rationalization of higher education administration as exemplified by the scholarship of A. J. Brumbaugh. For this reason, the incipient literature of institutional research, deeply imbricated in the political efforts to democratize higher education, transparently and conscientiously contemplated the criteria for its acceptance as a social science. In one of the first explicit endorsements for the scientific élan giving rise to institutional research, Edward M. Stout and Irma Halfter of DePaul University contributed an article to the Lins collection from 1962. The article, "Institutional Research and Automation," sketches the parameters for a research apparatus designed specifically for the study of higher education. In doing so, they also set priorities for institutional research to conduct studies of higher education as a social science that closely adhere to the National Research Council's statement forty years later.[5]

Significantly, Stout and Halfter conflated institutional research and research on higher education, regarding institutional research's "contribution to theoretical knowledge…[as] the 'main-line' investigation, with practical considerations being second." Thus, research at one particular institution was not a categorical bar to theoretical work:

> To merit the title "research," institutional research, just as scientific investigation in the natural or social sciences, implies not only empirical evidence and method but also the primary objective of true research: a contribution to theoretical knowledge. This is so even though the inquiry be pursued on a single institutional level. The investigation should produce a design that can be replicated and which can, therefore, be broadened to an inter-institutional inquiry.

Distinguishing institutional research *qua* social science from action research and evaluation, they set an ambitious goal for the field, claiming, "The statistical inquiry of institutional research, as is characteristic of any scientific investigation, should be expected to yield a search for principles with some degree of generality even at the single institutional level." Although their piece predates widespread computer automation in college and university administration by several years, their outline for the design of institutional research studies as scientific investigations provides sound insights with continuing relevance for technological disruption and machine processing today.

In a series of guidelines on automation for institutional research, the two maintained a distinction between the viewpoint of data processing for student information systems and the viewpoint of data processing for "the art of research design." Specifically, they state, "[R]esearchers insist on flexibility…The [research] problem and the steps necessary for its elaboration must have priority over machine solutions." At DePaul University, the team of institutional researchers claimed their efforts to organize research along these lines over three years yielded multiple benefits over time, including "refinement of hypotheses," "new lines of inquiry," and "a body of data" that was suitable for comparative analysis. Substantively, the authors recognized the portfolio of institutional research as a progressive iteration of studies related by their contributions to a theoretically based body of knowledge accumulated through systematic investigation.

The publication of the Minnesota report, proudly claiming its novelty and leadership for social scientific research on a college or university, prefigures the institution as the unit of analysis and the University of Minnesota as one observation or instance from which generalizable knowledge about higher education may be drawn. At that point of departure, institutional research no longer originates in an internal dialogue of self-study but an external dialogue among specialists regarding the "class of facts" that represent the "nature" of higher education institutions in whole or in part. After institutional researchers gathered at the first National Institutional Research Forum (NIRF) in the early 1960s, the exchange of methodologies and knowledge as recorded in the Lins collection of articles provides a testament to how quickly and effectively the practice of institutional research progressed toward the realization of a scientific field for the study of higher education. In essence, the discipline of institutional research emerged when the community of administrators in bureaus and offices published their research studies for peer review and scrutiny. By 1962, institutional researchers directly engaged in efforts to define "discoverable rules" from the paradigm for higher education research had grown organically from studies conducted by the bureaus, the inter-institutional committees, and eventually the nationwide professional meetings.

One contributor to the Lins volume, Philip H. Tyrrell of the Renssalaer Polytechnic Institute shrewdly noted that the practice of institutional research proceeds along spectra of investigations requiring a designed program of research. He proposed a definition of institutional research as "methodological study…of a college or university…[that] includes not only traditional data gathering, processes, and interpretation and the study of operational procedures, but also it includes those activities usually called 'education research,' a term whose many acceptable definitions all presuppose disciplined, scholarly inquiry into the processes of teaching and learning." Hence, the distinction between basic and applied research, or the domains of scholarships and institutional research, complemented each other in Tyrrell's formula.

He envisioned multifaceted activities for the discipline as evinced by the research program introduced by the offices: "there is not a spectrum of institutional research; there are spectra." His description of an office of institutional research, the administrative organ of basic and applied research, positions the agency as "a microcosm that facilitates, through its special kind of research, the activities of the macrocosmic, purposeful, life-liberating assembly of scholars who undertake those individual and collective tasks necessary to the 'creation of the future.'" The office of institutional research, "with this image of itself...both serves and is part of the intellectual community...in the study and implementation of findings concerning an institution's human and physical networks, e.g., in networks of characteristics which facilitate or impede individual or collective creativity."[6] While there is much to unpack in Tyrrell's aspiring portfolio of studies for offices of institutional research, he unquestionably identifies institutional research and educational research as a single institutionalized system of inquiry—a scientific discipline—to understand and influence excellence in higher education.

More profoundly, Tyrrell proposed to study any institution of higher education as "the center of confluence for many social forces." In his nascent theory, the institution as a unit of analysis is a setting in which cultural and material phenomena unite past, present, and future: "Into its [an institution's] human and physical networks are swept all known human history as well as the turbulent discoveries of the moment, and from these dynamic networks of interaction flow the hypotheses that help shape tomorrow." As such, colleges and universities take shape in the larger world of social and historical exigencies that defy the narrow motivations of reflexive self-study.[7] To the contrary, anticipating that institutional research offices must adopt portfolios of research for "the manipulation of events so as to attain ever-evolving objectives," Tyrrell envisioned a theoretical basis for the study of higher education that squarely defined colleges and universities in terms to engender generalizable knowledge.

More noteworthy, his theory of a social, material, and temporal confluence at institutions of higher education "preclude[d] the possibility of existence [for an institution] outside the main stream of history." The office of institutional research participates in "an institutional world of dynamic interaction" encompassing ethics, communications, talents, politics, and the advancement of systematized institutional knowledge. In effect, Tyrrell extended the basic premise of the Truman Commission that posited a higher education system as a participant in its larger social world conceived as either authoritarian or democratic. By referencing "social forces" and "human history," he conceptualized a world of abstract phenomena that underlie the nature of higher education and formed the class of facts uncovered by scientific inquiry.[8]

Tyrrell undoubtedly understood the college or university campus as an object of study that differentiated institutional research from other disciplines: "an established or commonly accepted educational setting, involving normal educational practices" (NSF), manifesting the phenomena of the larger social and historical forces that are subject to an institutionalized system of inquiry for generalizable knowledge. His dense article offered enough suppositions to support independent study among a large community of researchers that could sustain scientific inquiry in higher education for many years to come. Tyrrell's pregnant notions about the confluence of social forces and the storehouse of human history at colleges and universities as fodder for an institutional research program of the "unknown" and "the future" projected a rich and malleable paradigm for the scientific study of higher education.

An Open-ended, Compatible Total Information System

The National Research Council considered as one hallmark of a scientific community the progressive development of instruments and procedures to advance the discipline, noting that "scientific knowledge is a by-product of both technological activities and analytical activities." Thomas Kuhn directly links this technological and analytical refinement to the "three normal foci of factual scientific investigation," which may be characterized as: 1) facts of the paradigm refined by measurement and scope, 2) facts predicted by the paradigm and tested by measurements, and 3) facts derived from ambiguities and unresolved problems of the paradigm. In reference to the first, Kuhn observes, "Again and again complex special apparatus has been designed for such purposes [refinement], and the invention, construction, and deployment of that apparatus have demanded first-rate talent, much time, and considerable financial backing."[9]

As recent literature in the field of psychology attests, replication provides the best guarantee for the reliability and validity of scientific research as well as a requisite foundation for a healthy scientific community.[10] Scientific research in higher education calls for theory and practice to be tested and retested to reveal the variability of results, the reliability of analysis, and the validity of paradigms. For this to occur, however, institutional research requires instruments, or automation, on a scale and in a manner consonant with other social scientific practices. To progress from self-study to social science, institutional research had to overcome the limitations for replication that resulted from the lack of common infrastructure and instrumentation for the study of colleges and universities.

The representation of an entire era of institutional research as the Survey

Era attests to the significance of the survey instrument as a technological and analytical instrument in the dominant paradigm for the study of higher education prior to 1960. The survey instrument and the accompanying methods utilized to compile, weight, and analyze data may be regarded as one such "complex special apparatus" for the field. Take, for instance, the complexity of a survey research project conducted by Floyd W. Reeves and John Dale Russell on behalf of the North Central Association of Colleges and Secondary Schools in 1935. To produce a report on fifty-seven colleges, the survey team visited the sites, reviewed financial documents directly, and weighted the figures to allow for comparisons of institutions of different sizes.[11]

As the field of institutional research stood ready to embark on a new phase of scientific research in the early 1960s, the need to refine analytical methods and technological instruments was apparent to the growing cadre of practitioners. At a single institution, the survey instrument sufficed for the application of institutional research for reporting. Even so, Coleman Griffith's description of his efforts to transform data from multiple departments into "facts" for an entire institution encapsulates the rudimentary technological and analytical tools necessary to facilitate institutional research. The institutional research teams brought together by state committees and the North Central Association served to multiply the complexities involved in securing the reliability and validity of studies involving multiple institutions.

At the fourth meeting (1964) of the National Institutional Research Forum, the predecessor of the Association for Institutional Research, the sessions on the final day considered new technologies for institutional research.[12] The discussion reflected—as foreshadowed by Stout and Halter—a dispute over the path for computing and automation in higher education to facilitate self-study at institutions or scientific research in higher education. The techniques of data processing called for local solutions to homegrown business processes to support reporting for self-study and decision-making by the administrators. The "art of research design," to use Stout and Halfter's phrase, required a system of data management that empowered the modalities of institutional research that defined the inter-institutional planning studies advanced by accreditors and state committees in the previous ten years.

G. Truman Hunter of IBM presented his company's University and College Information System (UCIS) as a model for the data processing approach, "a framework which each institution can modify to create a management control system which will help those in charge solve today's problems and plan for tomorrow's needs." Claiming that the "IBM University and College Information System evolved from a total approach to the information needs of all elements of the institution," Hunter generally described the system's ability to manage student records, finances, and planning and development. Planning and development constituted one category, "becoming the most critical in all of administration," and empowered colleges and universities to deploy "effective planning and development activity for their own internal control."

Hunter added that "the modern data processing installation," for only student record management, would create a student "master record" to track "a complete person" from application to alumnus. The master record stored transactions for application, registration, financial aid, scheduling, testing, counseling, grade reporting, degree auditing, job placement, career services, and alumni donations. The financial module then provided similar capabilities to track performance budgeting, from manpower to purchase requisitions and plant maintenance. The planning and development features "most closely related the chief administrator of a college or university" promised to deliver scientific "knowledge and capability to the area of administrative planning" on campuses. Lacking regard for the distinction between data processing and research design defined by Stout and Halfter, IBM's Hunter naïvely concluded: "You people in institutional research should support the improved system of mechanizing student and financial record handling with modern data processing technology."

A description of the planning and development potential of IBM's UCIS fell to Vernon L. Hendrix of UCLA, who presented a paper on "administrative," or operations, research: "the systems approach...[that] seeks to find the best decision for the total institution or operation." In Hendrix's presentation, institutional research assumes its responsibilities under the auspices of "management control" and "decisions" for an "education system," defined as "any sufficiently autonomous and discrete educational institution, organization, or unit." Guided by IBM's data-processing mechanizations, institutional research primarily supported "decision-makers...since they are the ones with problems and objectives which can be valued and which must be obtained or maintained." The decision-makers then "define the objectives methods for measuring the achievement of objectives, and specify the measurement of the efficiency and effectiveness of alternatives when applied to objectives." Seemingly lacking knowledge of the origins of the field in scientific study and democratization, Hendrix neglected to consider the design of research, per se, for the accumulation of knowledge and the advancement of public interests concerning higher education.

The Hunter and Hendrix presentations clearly evidence the information technology solution for institutional research as enhanced planning and decision support by nonresearchers. Several commentators expressed skepticism for the technological apparatus of IBM and the operations research proposed by Hendrix. In particular, Keith W. Smith of Southern

Illinois University presciently counseled his colleagues, "I think the advent to total information banks, and the accessibility to them, are certainly a near reality. They are going to be in our institutions very shortly, for better or for worse." At the time, Southern Illinois University was implementing its own "total information system," an undertaking that necessarily anticipated improvements in college administration. Smith notes, for the better, "[T]he application of operations research techniques to decision-making and planning in higher education" may lead to better judgments "with data available immediately." For the worse, he intimated, the technological solution proposed a research system encompassing only the "total" operation of a single institution for its decision-makers.

In the latter scenario, the study of higher education in general may suffer because the community of institutional researchers may be displaced by local authorities with no sense of common purpose. In Smith's estimation, the outcome would then perpetuate the existing conditions: "the models that we create by our 'new technique' approaches could very well be cast in the form of our present obsolete organizations and practices of higher education." Decision-making requires trial and error; he said, "Freedom of choice permits us to explore new and suboptimal paths of the maze and to anticipate the unexpected and the accidental forces which will come." At the heart of his critique, decision-making rooted only in the particular concerns of one institution threatened to retard the operations of colleges and universities by perpetuating anachronistic policies and practices already adopted by the institution. Or, in another sense, optimization of existing policies and practices through operations research may result in improvements by degree for an institution but could not produce an improvement in kind for the nature of higher education.

Concurrent with the 1964 conference, the US National Science Foundation (NSF) and US National Institute of Health sponsored a research project that engaged eight universities for the development of "systems for measuring and reporting the resources and activities of colleges and universities." The project originally arose from discussions organized by the NSF in 1959 to address "the increasing need for accurate, current statistical data concerning the activities of colleges and universities." The project took over two years to organize and three and a half years to conduct. R. J. Henle of St. Louis University and Phillip Tyrrell of Rensselaer Polytechnic Institute, notably, edited the final report. The multiuniversity project and report came closest to devising an architecture for information systems in college and universities with substantive input from at least one institutional researcher (Tyrrell) who expressed an abiding interest in the scientific study of higher education.[13]

In 1967, Henle and Tyrrell published their 444-page report on the project to define the data architecture for a "total information system" in higher education, directly addressing the concerns raised by Stout and Halfter five years earlier. The abstract made clear the prioritization of institutional research for higher education in general alongside the comprehensive interests of institutional decision-makers:

> This study was designed to devise and test systems of measuring and reporting activities in colleges and universities so that such institutions could maintain records adequate both for their own purposes and for reporting to interested agencies. Data concerning manpower, students, facilities, and finances cover all fields of university activity and all major components of the university…Five general implications of the study are noted—(1) comprehensive attack on administrative problems of higher education warrants further application, (2) institutions should formulate their educational objectives and analyze their operations in the light of these objectives, (3) the guidelines expressed in this report may make possible the establishment of a body of evidence for evaluation of educational effectiveness over a long period of time, (4) formal analytical study of university structure from the standpoint of data communication is needed, and (5) any philosophy of the modern university must be infused with such wisdom as is within the capability of man, and practical procedures must be found to assist its realization.

Significantly, the report anticipated the need for a flexible data management system to incorporate data elements generated by the advancement of a social science for higher education. The five implications focus on a pervasive and permanent system to advance analytical study of colleges and universities to promote the educational effectiveness and wisdom of higher education administration.

Henle and Tyrrell explicitly linked their report to the forty-year movement to bring the spirit of scientific study to higher education research. Mindful of the need to present research in terms of theory, they proposed the creation of an information system specifically for the advancement of institutional research: "an information system, to be fully adequate, must be worked out within the context of sound educational theory." Three general recommendations in the foreword solidify the commitment to scientific principles. They first assert the "analytic and philosophical view of higher education" guiding the project "should be accepted as a basis for the development, on a national scale, of an open-ended, compatible total information system." Like the NRC many years later, they recommended a "permanent agency" to oversee the "future developmental work toward this kind of system." Lastly, they state the paramount interest in any information system for higher education "must be capable of being intermeshed…[so] that these systems should fit into the totality of the scientific community and other comparable communities."[14] In this final recommendation, Henle and Tyrrell root the proposal for a total information system to the vision of institutional researchers as a scientific community.

In another respect, the document provided a comprehensive digest for the vast number of variables and factors introduced by the institutional and planning studies of the prior forty years. The studies, however, had been so varied and inconsistent in terminology and methods that the burden placed on colleges and universities was "tedious, expensive and, in the end, largely unsatisfactory." The study aimed to create a comprehensive system to measure "all fields of university activity," including student, faculty, personnel, facilities, and financial data, and provide detailed recommendations for elements in a total information system for higher education. With an emphasis on the open-endedness and flexibility of a system on a wide scale, the study considered university data necessary to day-to-day operations, general quantitative reporting about the conditions of an institution, and "the gamut of projection and planning" from local administration to national interests. In this last goal, as in others, the report envisioned institutional researchers as part of a large community of scholars that transcended the province of decision-making at a single institution.

In an era before widespread adoption of sophisticated student information systems, the Henle and Tyrrell report exemplifies an approach to institutional research as a social scientific endeavor and made explicit the need to overcome "the lack of correspondence among the measuring and recording procedures and the cataloging of data by different agencies." Whether applied to day-to-day operations, reporting, planning, or effectiveness, the prospective specifications for an institutional research apparatus aimed to translate concrete transactions at individual institutions into data representing abstract concepts and a "class of facts" studied by a scientific discipline. As an institutional research apparatus, the technology drew an architecture for data management in which the "three normal foci of factual scientific investigation" (Kuhn) may take place in perpetuity. For these reasons, the Henle and Tyrrell report on a total information system for research on higher education epitomizes "the development of the scientific spirit" in higher education during the early to mid twentieth century in the United States.

Focused and Balanced Portfolio of Research of Importance to Policy and Practice

In the explicit examination of theoretical and technological underpinnings for a new social science for the study of higher education, institutional researchers began to perceive the scientific paradigm inherent to the portfolio of research established by the field by 1965. With minor variation, this portfolio continues to delimit the scope of research typically undertaken by such offices today. In 1938, Coleman Griffith drafted the basic premises for institutional research to perform data aggregation and fact-finding for submission to policy makers. In the 1950s, the University of Minnesota and the state committees demonstrated the advantages of institutional research for college and state planning. By the early 1960s, scholars had reached a threshold past which the conceptual framework for the study of higher education elevated the study of institutional effectiveness as a means to achieve the abstract concept of excellence. While more recent scholarship has proposed other classifications for institutional studies, the portfolio of institutional research enumerated in the different systems remains largely the same as that introduced by the first administrative offices prior to 1965. This is to say that the problems, class of facts, and discoverable rules congruent with a social science of higher education became manifest in the seminal work of early practitioners.[15]

Prior to 1965, institutional researchers and their advocates in the accrediting bodies in essence had formed the "golden triangle of institutional research," to use J. Frederick Volkswein's phrase. According to Volkswein, colleges and universities tend to divide institutional research questions and motivations under three formal categories: 1) "institutional reporting and policy analysis," 2) "planning, enrollment, & financial management," and 3) "quality assurance, outcomes assessment, program review, effectiveness, accreditation."[16] For the sake of brevity, these three categories may be refined by eliminating redundancy and identifying the primary objectives of institutional research: 1) reporting, 2) planning, and 3) effectiveness. Although Volkswein's schema interprets the three points of the "golden triangle" within the stunted vision of institutional research as operations research, apropos Hunter and Hendrix, the golden triangle nonetheless retains a tacit reference to the historical progress in the application of scientific method to the study of higher education by institutional researchers who upheld the "mainline" research objectives advanced by Stout and Halfter.

Contextually, each point in the golden triangle originates in contributions to policy making for the American system of higher education. The era of reporting "facts" as described by Coleman Griffith at the University of Illinois provides the basis for institutional reporting. Though preceding the postwar era of institutional and state planning, research conducted for the sole purpose of aggregating data and submitting facts without direct influence underlies the fundamental techniques of data manipulation and statistical aggregation. The deployment of institutional research to plan at the institutional and state level then represents a move to align departments with a common mission for the institution and, later, to coordinate institutions in a system of higher education for the public good.

As institutional leaders learned to understand their colleges and universities as parts in a whole, the possibility of modifying the "fit" of an institution with its system opened new avenues of research into the continuous improvement of higher education administration. The turn to "institutional excellence"—as Eckert described the contributions of the North Central Association committee—made institutional effectiveness a key component of the research triad to ensure that the "facts" and "fit" did not become institutional destiny.

One reason for the latent connection between institutional research past and present is that most research in higher education may be triangulated for institutional applications at each point in the golden triangle. For example, freshman retention often entails studies in all three phases: reporting, planning, and effectiveness. In order to comply with legal or funding requirements, the institution submits to the federal government and various other entities the number of students retained from the prior fall term's cohort of first-time freshmen (reporting). Subsequently, the institution may decide to translate its record of retained students into trend data for the retention rates of freshman student populations to project seat capacity for future enrollment or to estimate institutional full-time equivalent students for tuition revenue projections (planning). Lastly, the institution may decide that it needs to study significant differences between retained and nonretained first-time students in order to ascertain its commitment to institutional excellence and fulfillment of the educational goals of the students who attend the college or university (effectiveness). Each transition from reporting to effectiveness invites the institution to recognize its agency in the fulfillment of its particular mission and also in the social construction of higher education in general.

Each phase in the golden triangle of institutional research increases the complexity in "the art of research design"—from a cohort headcount at two points in time, to the calculation of annual retention rates for use in a formula to project future revenue, and to the measurement of continuous improvements for student outcomes—as adherence to the mission of the institution. Volkswein's point of emphasis on the application of the research, however, masks the corresponding rigor and scientificity of the portfolio of institutional research spanning the spectrum of research questions from descriptives to causality to processes and mechanisms (NRC). As an applied research, the two schemas for institutional research do not overlap in redundancy. Institutional research requires, at the least, a two-dimensional matrix that maps both the type of application and the nature of the scientific question suitable for the research at hand.

Figure 3 visualizes the institutional research performed by the first centralized offices of the mid-twentieth century along both spectra: the golden triangle from reporting to effectiveness studies and the three types of scientific research questions as defined by the NRC's *Scientific Research in Education*. The matrix results in nine modalities of systematic inquiry that an office of institutional research may deploy for the study of higher education. The itemized projects dated from the 1930s to 1960s in each modality illustrate the types of projects assignable to the nine modalities: 1938 for the University of Illinois, 1954 for the University of Minnesota, and 1962 for the Lins volume. Each modality in the matrix of institutional research may contribute to policy making based on the objectives of a particular project, from an individual program of an institution to the national system of higher education. This general framework productively conceptualizes the practice of the first institutional research offices as a "focused and balanced portfolio of research that addresses short-, medium-, and long-term issues of importance to policy and practice"—the NRC's fourth principle for scientific research in education.

FIGURE 3 | MODALITIES OF INSTITUTIONAL RESEARCH IN VOLKSWEIN'S GOLDEN TRIANGLE AND THE TYPES OF SCIENTIFIC RESEARCH QUESTIONS

	1. Reporting	2. Planning	3. Effectiveness
	Data Integrity and Submission Compliance	Operations and Resource Analysis	Mission and Outcomes Research
1. Descriptive / Correlates	1.1 Statistical and Qualitative Reports • FTE Staff and SCH per FTE Staff (1938) • Faculty and Student Loads (1938) • Student Demographics (1938) • Classroom Space Utilization (1938)	2.1 Correlations and Projections • Academic Program Unit Costs (1938) • Academic Program Cost Deviations and Budget Allocations (1938) • Curriculum Development Correlation to Number of Enrollments (1938)	3.1 Exploratory and Policy Research • Education Policy Research (1938) • Equity in Education Study (1962) • Correlation between Learning Outcomes and Pace of Curriculum Development (1954)
2. Systemic / Causal	1.2 Survey and Ethnographic Research • Student Evaluations (1954) • Follow-up Surveys with Graduates (1954) • Faculty Satisfaction Surveys (1962) • Applicant Choice of College (1954)	2.2 Benchmarking and Competitive Analysis • Academic Program Benchmarking (1938) • Enrollment Trend Projections (1954) • Faculty Salary Benchmarking (1962)	3.2 Outcomes and Intervention Assessments • Pre- and Post-Test Learning Outcomes in General Education (1954) • Inter-rater Reliability and Validity of Grading Practices (1954) • Change in Attitudes toward Psychiatry Associated with Program Intervention (1954)
3. Mechanism / Process	1.3 Electronic Automations and Machine Forecasts • Enrollment Forecasts with Variable Parameters (1954) • Predicting Academic Success (1954) • Automation of Research Processes (1962)	2.3 Predictive Modeling and SEM • Effect of Relaxing General Requirements on Course-Taking Behaviors with Non-Randomized Control Group (1954) • Predicting Medical School Success to Better Target Admissions (1962)	3.3 (Quasi-)Experimental Research • Learning Outcomes by Physics Students via Lab Experiments or Demonstration with Semi-Randomized Control (1954) • Pre- and Post-Test Learning Outcomes in Independent Studies with Control Group (1962) • Predicted vs. Actual First-Year GPAs to Identify Grade Inequities by Dept. (1962)

Modalities of Institutional Research

In its earliest form of reporting, institutional research organized to aggregate statistical and qualitative information based on ad hoc specifications determined by unsystematic motivations of internal clients—as at the University of Illinois in the 1920s and 1930s. At the second stage of reporting, the practice of institutional research gains a modicum of standardization with an investigator employing common research instruments such as surveys, focus groups, or ethnographic studies. Evident in the studies conducted by the University of Minnesota in the 1940s and 1950s, investigators then define variables in advance and determine the breadth of measurable phenomena necessary for a study, including psychographic or attitudinal characteristics of students, faculty, and others in the educational setting of higher education. At the third stage of reporting, routine or periodic research studies give rise to general standards for the phenomena of educational settings, and the operations of the institution tend toward greater automation in data collection, as foreseen by Stout and Halfter in 1962. Significantly, the difficulty of the reporting procedures increases at each level of scientific rigor, but the institution itself may not engage in more than casual observations about its plans or performance, as Griffith's early publication suggests.

When colleges and universities like the University of Minnesota in the 1950s progressed into the second stage of reporting, they discover rudimentary correlations and projections from historical statistics that facilitate internal planning. Insights drawn from intra-institutional comparisons of units or departments eventually reach a limit, resulting in the need for institutional research and planning on a broader state level, as exemplified by California. Depending on the degree to which conditions in general progressed toward standardization and automation for the individual states,[17] the benchmark analyses drawing on inter-institutional comparisons enabled researchers to understand colleges and universities as members of a system of higher education—or "between college" research and analysis. At the third stage of planning, institutional research contemplated predictive analytics or structural equation modeling—utilizing student record level or "between student" methods of statistical analysis as found in a few articles from the 1962 Lins volume—to refine its understanding and explanations for the efficacy of higher education in general. In this manner, institutional research and planning progressed from the alignment of programs and units under an institution's control, to the coordination of institutions within a larger (public) system, and eventually to the manipulation of institutional policies to plan for alternative futures for an institution.

After the second and third orders of planning became commonplace through statewide and collaborative studies, institutional research then extended its scope to the consideration of institutional excellence locally or in higher education in general, as the work of Eckert and Brumbaugh on behalf of the professional associations reveals. The generalizability of institutional research from effectiveness studies depended largely on the degree to which investigators designed replicable and rigorous studies. At the first order, institutional research engaged in policy research and student initiatives that favored improved outcomes specific to the institution, such as the University of Minnesota, or a system of higher education, akin to the unit cost study by California and the western states team. In the second order of effectiveness studies, institutional research attempted to identify factors or independent variables that logically signified the attainment of desired outcomes from policies, practices, and intentional interventions defined abstractly.

Lastly, in the third order of effectiveness, the studies purposely engaged theoretical terms and design research based on sound social scientific principles to elicit findings and conclusions about the processes and mechanisms for the fulfillment of institutional missions and outcomes for higher education in general. Under the umbrella of effectiveness, mid-twentieth century studies sought concrete measurements such as headcounts, unit costs, and plant utilization to inform policy research for entire states like California, while studies involving abstract concepts such as learning outcomes, student resilience, and predicted versus actual metrics had greater valence for institutional policies, as found in the University of Minnesota and Lins volumes.

Leaving aside the mastery of subject matter in each modality of the matrix of applied and basic research principles in figure 3, this system of organization and classification for institutional research suggests why the first administrative offices of institutional research were able to explore meaningful and significant questions for higher education in general. Mundane requests or reporting for institutional data exist in a system of inquiry progressing from descriptive statistics to more and more complex understanding of underlying factors that influence planning and effectiveness in higher education. At its origins, institutional research as research on higher education was "a continual process of rigorous reasoning supported by a dynamic interplay among methods, theories, and findings." Separately, as Tyrrell scintillatingly suggested, higher education institutions served as sites of research for a multitude of social phenomena and more multitudinous relationships of such phenomena with each other. When arrayed into a scientific enterprise for the study of higher education, the portfolio of research had the potential to give rise to "a healthy community of researchers...guided by a set of fundamental principles."[18]

Generally, the modalities in reporting, planning, and effectiveness remain the same today. The degree to which scientific research principles guide institutional research at a college or university roughly correlates with specializations that favor centralization of institutional research in administrative offices. The use of student information and enterprise resource planning systems and the measurement of higher education phenomena according to specifications for the Integrated Post-Secondary Education Data System (IPEDS) and other external agencies force most colleges and universities to establish institutional research functions to reach at least two orders of reporting complexity. As Stickler's study on behalf of the land-grant colleges and state universities discovered, the lower-order modalities of institutional reporting and planning may be carried out by ad hoc committees and decentralized personnel when quality and consistency matter little to the leadership. Higher-level competencies for reporting, planning, and effectiveness, however, required centralized offices with staff that had been trained for social scientific research, as many of the earliest institutional researchers were. To the degree that institutional excellence—or continuous improvement toward the mission of higher education—animated the research questions, an institution required extensive knowledge of higher education literature and the scientific training to design studies of the processes and mechanisms that theoretically would enhance institutional effectiveness and student outcomes.

Many institutions today, regrettably, seek no more than a basic competency from their institutional research offices or functions. Paradoxically, the most common functions of institutional research offices—lower-order reporting and planning—require the least rigorous standards and oftentimes shape broad policy research outside of the direct control of the college leadership. The least common functions of institutional research offices—automation, predictive modeling, and quasi-experimental research—require rigorous standards to yield results directly applicable to the policies and practices at a single college. Presently, the three higher-order modalities of planning and effectiveness entail "big data" management, advanced statistical methods, and the refinement of scientific research questions—skills now attributed to data science for student success. No wonder, then, that higher education leadership now looks to data science for student success: the new field exemplifies the spirit of scientific research on higher education that first motivated and brought together the earliest practitioners of institutional research.

Just as Scientific Investigation in the Natural or Social Sciences

To this point in the field's history, the practitioners of institutional research in administrative offices at colleges and universities enjoyed an intellectual freedom to pursue the possibilities of their field with full regard for the mission of higher education. In many respects, these institutional researchers proved themselves far ahead of their time in the vision they demonstrated for the future of the profession before the widespread existence of key technologies: student information systems, statistical software for the social sciences (SPSS, R, and the like), spreadsheets, visualization software, intranets, color monitors, and on and on. The praxis of institutional research revealed to several scholars what was necessary for the design of computing technology to provide the most value to college and university administration as well as the "complex special apparatus" necessary to advance institutional research as a social science. Ultimately, others recognized the need for an authentic institutional research paradigm to empower a scientific community for the study of higher education settings. In a manner, the original authors of institutional research literature exemplified the best principles of a scientific community: engaged in publications and conferences for the exchange and scrutiny of results, generalizing standards and definitions about the nature of higher education institutions, and imagining technological apparatuses to enable the replication of studies.

Stout and Halfter's premise to hold institutional research to standards "just as scientific investigation in the natural or social sciences," Philip Tyrrell's theoretical statement on "the spectra of institutional research," and Henle's architecture for a "total information system" for measuring college activities supplied the basic outlines for a stable paradigm to advance scientific investigations into higher education. Institutional researchers provided parameters for the scientific study of higher education both between and within institutions—an applied-basic method for institutional research. This framework for institutional research as a social science remains within reach today, reflected in the application of data science for the study and improvement of college student success. The complement of research activities and interventions undertaken by data science of student success easily fits into the nine modalities of institutional research defined by the golden triangle of institutional research and the three modes of scientific research in education stated by the National Research Council. These activities include automation, the aggregation ("intermesh") of disparate information systems from multiple institutions, the application of social scientific research designs and analytics to advance an understanding of the causes and mechanisms in student success, and a framework for planning both at the level of institutions and wider regional considerations from the aggregated data sets of student records.

For good reason, then, higher education executives now accord favor for data science of student success as a means to reengineer college administration, much like the favor their antecedents granted to institutional research sixty-five years ago. The emergence of data science for student success in the past few years suggests that institutional research continues to spur the organic generation of scientific research questions regarding institutional excellence and student success. Despite the evident overlap in research modalities, however, the vast majority of college executives do not seem to regard the data science of student success as analogous to institutional research. For this reason, significant associations like the National Association of System Heads and the American Council on Education do not regard centralized offices of institutional research as capable of scaling up to include these advanced solutions. Thus, the recent trend to outsource a key administrative responsibility to vendors of data science raises a question: what happened to the promise of centralized offices of institutional research after 1965?

6 | PRODUCTION OF KNOWLEDGE WITHOUT PERVASIVE AND LASTING SIGNIFICANCE

Another Unnecessary Appendage to the Administrative Bureaucracy

In 1960, institutional researchers first convened the National Institutional Research Forum (NIRF) in conjunction with the American Association of Higher Education. Initially organized by direct invitation, the first two meetings largely "excluded practitioners from state colleges, liberal arts institutions, and junior colleges." The effort to form a narrowly defined community from research universities met with an opposition that successfully organized a more open community, the Conference on Institutional Research in Higher Education. NIRF organizers bent to the will of the larger community of institutional researchers and subsequent meetings included those engaged or professionally interested in the practice of institutional research more broadly. At the third meeting, the forum organizers formed a special committee to consider the establishment of a permanent association. Attendees at the fourth forum endorsed the organization of a professional association and assigned a new committee the responsibility of drafting a constitution. Institutional researchers in attendance at the fifth forum adopted the proposed constitution and formalized their gathering as professionals. The Association for Institutional Research formed in 1965 with 382 charter members, seemingly as fulfillment of the promise of institutional research in higher education over the prior forty years.[1]

The fourth annual meeting of the NIRF in 1964, where attendees endorsed the formation of a permanent association, also featured James Doi's summary of a conceptual framework for institutional research. Doi noted that, in contrast to discussions about the "generalized role" of institutional research, the presenters at the conference tended to focus more so on "the status of the director of [institutional research] in the institutional hierarchy, his role, and the style of operation." To Doi, the variations in understanding for the scope of institutional research largely depended on the commitment of an institution's administration and faculty to "scientific" administration and the "reliance on knowledge as the basis for decision-making."

Despite what the institutions or institutional researchers settled on as the role or function on the administrative office, Doi noted that the most likely conditions in which a director may fail were as follows:

> Not infrequently an institution will appoint as [institutional research] director an individual with competency in certain kinds of studies that are of immediate interest to it—for example, budget analysis and cost studies, or enrollment projections and student characteristics, or curriculum analysis and educational experimentation. Within a two- or three-year period, studies of a given type should become a matter of routine and the institution reasonably well informed of the situations that encompass them. Other problems in other areas requiring analysis may then come to the forefront. The director of [institutional research] should be able to provide the knowledge and leadership in the study of such other problems, if not, the administration will have no other recourse but to regard the office of [institutional research] as a repository of more or less routine, perhaps even unimportant, studies....As a minimum...[the director] should acquire knowledge of the kinds of studies developed by others engaged in research on higher education and of their relevance and applicability to the problems faced by his institution.[2]

Continuous improvement for a single director applied more generally to institutional research as a profession and as a social scientific discipline. Doi's description of the stagnation of directors' capabilities complements his five propositions for the development of the profession in general and encapsulates how a restrictive definition for institutional research may serve to stunt its further progress.

Although Doi had the operations of a single institutional research office in mind, his recommendation for the relentless acquisition of knowledge and the ambition to take a leadership role in the study of higher education came root and branch from the initial purpose behind the organization of such offices. Conversely, if the ability of institutional research to contribute to scientific research diminished, the accumulation of knowledge about higher education became arrested, and the officers failed to seek leadership roles as policy makers and decision-makers on campus, the profession as a whole must decline. In short, Doi provided a blueprint for the conditions under which the development and extension of institutional research as a field of study may be arrested.

When Tyrrell warned institutional researchers in general about the potential for others to reexamine the "concepts, assumptions, and strategies" of the profession, he clearly intended for his colleagues to take up the challenge in his program for a "spectra of institutional research." He did not consider, however, that skeptics for the scientific spirit among institutional researchers and higher education administration extended deep into the ranks of professionals that Tyrrell likely regarded as his colleagues: institutional researchers who held or aspired to faculty status at their institutions. Nor did he anticipate that a new association formed to represent the interests of the profession could be led by a faction of institutional researchers who held antipathy for the scientific ambitions of the original pioneers of the profession.

Yet, in fact, a growing cadre of both faculty and administrators came to regard institutional research as a peril that threatened institutional autonomy and academic freedom on campuses. For these stakeholders in higher education, the most important question regarding institutional research was how to prescribe a more defined "nature," "role," and "function"—three terms that inform and motivate many later writings about the profession— for the offices on campus. Doi observed in his remarks on a conceptual framework for institutional research, "An office of [institutional research] is perceived by many faculty members as another unnecessary appendage to the administrative bureaucracy." In 1966, the same year that the Association for Institutional Research held its first forum, two political scientists published a work detailing the threats that centralized institutional research posed on campuses and advocated for institutional research to become re-oriented to promote the perspective of faculty.

In addition to the local threat of institutional research on the individual campuses, faculty who studied higher education came to recognize institutional research as a competitor in the production of knowledge about higher education and higher education administration in general. These emerging opponents to institutional research sought to distinguish the practices of institutional research from practices of faculty scholarship. To bolster the division between institutional research and scholarship on higher education, the proponents of the faculty point of view drew hard distinctions between applied and basic research. With this distinction, a new paradigm for institutional research advocated institutional research as 1) an administrative staff function, 2) divorced from scholarship on higher education, 3) circumscribed within each particular institution, and 4) effectively decentralized in an "elaborate profusion" of local units and decision-makers. Within a decade, the paradigm for institutional research offered by these opponents to centralization became commonplace in higher education scholarship, in the official documents of the Association for Institutional Research, and in the practical organization of the institutional research offices at colleges and universities.

Bolstering the Point of View of the Faculty

Francis E. Rourke and Glenn E. Brooks acknowledged in their 1966 work, *The Managerial Revolution in Higher Education*, "Institutional research lies at the heart of the trend toward the use of modern management techniques in higher education." The observation merely paralleled what many knew already and what Doi observed in his summary comments at the 1964 NIRF meeting. Nevertheless, many institutional researchers and scholars expressed considerable favor for the publication by Rourke and Brooks as an original contribution. In one of the earliest statements on the role and nature of institutional research from the Association for Institutional Research, two of its first presidents lauded their work as "[a]n excellent review of institutional research and computer usage in colleges and universities." Forty years later, Donald J. Reichard, a contributor to the 2012 *Handbook* published through the AIR, considered the work on par with the ACE publication by A. J. Brumbaugh in 1960, crediting its chapter on institutional research as one of the sources for "the establishment of effective institutional research units." In the intervening years, publications released through the Association for Institutional Research routinely praised the unoriginal scholars.[3]

Despite the emphatic embrace, the chapter on institutional research largely constituted a censure of the profession. Two professors of political science with no discernible connection to institutional research, Rourke and Brooks showed little respect for the growing body of literature and dialogue about institutional research evident from the proceedings of the first National Institutional Research Forums during the early 1960s. In a corresponding article with the same title published in *Administrative Science Quarterly*, the two authors characterized institutional research as a dubious enterprise masquerading under the moniker of science: "many of the studies undertaken in the name of institutional research today are not so much designed to answer questions as they are to win support for findings which administrators know about from reports published by other schools, but which they hope to see applied to their own campuses." Taking aim at the pretensions of the NIRF meetings, they categorically dismiss the potential of the field to become more than a political weapon in the hands of centralizing administrators: "While the ideology of institutional research thus stresses its importance as a 'basis for decision' [the title of the 1962 Lins volume], in actual practice such research also serves as a means of implementing courses of action already decided upon."[4] Dismissing the extent literature as "ideology," their scholarship relied almost entirely on an analysis of survey research that they conducted to confirm their suspicions of the new profession.

From beginning to end, then, the chapter on institutional research in their much-lauded book emphasizes the many "perils" posed by institutional research to institutional autonomy, to faculty, and especially to other administrators. According to Rourke and Brooks, the profession posed suspect challenges to an institution, both faculty and administration:

> The fact that the faculty should look with suspicion upon the establishment of an office of institutional research in a university hierarchy is not surprising, in view of the common propensity of academic man [sic] to look with alarm upon any apparent extension in the power of university administration. What is not so generally recognized, however, is the extent to which the advent of such an office may arouse anxiety within the ranks of university administration itself.

The litany of perils is too numerous to cite in full, but the key discouragements for administrators, often contradicting each other, were "[institutional research] techniques are 'burglar's tools' which might eventually allow outsiders to gain entry into aspects of university decisions"; "an office ordinarily has very little opportunity to develop into an instrument of long-range planning, helping a university president to look ahead and anticipate...five or ten years [in advance]"; "a division of finance...may well suspect that the new institutional research unit will pull some power from its own jurisdiction"; "the centralization of information—and administrative power—in the [institutional research] office"; "the prospect for having wide publicity given to certain disadvantageous information"; and "the director [who] took it upon himself to write a sharp letter of protest against [the college president's] proposal."[5]

In effect, in as much as the "managerial revolution" made such offices a necessity on campus, institutional research presented a prisoner's dilemma for both faculty and administrators. According to Rourke and Brooks, the practice of institutional research threatened the administration, if not the institution itself, and the leadership of presidents, finance officers, and all others who may be placed at a disadvantage if one office served to centralize "data." Institutional research and new management techniques in higher education organized on a state, inter-institutional, or scientific scale threatened the autonomy of administration and the academic freedom of faculty, they repeatedly intimated. As a solution, the authors proposed that institutional research narrow its field of study to academic programming and that research on business operations fall to the functional units at local institutions.

In the first respect, they recommended that institutional research offices of the future be "distinct apart from the business side of operations," effectively breaking with the origins and trend to centralize administrative research, and be subject to "an academic orientation...bolstering the point of view of the faculty." In the second respect, they argued, "Under this arrangement, management problems connected with student registration, employee payrolls, and the utilization of physical facilities are not the responsibility of the office of institutional research." In the final analysis, Rourke and Brooks argued for a division of labors for institutional research functions that tethered institutional research to local faculty's control and stovepiped administrative research in the respective units of an institution.[6] Thus, despite the guise of opprobrium attributed to institutional research as "at the heart" of a management revolution in higher education administration, Rourke and Brooks overtly endeavored to contain the threat of both institutional research and new administrative powers over the direction of higher education.

Fortunately, Rourke and Brooks wrote in support of their recommendation, the survey research showed that many institutional researchers favored a narrow conceptual framework: "Most IR directors appear to accept a limited conception of their own research function within the university." They were not entirely wrong in that institutional researchers genuinely held concern for their relationship to faculty and administrators. At the 1964 NIRF meeting, several participants expressed concern for the relationships with faculty and the participation of institutional researchers in policy implementation as administrative officers.

Doi noted in his address that some institutional researchers still adopted the role "to search for and report only the facts," as advocated by Coleman Griffith in the 1930s. Joe L. Saupe of Michigan State University flatly claimed, "Institutional research cannot become a true discipline in any traditional sense." To the extent that institutional researchers needed academic specialization, Saupe added, "[W]e have these resources in the form of faculty members in academic departments." Carl E. Wedekind of the University of Pittsburgh argued that institutional research offices be equally faculty-oriented, and "serve the faculty as well as the administration of the institution." To that end, Wedekind urged his colleagues to "avoid involvement in the implementation" of policies as much as possible in order to avert developing an "administrative image."[7] At the time Rourke and Brooks published their jeremiad on the managerial revolution, the direction of the profession of institutional research remained an open question subject to the direction of the Association for Institutional Research and its agenda at the annual forums.

Institutional Research as a Function with a Minimum of Specific Implications for Organization

At the first forum held after the organization of the Association for

Institutional Research in 1966, the leadership of the new organization seemed to work toward the goal outlined by Carl E. Wedekind. In the first President's Address, John E. Stecklein from the University of Minnesota defined "the role of an institutional research office...as a major point of intersection of faculty and administrative concerns." Institutional research offices "survive and thrive," he suggested, when they encompassed the point of view of faculty as well as administration. Institutional research's contributions to an administration could not be applied effectively if they are "applied in a vacuum that excludes faculty concerns about institutional goals and educational values." For institutional researchers to avoid being "identified solely with the mundane, routine data collection and tabulation," they had to engage in "more basic [academic] research devoted to a better understanding and critical evaluation of fundamental educational policies." Embracing the perspective of faculty and the values of academic research, institutional research as a field of study may "bring the temper of educational values into the forging of economy and efficiency tools."[8] Stecklein in essence called for institutional researchers to adopt voluntarily the perspective of faculty as recommended by Rourke and Brooks the same year.

At the third forum following the formation of the association, the president clearly signaled that institutional researchers may not be prepared to adhere to the general advice that they refrain from policy- and decision-making. In his address, L. E. Hull recalled an exchange at one of the first forums in which the president of a state university recommended "that the proper role of institutional research was to give advice to the president and central administration." Many institutional researchers in attendance, according to his account, objected to the suggestion and "maintained that the proper role of institutional research was solely that of providing objective analysis, not to propose a solution." Hull then went on to advocate that institutional researchers not only advise presidents on policy matters, but also become increasingly involved in "the creation of policy and planning documents...[and] providing advice to outside groups."[9] In his remarks, Hull evinces the integral policy role for institutional research envisioned by prior presidents as opposed to the ancillary staff role advanced by suspicious faculty.

At the fifth meeting of the formal association, the president openly considered the need for the profession to contribute to basic research in their capacity as institutional researchers, not research faculty. Thomas R. Mason from the University of Colorado in a short address titled "Communication in Institutional Research: The Purpose of the Association" assessed the social and political unrest on American campuses in 1970 that "confront[ed] those of us working in institutional research with the necessity to reexamine and re-evaluate our role." In his estimation, "The old debate over whether institutional research should focus upon more basic research, on the process of education, or upon the administrative processes is coming back into focus, and the issue merits reconsideration." Mason counseled his colleagues to put aside the division between the study of administrative and educational processes to work toward "the resolution of the difficult problems measuring educational effectiveness." To that end, he proposed that the Association for Institutional Research join an effort led by the Western Interstate Commission for Higher Education to form "a basic research group to pursue the problem of assessing the outputs of higher education and to probe more deeply into the economics of higher education."[10]

The implication of Mason's address was that institutional researchers should no longer regard themselves as neutral participants in the formation of policy in higher education. Institutional researchers—precisely because of their roles in administration—were uniquely qualified to conduct basic research on educational effectiveness as the intersection of student learning (educational processes) and resource allocations (administrative efficiencies). In other words, the fifth president suggested that the profession move beyond the tenuous balancing act between faculty and administrative perspectives to adopt its own research perspective on higher education. Moreover, in Mason's estimation, the mission of the Association for Institutional Research entailed direct contributions to basic research and policies for higher education in general.

Nonetheless, opponents to further involvement of institutional research in policy making and basic research on higher education thrived at the highest levels of the association. At the fourth forum of the association, following Hull's presentation on the potential role for institutional research to take greater initiative in policy making, Joe L. Saupe, fourth President of the Association and Director of Institutional Research at the University of Missouri, claimed that the first three presidential addresses "could not be topped." He subsequently turned his presidential address into an exhaustive presentation on "the assessment of program quality." The copious details of his presentation suggested that higher education quality assessment required a hopeless level of contextualization, in effect satirizing those who regarded centralized offices of institutional research as key agencies in quality assessment.

The brief conclusion to his presidential address served to reaffirm Saupe's assertion from the 1964 NIRF meeting that institutional research was not a discipline and that faculty had to provide the disciplinary expertise to evaluate the activities of higher education. Noting first that college classes had met "for one or two hundred years without such a program of quality assessment," he asked, "Where should the responsibility for quality assessment lie?" His answer was "with the department faculty."

In a subordinated role, "Central offices, for example, the office of institutional research, may serve to coordinate the effort and serve as resources to departments." In sum, Saupe's presidential address delivered a bitter rebuke about the limits of institutional research as a "fact-finding" agency with no policy-making implications or expertise for faculty's sphere of activity.[11]

In November 1970, on the heels of Mason's statement for an enlarged role for institutional research, Saupe then cowrote with James B. Montgomery, the second president of the Association and Director of Institutional Research for the University of Tennessee, the AIR's first official "prepared statement on the nature and role of institutional research" for college faculty and administrators.[12] The statement borrowed "extensively" from Saupe's prior engagement at a workshop on institutional research for the West Virginia Commission on Higher Education in 1968. For this reason, "The Nature and Role of Institutional Research: A Memo to a College or University," reflects in many respects the prior opinions that Saupe had staked out in regard to the future of institutional research.[13]

Although Montgomery's contributions at the annual forums in previous years suggest he favored a local role for institutional research in policy making and planning far more than Saupe, the one commonality both seemed to share was a lack of regard for institutional research as basic research. His second presidential address, delivered in 1967, focused on "two basic types of studies for the future" open to institutional researchers: operations management and academic development in the local institution. He allocated little time to the consideration of "experimental" research—meaning basic or academic research—except to note the lack of effort and success by institutional researchers. In 1970, he again spoke on "an effective role for institutional research" as operations management and academic development research, dismissing outright the possibility of "a grandiose study" regarding student learning outcomes "under the quarter or the semester system…the controls necessary for it are such as to preclude one."[14] Echoing Saupe's sentiments on program quality assessment, Montgomery perceived the contextual setting of higher education as a barrier to a common, scientific system of inquiry.

Endorsed in the preface by then-president of the Association for Institutional Research, Sidney Suslow from the University of California, Saupe and Montgomery's memo notably begins with the assertion that higher education always practiced institutional research functions—the real question then was whether the institution organize these function under a central office. Briefly considering how institutional size and public accountability influences the decision to create a dedicated administrative unit, they addressed their memo to a college or university that "considers whether or not and how to formalize the institutional research function."

Framed in this manner, they encourage college leaders generally to relegate the decision to create an office of institutional research to a question of decentralization or centralization rather than in terms of the rigor, reliability, and validity of the studies undertaken.

Introducing the considerations involved, they offered a definition for institutional research proposed by Paul L. Dressel at Michigan State University in an unpublished mimeographed essay from 1966: "Institutional research involves the collection of data or the making of studies useful or necessary in (a) understanding and interpreting the institution; (b) making intelligent decisions about current operations or plans for the future; (c) improving the efficiency and effectiveness of the institution." As context, the authors forwarded the views of John Dale Russell who emphasized "the need for an administratively oriented office," Nevitt Sanford, who "called for studies by a research organization free from administrative needs," and Rourke and Brooks, who characterized the function as "'a variegated form of organizational self-study.'" These three views, Saupe and Montgomery claimed, "span the range of definitions in the literature," despite the fact that only the first derived directly from an institutional researcher with a connection to the substantive yet inconclusive discussions held at the forums in the prior ten years.

The two former presidents of the Association for Institutional Research then proposed, as their own contribution, a more diminished definition and role for institutional research: "institutional research consists of data collection, analyses, reporting, and related staff work designed to facilitate operations and decision-making within institutions of higher education." Described entirely in terms of "staff functions," as opposed to line (executive) or faculty responsibilities, the memo continues with descriptions that make clear that institutional research collects, tabulates, and reports "the facts...[that] hopefully are used in decision-making." Under "related staff work," the memo stresses that the institutional researchers "should not be called into political situations" of policy-making or administrative decision-making, but if necessary "with proper considerations for the priorities on his time" and degree of "expertise on higher education." Even then, the "objectivity and detachment characteristic of all scientific endeavor" required the institutional researcher "to remain in a staff role, separate from policy determination and decision-making."

Having minimized the role for institutional research as an administrative staff capacity apart from policy making and decision-making, Saupe and Montgomery then delimited the potential for institutional research to contribute to "pure" or "basic" research on higher education. Citing the keynote address at the first forum organized by the Association for Institutional Research in 1966, the two collaborators addressed a concern that the field had "produced little of lasting significance." In response, rather than enumerate the success of the functions as practiced generally in higher education since the first American colleges incorporated or the progress of the field since its organization as a centralized administrative unit during the preceding fifty years, Saupe and Montgomery sought to correct the expectations of those with less familiarity for the profession:

> The critics seem to confuse institutional research, as we view it, with the more basic research on higher education carried out in the centers for the study of higher education and by scholars in higher education and related subject fields. Certainly the more fundamental research is essential and practicing institutional researchers would be proud to have the general researchers included with them in a broader category of those committed to institutional research. But institutional research is specific and applied and the other is general and theoretical, institutional research should not be expected to produce knowledge of pervasive and lasting significance, though on occasion it may.

Invoking a hard distinction between basic research and applied research on higher education, Saupe and Montgomery effectively circumscribed the knowledge yielded from institutional research to nongeneralizable and ephemeral findings. They in essence provide a paradigm for the practice of institutional research that categorically embeds its studies and findings in the particularity of each institution and the extemporaneous requests for data or facts. When such requests demanded academic prowess, whether to perform basic research or to perform program quality assessments, the two former presidents asserted that institutional research functions should defer to the expertise of faculty or faculty committees.

Their explanation for the nature of institutional research knowledge complemented their understanding of practitioners as rooted to the particularity of each and every institution. The consequences of the definition of institutional research and the scope of institutional research cannot be overstated. As an activity that produced parochial and unstudied "facts," institutional research did not produce something akin to the accumulation of knowledge or, therefore, a community of scientific researchers dedicated to the discovery of the next unknown in higher education. When they returned to the question of how a college or university may "formalize the institutional research function" into a single office, they demurred: "This memo, while referring frequently to the 'institutional researcher,' has focused on institutional research as a function with a minimum of specific implications for organization. There are many organizational options available. These range from utilizing existing personnel in existing units to the creation of an office of institutional research with a director and staff...Clearly, no prescription for success can be suggested here. Too much depends upon the size, style, and needs of the individual college or university." The two former presidents of the

Association for Institutional Research, to the contrary, offered one explicit conclusion: the organization of a centralized office for institutional research could not "be undertaken intensively without a considerable expenditure."

In the first official document released by the Association for Institutional Research to advise colleges and universities that had not yet established institutional research offices, Saupe and Montgomery effectively laid the foundations for the stagnation of institutional research and its shift away from the scientific study of higher education as a centralized administrative unit. The underlying and contradictory arguments for the nature of institutional research stated that it should not be regarded as a scientific endeavor and that it should not be involved in "policy determination and decision making" in deference to the spirit of "all scientific endeavor." In short, the AIR soon after its establishment adopted the position that the professionals under its auspices contribute to neither basic research nor decision-making directly. Institutional researchers report the facts—insular and fleeting—if sometimes informative to others who hold responsibility for policy making and decision-making. At the same time, the AIR expected practitioners to "anticipate problems or issues before they occur," though unable to organize with colleagues for the accumulation of knowledge and contribute to "developments and research in higher education generally." Unlike the aspirational statements first published by practitioners in the late 1950s and early 1960s, the new association conjured the worst of all possible worlds for institutional research.

The Typical Higher Education Program May Be the Least Desirable Preparation

In the most recent *Handbook of Institutional Research* (2012), Donald Reichard delivers the history of the profession with a nod to the "debate" on the scientific potential of institutional research. In four brief paragraphs referencing the same authors from the 1960s cited by Saupe and Montgomery, he provides no substantive review of arguments in the "debate." He concludes with reference to a work from the early 1970s by Paul L. Dressel, who "as the founder of the Office of Institutional Research at Michigan State University, took the middle ground." Presumably, since the section ends after a literature review of a debate with documents from forty and more years ago, Reichard credits Dressel with the final word on the scientific or scholarly potential for institutional research on higher education.[15]

Paul L. Dressel edited the first handbook for institutional research, published in 1971. The various chapters in the handbook describe aspects of the work that can be done for a particular institution "to probe deeply into the workings of an institution for evidence of weaknesses or flaws," a purpose and program of research with negative connotations alluding to the peril of scrutiny. He categorically dismisses commonalities between institutional research and academic scholarship on higher education:

> Institutional research is different from the research of faculty members in a number of ways. It does not share the mantle of academic freedom; it is primarily utilitarian and therefore has a distinctive set of values; and its ultimate success depends less on the research findings than on the promotion of action to alleviate functional weaknesses and to increase the effectiveness of the institution.

At the conclusion, he surveys the future and presents institutional research with a choice among three options: a) applied research for the effectiveness of the college, b) operations research regarding efficiencies and resource allocations, and c) data coordinators for other offices and faculty committees that conduct their own institutional research—the last, corresponding to the proposal of Rourke and Brooks.[16]

Given his stature and influence over the practice of institutional research in the past forty years as "the middle ground," Dressel's ideas perhaps deserve more scrutiny than any other author of his generation. While such an endeavor is beyond the scope of this work, Dressel's definition for institutional research served a specific purpose in his larger body of writings on scholarly research on higher education. When viewed through the prism of his dual efforts to define two professions at once, the middle ground he offered doubled as a wedge—basic research versus applied research—to drive between institutional research and research on higher education.

His credentials as an institutional researcher notwithstanding, as a faculty member of the College of Education at Michigan State University, Dressel also contributed to the foundation of the Association of Professors of Higher Education, today known as the Association for the Study of Higher Education (ASHE). As the title of the third meeting of the association attests, *Higher Education: A Developing Field of Study*, the new association thoroughly considered the path forward for scholarship and research on higher education as a field of study. One of the pressing questions many members, including Dressel, sought to answer was how "to distinguish between [a higher education department's] role and that of an office of institutional research."[17] At the same meeting, Dressel contributed a summary of his forthcoming work, *Higher Education as a Field of Study*, cowritten with Lewis B. Mayhew, another member of the new organization for professors of higher education.

Over his career, Lewis B. Mayhew became a noted critic of the "the research demands and a corporate-style bureaucracy" in higher education.[18] Given his reputation and relative lack of institutional research experience, Mayhew surprisingly delivered the keynote address at the 1966 forum, the first held after the organization of the Association for Institutional Research. His caustic address chided institutional researchers because, in his estimation, the newly organized profession had "yet to make a major impact on the main course of thinking about higher education." After listing a sample of works that epitomized such impacts in his estimation, Mayhew concluded, "When one thinks of what is really known about the central structures of higher education the names which most quickly come to mind are not, with a few exceptions, those men devoting their full professional talents to institutional research and to the accumulation of information about the enterprise." Although he went on to suggest strategies for institutional researchers to become more relevant, Mayhew's condemnation of the profession set a lasting impression on the association.[19] Only a few years later, Saupe and Montgomery cited Mayhew's keynote address to support their dismal outlook for institutional research as the production of knowledge with no "pervasive and lasting significance."

Mayhew does not explicitly state his motivations for attending the forum or delivering the first keynote address following the formation of the Association for Institutional Research. If he intended to acclimate the new association to the faculty perspective or inspire institutional researchers to pursue significant contributions on their own is not made clear by his presentation. As the association leadership sought to inspire the profession to take on greater roles in policy making and basic research, however, he joined Dressel in writing what became a touchstone for faculty scholars on the measure of their progress to form a distinct discipline on higher education.

To the extent that their work examines institutional research, Dressel and Mayhew typically consider the field when seeking to draw distinctions from higher education as a field of study, by which they meant a field of study for faculty researchers. In a section entitled "Institutional versus Pure Research," Dressel and Mayhew clearly delineate institutional research in order to promote their agenda for research on higher education as field of study. The key passage reads:

> Institutional research is directed to problems and decisions within institutions or systems of institutions...Research on higher education, in contrast...may be conducted for many reasons: individual curiosity, increased personal understanding, theory development or validation, basis for policy formulation, arousal of interest and concern, or influencing the opinions and the decisions of certain groups in the higher education enterprise.[20]

The imperative to distinguish between institutional research and scholarly research is readily apparent in these words, but the logic for the distinction is lacking in the entirety of the work. For instance, whereas individual curiosity and search for personal understanding motivates basic research on higher education, "[a]n institutional researcher…who becomes enamored of doing research for the sake of enhanced personal insight and increased stature among his fellows is not fulfilling his [sic] obligation." In lieu of considered analysis, at key points in the work, the authors simply invoke institutional research when they wish to define institutional research as the contrast for research on higher education by faculty.

Dressel and Mayhew do not explain why research within an institution or system of institutions may not be directed for the very same reasons as faculty research on higher education. Do not institutional administrators have a stake in influencing opinions and decisions of certain groups in the higher education enterprise? Does an institution not have a stake in the basis for policy formation? Would not an institution benefit from theory development or validation before taking an action to improve its operations? Is not increased personal understanding or even curiosity the prerequisite of research and development for a college and university? More problematic, of course, is the question: is not faculty as a key stakeholder in the governance of colleges and universities directed to problems and decisions within institutions or systems of institutions? The last question, while widely apparent in the literature, like the prior questions is not addressed to explain how institutional research and faculty research differ fundamentally as applied and "pure" research.

In a lengthy monograph on the requirements for research on higher education to become a field of doctoral-level study in the American academy, the authors note, "Higher education as a field of study is sufficiently complex as to require great strength from a number of [other] fields." In contrast, "The intelligent institutional researcher can quickly learn on the job most of what he needs to know about higher education problems." The difference between institutional research and research on higher education is most starkly evident in one line of the work: "Institutional research requires such a range of knowledge and proficiencies that the typical higher education program may be the least desirable preparation." Consequently, Dressel and Mayhew preconceived institutional research as wholly foreign to higher education programming, and the advancement of institutional research posed little concern to scholars of higher education interested in the field's development into a discipline.[21]

When considered in the context of the parallel development of administrative institutional research and higher education as a field of study, what appears to be Dressel's "middle ground" for the role of institutional research in higher education reflects his solution to the problem for professors of higher education programs to legitimize their own field of study. A full comparison of statements regarding the differences between institutional research and research on higher education in Dressel's works would certainly provide more comprehensive and nuanced insight into Dressel's use of the distinctions between institutional research and research on higher education. In its most basic form, however, it is enough to know that "in the nature of things," Dressel did not perceive the nature and progress of institutional research as integral to the nature and progress of higher education as a field of study. Quite the opposite, according to Dressel, higher education as a field of study is measured by its difference and distance from institutional research as a practice.

Montgomery and Mayhew's contributions aside, the Association for Institutional Research has repeatedly credited Paul L. Dressel and Joe L. Saupe with the definitive statements on the role and nature of institutional research since the early 1970s. While Dressel serves as a touchstone for distinguishing institutional research from research on higher education, Saupe updated his statement on the role and nature of institutional research for the association in 1981.[22] Dressel and Saupe worked together at Michigan State University's institutional research office during the 1960s prior to the prominent role each played in drafting the early documents for the association. Together, following the lead of Rourke and Brooks, the two Michigan State University colleagues formalized a consensus paradigm and historical emplotment for the practice of institutional research that has perdured for nearly fifty years.[23]

Their writings set down four fundamental tenets for the practice of institutional research that influenced the practice and organization of institutional research in subsequent years. First, institutional research is "a function" of administrative staff (Dressel and Saupe). Second, "institutional research is different from the research of faculty members" (Dressel), and they warn not "to confuse institutional research, as we view it, with the more basic research on higher education" (Saupe). Third, the purpose of institutional research is "to probe deeply into the workings of [a single] institution" (Dressel); thus institutional research is "specific and applied…and should not be expected to produce knowledge of pervasive and lasting significance." (Saupe). Fourth, as "a function," institutional research may be performed by nonspecialists and faculty committees (Dressel) and, generally, "carried on in institutions whether or not individuals or organizational units are specifically assigned to institutional research" (Saupe). In a short time, the consensus paradigm appeared to be a settled question in the subsequent literature under the control of scholars of higher education and the Association for Institutional Research.

Lest Institutional Research Serve to Diminish Personal and Departmental Autonomy

Rourke and Brooks's riposte to "the heart" of the managerial revolution in higher education epitomized a reactionary vision for institutional research taking shape among scholars, as the two readily acknowledged. Yet they were in no position to influence the direction of the profession or its association. Institutional researchers, such as their champions Paul L. Dressel and Joe L. Saupe, who held faculty status in the education departments of their universities, shared similar concerns regarding the lines between the spectra of research on higher education taking place throughout American society. In this context, the prodigious output on "the role," "the function," and "the nature" of institutional research by researchers on higher education since 1965 reflects the enduring concern among scholars who feel compelled to distinguish institutional research from their own research on higher education. Unsurprisingly, a key passage in these writings on the "nature" of institutional research lingers over the question of how administrators' institutional research fundamentally differs from faculty's research on higher education as the distinction between applied research and basic research.

For example, the authors of "Institutional Research: A Review of the Literature to 1972" neglect statements from prior decades on the overlapping domains of applied and basic research. Instead, they offered a definition that recites Dressel and Saupe's position on "[t]he distinction between institutional research and research on higher education," asserting that "research on higher education is a more comprehensive concept than is institutional research." After a summary review of the connection of institutional research to self-study, the authors conclude, "Thus, institutional research is research about a particular institution of higher learning by those within the institution for the express purpose of aiding in the administration of the institution." Echoing Dressel and Mayhew, the authors of the literature review then warn practitioners that greater aspirations are illegitimate: "[I]nstitutional research differs from scholarly research. It can only be justified if it aids the institution and those who are responsible for its operation."[24] Whereas Stickler, writing on behalf of the land-grant colleges and state universities, demonstrated that the imperatives of particular institutions proved detrimental to the rigor and scientificity of institutional research, the consensus paradigm hailed the inward focus as the proper sphere of institutional research and the fulfillment of institutional self-study.

In a sudden reversal with the past, long-time observers of institutional research took note of the new direction for institutional research. In an evaluation of the recent turn to reporting facts without further analysis, the president of Radford College labeled institutional research an "evolving misnomer" unworthy of the term, "research."[25] Doi noted in 1979 the absence of historical memory regarding the early contributions and origins of institutional research in the 1950s. While a few lamented the transformation, many scholars welcomed this new development in the trajectory of institutional research as a profession. In fact, the antipathy for institutional research became *de rigueur* in the publications professing to advance the field, and Dressel and/or Saupe diligently stood by to support the consensus paradigm when others questioned the lack of professionalism in the new field.

For instance, in the 1979 edition of *New Directions for Institutional Research* entitled, *Professional Development for Institutional Research*, Dressel expressed "dismay" when he "found increasingly that some individuals regard higher education programs as effective training for institutional research." His certainty that institutional research differed from research on higher education never wavered; he affirmed his position that doctoral programs in higher education abandon all hope for the professional development of institutional researchers. Dressel, more to the point, freely expressed his motivations for discouraging the professional development of institutional researchers among his peers. In the concluding article to the collection, the editor noted, "Paul Dressel is concerned lest institutional research serves to diminish personal and departmental autonomy, and he offers cautions about 'overprofessionalization.'"[26] In sum, the ideological interest in faculty and academic programs openly eclipsed the professional needs of institutional researchers in Dressel's scholarship.

Similarly, though not cited as an editor or a contributor to a single article in the volume, Dressel's name appears under the list of authors for the 1980 work *Improving Academic Management: A Handbook of Planning and Institutional Research*. Other contributors nonetheless parrot Dressel's concerns for "personal and departmental autonomy" in the college and university. The second article in the collection advocates for "an adversarial model" that pushed institutions to adopt "decentralized research capabilities and planning responsibility" in order to empower individual departments to "self-consciously guide the interpretation of factual data." A later contributor explains more fully why institutions must decentralize institutional research functions:

> Typical institutional research into...[teaching-learning environments] is not collaborative at all. The researchers or a few higher ups decide what to ask, how to ask it, and what the resulting data say. Then they report *their* [emphasis in original] findings, not ours. The upshot is that we are uninterested or distrustful. These are not our kind of evidence about our

concerns. Our thinking did not go into the analysis. And besides, those institutional researchers are probably under the president's thumb.

In explicit terms, the author goes on to explain why the faculty perspective—"our thinking"—failed to yield a community for the scientific study of higher education administration *qua* institutional research. "The organization of colleges contradicts the goal of an effective learning community about teaching and learning," he exclaimed. "College members are separated into contending camps, not integrated into a mutually supportive community."[27] Faculty's widespread suspicion of institutional research seemed to push scholars to abandon decorum and collegiality even when ostensibly publishing a handbook for the field's practitioners in higher education administration.

7 | IN A PRE-PARADIGM STAGE IN PERPETUITY

Institutional Research Is Not a Science, and It Does Not Need to Be

Writing in 1978, Cameron Fincher, a faculty member in education in the University of Georgia system for over fifty years and director of its Institute for Higher Education for thirty years, praised the 1966 work by Rourke and Brooks. Conversely, he dismissed Henle's 1967 report on a total information system as an artifact of a prior era preoccupied with "scientific and technological progress" for higher education management: "The Henle Report (1967) can be read, in retrospect, as a manifesto for managerial control, public accountability, and governmental supervision." A frequent contributor to the AIR forums in the late 1970s and early 1980s, he regarded the "predictable crises" in institutional research as a consequence of its maturity, its "young adult years," drawing an analogy with corresponding "growth stages" in developmental psychology.

"Questions asked about the maturity of institutional research need not receive flattering answers but they should be asked openly and frankly," he begins. Though regarding the field as a "professional specialty," he assayed the immaturity of the field in terms of its lack of specialization, inability to elevate its status, its standards of preparation for new professionals, and the unsophisticated communications among existing practitioners. Given the many unflattering blemishes of these "young adult years," though similar in character to "the path of growth and development that other professional specialties have followed," it was inevitable that there "will indeed be 'predictable crises' that should concern practitioners of the art."[1]

In his analogy with the predictable crises or passions of the young adult, Fincher deliberately chose to describe institutional research as an "art." In a 1985 article, "The Art and Science of Institutional Research," he dismissed as undesirable and unattainable any aspiration for institutional research to become a social scientific study of higher education. Appealing to the consensus paradigm, he argued that the "origins of institutional research are embedded...in institutional functions and activities" of the autonomous colleges and universities, naming history as the closest approximate, since "no concept of systematic research" guided the pioneering efforts. Given this perceived origin, he unequivocally denied science as a meaningful archetype in his abstract: "Institutional research is not a science, and it does not need to be. It is a practicing art with commendable promise as a professional technical specialty in policy-related research." Appearing in an edition of *New Directions for Institutional Research*, those in a position to influence the direction of the field welcomed his further elaboration of the consensus paradigm defining institutional research as an art. With respect for his career-long effort to clarify and advance the art of institutional research within the strictures of the consensus paradigm, the Association for Institutional Research conferred all three of its honors on Cameron Fincher during his lifetime: the Outstanding Service Award (1980), John Stecklein Distinguished Member Award (1983), and the Sidney Suslow Scholar Award (1995).[2]

Occasionally, however, an outsider to the consensus paradigm emerged to challenge the undisciplined drift of the profession. In 1990, Frans Van Vught, a European scholar in higher education, attended the Annual Forum of the Association for Institutional Research to argue the need for a scientific basis in institutional research. Correctly identifying the lack of the scientific élan among the association's leadership, Van Vught urged institutional researchers "to develop such a scientific base for itself, or to drift away from the fundamental values that belong to the academic attitude to which institutional research is oriented." At the time of his presentation, Van Vught surmised that a "scientific base will increase the legitimacy and the academic standing of institutional research." His concern rested with the ability of institutional researchers to affect change at their institutions when faculty and professionals from other sciences may easily question the stringency of institutional research: "the low academic standing of institutional research may create legitimacy problems." In concert with early practitioners in the United States, Van Vught characterized the specialization, stature, and legitimacy of the profession as features directly influenced by the deliberate application of the principles of science rather than as a natural process of maturation for an art form that must be indulged, as Fincher advised.

Van Vught squarely placed responsibility for the lack of a scientific basis on the profession and the association, whose membership had grown to nearly two thousand five hundred members by 1989–90. He observed that the noticeable decline in the prestige of institutional research over the previous twenty-five years paralleled the decline in regard for professions in general. His colleagues differed from other professionals in that "the complacency of institutional researchers concerning the professional status of their field" stood out. To remedy the situation in which institutional research found itself, he recommended "the empirical-analytical approach of social science research" entailing theorization, falsifiability, empiricism, and universality. If institutional researchers and their association chose to disregard the power of scientifically based knowledge accumulation, its practitioners risked becoming members of a "minor profession" or one that would cease to be regarded as a profession whatsoever. Whether knowingly or not, by fixing the start of a progressive decline for the profession in 1965, Van Vught offered an indictment of the AIR and the scholars of higher education who shaped the consensus paradigm during the prior two decades.[3]

Van Vught's presentation itself proved to be unremarkable in that he failed to redirect the drift of the profession or spur a reevaluation of the basic tenets of the consensus paradigm advanced by American scholars— unremarkable with one exception: the devoted defense marshaled by the AIR's leadership in support of the unscientific aspirations for the field and undisciplined organization of professionals as defined by Dressel and Saupe. Among the handful of responses to Van Vught's challenge by members of the association at the forum, a former president of the AIR invited a scholar of higher education with no evident experience in institutional research to speak. George Keller, an education scholar from the University of Pennsylvania, describing his experience working with the AIR leadership, expressed his astonishment with the coordinated effort to rebuff Van Vught: "I now have a sense of what it's like to have the National Rifle Association or the American Association of Retired Persons lean on you." The inelegant allusion appears to have been intended as a sign of endorsement, and Keller went on to dismiss Van Vught's argument explicitly as if to provide the formal counterargument to the European on behalf of the association's leadership.

Echoing Fincher from five years earlier, Keller tersely advised attendees that institutional research is "an art, not a science." Seemingly without recognizing his confirmation of Van Vught's argument, he went so far as to dispute the value of science in general: "We have come to believe that science is somehow a higher activity than statesmanship or craftsman-like behavior." In deference to the consensus paradigm, Keller explained, "For better or worse, institutional researchers seem to be married to institutions of higher education."[4] Internally, the forces of centralization and decentralization driven by technological innovations pulled institutional research functions in every direction, largely outside the control of practitioners. Externally, in his longest section, he enumerated the unwieldy changes at foot in demographics, socioeconomic conditions, international economics, culture, religion, politics, and higher education per se. Contra Van Vught, Keller aimed to dispel the illusion of control for a profession such as institutional research.

George Keller's response to Van Vught was only one in a series of refutations released under the auspices of the Association for Institutional Research in the following years. These publications reasserted the categorical difference between institutional research and research on higher education as the distinction between applied research and basic research. As an applied research, institutional research was irredeemably embedded in the particular institution and subject to the undisciplined needs of decision-makers at every turn. Mindful of the need to maintain some semblance of professionalism for members of the Association for Institutional Research, however, later scholars offered more nuanced assessments to fabricate models of maturation or specialization for the profession. Nonetheless, the scholarship on institutional research redoubled its commitment to the role and nature of institutional research defined in the consensus paradigm, while the profession continued its drift toward the outcome foretold by Frans Van Vught.

Any Component of the College or University May Have a Responsibility for Institutional Research

George Keller's opposition to the regard for or practice of institutional research as a social science invoked the skepticism for professionals in general, as Van Vught characterized the era. Keller, an invited speaker at the forum, counseled the attendees that "many of the finest people in the social sciences are coming to believe that the social world may not be as susceptible to scientific lawfulness." Institutional research, he inferred, would be misguided by the pursuit of scientific discipline. Moreover, the advancements of computing technology drove institutions to decentralize their institutional research functions in an "information feudalism" in which the institutional researcher, as a "staff role," would have to partner with the faculty and "local unit heads." In the emerging conditions created by information systems, institutional research required "different loyalties" and "different outlooks" to help "individual deans sharpen the data…for their partisan management needs." Recalling the adversarial environment of higher education advocated in the consensus paradigm, institutional research served ideological ends despite the best intentions.

For this reason, institutional researchers controlled "only part" of their future as a profession because the local executive officers and faculty deans would determine what "information their institution should have." Keller concluded that individual professionals had little control over the direction of their profession due to the influence of computer technology and their subordination as a staff role to administrative decision-makers. Understanding decentralization as the more dominant force internally, he warned, "[Y]ou face a tearing asunder of your profession, a feudalization of your profession."[5] Thus, while on the one hand he criticized the association's "passive and laissez-faire attitude" to envisioning the future of higher education and its lack of standards for professional training, he counseled the professionals before him to resign themselves to the feudal tutelage demanded by the irrepressible political partisanship of higher education administration.

In several negative respects, Van Vught and Keller's projections for the profession of institutional research paralleled each other. Neither considered institutional research as a viable profession if organized as "an art" under the direct control of local administrative directors and deans. Van Vught naïvely held out hope that American institutional researchers would take responsibility for the future of their profession. On the other hand, scholars of higher education who had little to no direct responsibilities as institutional researchers, like George Keller, commanded the podium when questions of the role and nature of institutional research came into question. Although the sentiments expressed by Van Vught episodically surfaced in subsequent forum meetings or publications, the Association for Institutional Research consistently advocated for the undisciplined and nonprofessional characterizations first advanced by Rourke, Brooks, Dressel, and Saupe.

Two months prior to Van Vught's presentation at the 1990 Annual Forum, the AIR leadership enlisted Joe L. Saupe to update his earlier policy paper, "Functions of Institutional Research," the third iteration of the document that he originally cowrote with James Montgomery for the association in 1970.[6] "Although the basic nature and functions of institutional research have not changed," as Saupe introduced the new edition, he agreed to submit a new version, reviewed and revised with the endorsement of the AIR's publications board and executive committee. Little, of course, had changed in Saupe's opinion from 1964, when he asserted that institutional research could not be a discipline. The timing for the third release of his dismal conceptual framework for institutional research thus can be read as a prebuttal to Van Vught's anticipated presentation at the upcoming forum.

The title of the revised statement distributed by the Association prominently announced, once again, that institutional research be regarded as a function and not a profession. The first section on the "nature and purpose of institutional research" then leads with the distinction between applied and basic research, stressing that institutional research be "distinguished from research on postsecondary education which has as its purpose the advancement of knowledge about and practice in postsecondary education generally." As an applied research, "within an institution of higher education to provide the information which supports institutional planning, policy formation, and decision making," the proper sphere of investigation was the "individual college, university, or system." Saupe relegates the "translation of...various items of data into information useful to planners and decision makers" to the domain of "management information," by which he meant not generalizable knowledge with "pervasive and lasting significance." As a function for decision-making, the "place" of institutional research was "in the individual academic and administrative units of the college or university." Although some institutions organized certain functions in a central office, he placed a special emphasis on the decentralization of the functions among the unit heads: "Any component of the college or university may have a responsibility for institutional research."

In a restatement on the subordination of institutional research, as applied research, to research on higher education, as basic research, Saupe asserts, "the purposes of institutional research and research on higher education differ." While the two may contribute to each other, "[t]he problems, methodology, and results of the general research can be applied and particularized in institutional research," whereas "the findings of institutional research may merit generalization through broader studies" by scholars of higher education. The bonds of administrative institutional research to its particular institution can only be broken by the generalizations of basic research by higher education scholars. Thus, the twofold subordination of institutional research to bolster the perspective of faculty—as both unit heads and basic researchers—remained at the nucleus of his instrumentalization of institutional research as a function in higher education administration.

In the twenty years following Saupe's first position paper on behalf of the Association for Institutional Research, the applied-basic distinction had become the dominant rationale for delimiting the "function" and "role" of institutional research. The year following Van Vught's presentation, the 1991 Annual Forum of the Association for Institutional Research featured a presentation entitled "Science and Institutional Research: The Links." Two political scientists who had no prior experience in the field of institutional research attended in order to dispel "the misconceptions about the 'research' in institutional research." Endowed with a proper social scientific education, E. Bernadette McKinney and John J. Hindera educated the attendees, "In science there is no intent to solve practical problems, only attempts to contribute to knowledge." Logically concluding from the premise of their ideology of pure science, the authors endeavored to help institutional research practitioners to understand that "[i]nstitutional research is more an art than a science." In other words, "research" was a misnomer, and the link between institutional research and science was, therefore, an error in judgment.

Applying concepts from Thomas Kuhn's philosophy of science, the authors further claimed that "institutional research is in a pre-paradigm stage; no body of scientific theory controls the kinds of questions that can be asked or the kinds of answers sought."[7] The reason traced directly to its performance as an applied research for a single college or university, driven by the demands of decision-makers. McKinney and Hindera conclude that the conditions for institutional research to move beyond the "pre-paradigm stage" were insufficient and suggest, in resignation, "If institutional research were not so dependent on the perceptions of those within a particular institutional context, it might be possible for a discipline to emerge…For the most part, others set the agenda for institutional research…There is little incentive for this [to] change."[8]

The presentation enthralled the AIR Forum Publications Committee members who "judged [the presentation] to be of high quality and of interest to others concerned with the research of higher education." The irony, of course, was that the authors explicitly distinguished the concerns of institutional research from the concerns of research on higher education. The committee exposed its obligation to the latter. Subsequently, *Research in Higher Education* published the paper in its 1992 edition promoting contributions from the Annual Forum of the Association for Institutional Research. The article has stood for over twenty-five years as the last word from the flagship journal of the association on the links between institutional research and science.

In the wake of Van Vught's presentation, the distinction between applied and basic research reaches an inflection point in the effort to draft a code of ethics for institutional researchers in 1992. In a dispute on the use of the terms "profession" or "craft," the AIR committee charged with drafting the code of ethics noted that:

> "[Professional] occupations share several important characteristics: (1) a well-defined body of knowledge that is rigorously taught, (2) a gate-keeping function to define who may practice the occupation, so as to protect the public from improperly trained practitioners and untrained pretenders, and (3) an enforced code of behavior and practice. Institutional research does not qualify on any of these criteria."

In its rationalization on the statement of competence, after citing a short list of common if not universal institutional research functions, the committee lapsed back into institutional particularity and concluded: "what constitutes competence in institutional research at one institution may be quite different from the criteria of another." With the direction of institutional research as a practice firmly under the control of nonpractitioners, "There is no agreed-upon theoretical definition of institutional research and consequently no consensus about the content of the body of knowledge that one ought, in the abstract, to acquire in order to practice institutional research." In short, the authors argue, institutional research always lacked the qualifications of a profession, qualifications that Van Vught simply had assumed to be the original status.

The AIR committee also weighed in on institutional researchers' ability to contribute research on higher education. In response to correspondence to the committee on the question of whether the practitioners should conduct studies "with broader applications" and generalizable knowledge regarding "human and institutional behavior," the committee informed the members of the Association for Institutional Research where the responsibility "properly belongs": "We by no means discourage that kind of research. But note that it properly belongs to the domain of the scholar, typically must meet the tests of scholarly protocols and reproducibility, and is normally reported and subjected to peer criticism in refereed journals."[9] In substance, the committee did not regard institutional researchers, in respect to their own profession, as competent or empowered to develop a "well-defined body of knowledge that is rigorously taught" because that responsibility fell to the decision-makers at the local institutions and the scholars of higher education in academic departments. Therefore, the committee concluded, institutional research should be regarded as a craft and not a profession.

The theme that emerges from the slew of publications marshaled by the AIR as a direct or indirect refutation of Van Vught's thesis is that institutional researchers may be considered a community of artists or craftspeople but not scientists or professionals. They should not presume to contribute to generalizable knowledge while taking great care to please consumers of institutional research "within a particular institutional context." Twenty years following the interventions of Dressel and Saupe in the direction of the field, the consensus paradigm clearly kept scholars of higher education and the leadership of the Association for Institutional Research spellbound. At the heart of the new scholarship, the proponents popularized the notion for institutional research as applied research artfully performed rather than basic research scientifically conducted. The utilization of applied and basic research in this manner significantly severed all ties with the literature on institutional research prior to the organization of the Association for Institutional Research. And yet nothing was more self-evident to the association's scholars and leadership.

An Elaborate Profusion throughout the Institution

In the years following Van Vught's challenge, the nature of institutional research seemed to be a settled debate—it is applied research, not basic research, and an art, not science. The dismal forecast for the field offered by McKinney and Hindera at the 1991 forum, bluntly demonstrated the conclusions to be drawn from the sharp dichotomy of research interests. Though political scientists may welcome the conclusions to be drawn regarding institutional research, the practitioners in the field required more purpose. Consequently, later scholars of higher education turned their attention to more nuanced descriptions of institutional research functions and roles in order to address the question of professional development or drift with more compassion—or ambiguity. They described the practice of institutional research in terms evoking a progressive or developmental narrative. The question of whether institutional research is, was, could remain, or could ever be regarded as a profession nevertheless needled their scholarship. None, fundamentally, broke from the paradigm for institutional research defined by Dressel and Saupe decades earlier.

Two prominent scholars of higher education who specialized in studies on the field of institutional research after 1990 are Patrick T. Terenzini and J. Frederick Volkswein. Like Cameron Fincher, both have the distinction of receiving all three major awards conferred by the Association for Institutional Research: Outstanding Service Award, John Stecklein Distinguished Member Award, and Sidney Suslow Scholar Award. In addition, both served as directors of institutional research at the State University of New York at Albany before joining the Center for the Study of Higher Education at Penn State University as tenured faculty later in their careers. Both also worked as editor-in-chief for *New Directions for Institutional Research*, the quarterly publication released by Josey-Bass. Terenzini held the position between 1985 and 1995 and then Volkswein between 1995 and 2005. In their capacity at the journal, they influenced publications on the role, function, and nature of institutional research for twenty years. Their own scholarship on the subject, then, must be regarded as a body of literature worthy of critical study regarding the nature, function, and role of institutional research.

The summer 1990 edition of *New Directions for Institutional Research*, titled *Organizing Effective Institutional Research Offices*, addressed the subject directly. Published during Terenzini's editorial tenure around the same time as Van Vught's May presentation to the Annual Forum, the volume leads with an article by Volkswein on the "diversity of institutional research structures and tasks."[10] Though not explicitly invoking the distinction between applied and basic research, Volkswein opens the basis for his analysis as a contrast between "the heavy demands" on institutional researchers in their administrative role and the "personally and professionally rewarding" studies that originally led them to graduate education or the field. Volkswein surveyed offices in the northeast region's association for institutional research to explore an identity crisis for the profession that coincided with the "proliferation" or decentralization of institutional research functions during the 1980s.

As Rourke and Brooks did twenty-five years earlier, Volkswein discovered a wide range of office sizes, responsibilities, reporting lines, and education levels among the officers. Although office size and staff experience correlated with the performance of "a more complex array of tasks," the predictive power of their model fell short of expectations "due to the wide diversity of organizational arrangements and tasks." In other words, the particular institutions determined the function and role of the institutional research offices: "Viewed holistically, these data suggest that the field of institutional research…is less a unified profession than an evolving ecology of very different organizational arrangements." Essentially, Volkswein affirmed that the field may not be regarded as more than a function, capably performed by decentralized agents throughout the institution by nonspecialists.

Volkswein proceeded to offer a system of classification for institutional research offices that establishes a hierarchy of organization and activities according to the size and decentralization of the functions. He cites the literature on "organizational life cycles [that] identifies four stages of organizational development that parallel human development." Volkswein then characterizes institutional research offices in terms consistent with the life cycle of an organism: infancy and childhood, adolescence, adulthood, and maturity. Like a human newborn, an institutional research office may then expect to go through phases of a life cycle determined by some underlying ontogeny or organic process. Reminiscent of Fincher's facile application of human developmental psychology to an analysis of the field, Volkswein introduces more formal tools from organizational theory to assess the maturation or development of institutional research—as a function, not a profession.

At the infantile stage, institutions establish one-person "craft" offices that are "burdened by the demands of routine reporting and a modest amount of number-crunching for the institution." At the childhood stage, offices of up to three persons formed "small adhocracies…characterized by a flat hierarchy, simple structure, and little specialization…Similar to the infantile stage, small adhocracies remained "responsive to their administrative hosts." The "professional bureaucracy…[c]onsisting of at least four (but usually more) professionals" performed "a number of sophisticated research projects each year." Volkswein characterizes staff from such offices as the active contributors "to organizations such as the

AIR and NEAIR." In the final stage, "an elaborate profusion...[of] institutional research activities and expertise proliferate throughout the institution" to service "an analytical environment" with such complexity that institutional research is conducted by "different offices reporting to different parts of the administrative hierarchy."[11] Whereas the consensus paradigm insisted that colleges and universities performed decentralized institutional research long before the advent of the offices, Volkswein's organizational developmental theory identifies the most mature stage of development as an elaborate profusion, or decentralization, of institutional research functions.

Questionably, Volkswein discerned this fourfold classification despite the fact that only 23 of 141 institutions qualified to be more than "adolescent" stage offices with four or more staff members in the office. Over half had less than one full-time equivalent staff member (twenty-five offices) or one full-time staff member (sixty-four offices). In effect, he imposed a schema that pigeonholed more than 80 percent of offices of institutional research in an infantile or childhood stage of development (figure 1 in his article). More notably, Volkswein's developmental classifications do not apply solely to the offices of institutional research but to institutional research regarded as a decentralized function. The maturity or development of the institutional functions does not necessarily correlate with the capacities of the office dedicated to the study of its effectiveness or excellence. Thus, Volkswein's application of a developmental theory for an organism to the establishment of institutional research functions leads to several outcomes that reinforce the barriers to a "unified profession" and calls into question why most institutions would even consider centralizing such functions in an office.

Similarly, the developmental theory implies that the latter stages for institutional research offices encompassed and mastered the earlier stages. Volkwein's schema scales with the size, not the quality of the institution. Craft offices are found on campuses of fewer than five thousand enrollments, small adhocracies on campuses of five to ten thousand, and professional bureaucracies and elaborate profusions at the larger doctoral and research universities. The largeness of the institution inherently advances the practice of institutional research, not its efficiency or effectiveness to educate college students. In this respect, the largest universities such as Pennsylvania State University, where both Terenzini and Volkswein taught, exemplified the most mature form of organization for practitioners in the field. The singular preoccupation with the size of the institution neglects to consider the maturity of institutional research practices according to the scientific methodology or community involved, the democratization of public institutions or state systems to serve citizens, and the institutional excellence of the college or university.

Moreover, knowledge or expertise for institutional research flows unidirectionally from the later stages to the earlier stages—or, typically, from large research institutions to small teaching-centric institutions—reinforcing the distinction between basic research on higher education in general and applied research for a particular college or university. In effect, generalizable knowledge about higher education retains its stature as the most sophisticated or "purist" type of research. The applied knowledge of the professional adhocracies, while suitable for contributions to the professional associations for institutional research or higher education management, does not rise to the same level of generalizable knowledge or professional expertise from the elaborate profusions. Practitioners in the adolescent adhocracies and infantile craft offices, it goes without saying, offer little to the seasoned practitioners at the later stages of development.

Lastly, Volkswein affirms Saupe's assertion that the responsibility for institutional research largely rested with the functional academic and administrative units of the college or university. In the paradigm for institutional research advanced by Dressel and Saupe, special emphasis is placed on the practice of institutional research functions at the first institutions of higher education in America. Centralization of functions in an administrative office is a relatively recent occurrence in the arc of this historical narrative. Volkswein formalizes the sequence as a developmental structure in which institutional research functions begin and end as "naturally" decentralized activities interrupted by a period of centralization spurred by the immature growing pains of the institution. In this respect, after a temporary interregnum in the cocoon of an office, institutional research functions return to their origins as an "elaborate profusion" in the mature, partisan units of a college or university.

In a 2008 review published under the *New Directions* series, Volkswein affirmed the lasting value of his schema while cautioning readers not to read too much in his divisions: "in generalizing about the practice of institutional research…we know that organizational arrangements are highly variable from campus to campus and state to state." Although he showed more favor for the office structure of "a professional bureaucracy," nearly twenty years following his first article, he re-asserted that an "elaborate profession" of institutional research functions in the departments and units of the college or university remained the most mature style of organization in his schema. His follow-up survey research, nonetheless, showed that a substantial majority of colleges and universities established no more than "infantile" or "adolescent" offices of institutional research in the intervening years. His effort to classify offices of institutional research therefore yielded no clear favor for institutional research aside from its decentralized practice in large universities, despite practitioners' efforts to secure the legitimacy and stature of maturity.[12]

In his own right, beyond his influence as an editor, Terenzini contributed to the literature on the nature of institutional research on the heels of Van Vught's presentation. In the 1993 edition of *Research in Higher Education*, featuring presentations from the prior annual AIR forum, he provided a brief review of prior articles on the nature of institutional research and then recited the incontestable reasons that "differentiate institutional research from research on higher education." Terenzini proposed "a conception of institutional research that grows out of existing definitions" while claiming to refine the prior literature for broad application to the evolving functions of institutional research. Terenzini's analysis, in effect, immediately betrays his commitment to the presumption that institutional research is an applied research on a particular institution, and he organizes his conceptual framework for the tiers of "organizational intelligence" in a manner to shore up the consensus paradigm.[13]

In tier 1, "technical/analytical intelligence," Terenzini lumps together basic data aggregation routines, methodological "skills" to perform social scientific quantitative and qualitative research, and technical know-how to work with mainframe and personal computers. Echoing Dressel's assertion that institutional research has no basis in the doctoral programs of higher education or the collective wisdom of local faculty, tier 1 institutional research intelligence offers only "data without information, processes without purposes, analyses without problems, and answers without questions." Additionally, in drawing so many activities into one tier, Terenzini closely aligns tier 1 spheres of activity with the portfolio of institutional studies evident since the foundational contributions of Coleman Griffith, the University of Minnesota, and the Lins volume prior to 1965. In doing so, he described tier 1 intelligence as "fundamental and foundational" but nonetheless dismissed the tier as meaningless without the other two forms of intelligence.

At tier 2, "issues intelligence," Terenzini identifies institutional research with problem-solving activities for "middle- and upper-level administrators in various parts of the institution." Issues intelligence combines general "understanding how institutions function and how decisions are made...[with] how to work successfully with other people (both individually and in groups) to accomplish some goal." Tier 2 intelligence clearly factors into the ability of institutional research to contribute to institutional policies or budgeting for "annual and strategic planning activities." Again, however, Terenzini defines tier 2 in only a formal sense, "content without processes and questions without the tools to answer them," that also renders issues intelligence "insufficient...for the effective functioning of an institutional researcher." Tier 2 thereby provides the conventional argument for the prevailing subordination of institutional research to a particular institution and its internal political contests between deans and unit heads—its applied component—while positioning research—its theoretical component—as deficient for basic research on higher education.

Tier 3, "contextual intelligence," Terenzini therefore reserves as the crux of effective institutional research, "the crowning form of organizational intelligence." Herein, context serves as shorthand to suggest that institutional research must be deeply informed about the culture and history of one particular institution in order to perform at its highest levels. Context intelligence is "organizational savvy and wisdom" that endows the institutional researchers with "the knowledge of how business is done in *this* [his emphasis] particular college or university and who the key players are in both organizational and governance units." Acquired "*only* [his emphasis] through on-the-job training," context intelligence requires years of dedication to a single institution "that earns institutional research and researchers legitimacy, trust, and respect." True to both Saupe's and Dressel's assertions from twenty years earlier, Terenzini relegates institutional research to the production of knowledge without pervasive or lasting significance that is dearest to deans and unit heads in their administrative posts and offices.

Like Volkswein, Terenzini had the opportunity to revisit his conceptual framework at the 2012 Annual Forum where the Association for Institutional Research awarded him the John Stecklein Distinguished Member Award.[14] Once again, *Research in Higher Education* featured his presentation from the closing plenary session as a significant contribution to the literature on institutional research. Though acknowledging that his three tier systematization of organizational intelligence called for revisions, the subtitle of his presentation, "Plus Ça Change," signaled his conclusion that much remained the same. He acknowledged this judgment when he expressed his indebtedness to the mentorship of Cameron Fincher for his original "conception" of institutional research. In the conclusion, he quoted Fincher's article on the "art and science of institutional research" from 1985 as the continuing "challenge over the next decade": "'The merits of institutional research depend not on its scientific underpinnings, but on its relevance and influence in decision and policy making.'"[15]

At first blush, Terenzini's categorization of institutional research as a combination of technical/analytical, issue, and context intelligences appears to offer a framework within which a body of knowledge may accumulate or a profession gain stature. In the years since his original presentation, many institutional researchers and academicians reference his categorizations as an interpretative tool in presentations and in the practitioner literature. In the final analysis, however, his framework for organizational intelligence confines the contours of the field within the purview of each particular institution, effectively undermining the foundation for professional development. In effect, Terenzini presents a recondite explanation for the native limitations of institutional research as "fact-finding" (tier 1), unable to accumulate "knowledge of pervasive and lasting significance" (tier 2), and its practitioners' ongoing struggle to be regarded as professionals until many years have passed under the cultural tutelage afforded by one single college or university (tier 3). Unwittingly, his affirmation of the three tiers in 2012 placed the dubious facets of his allegiance to the consensus paradigm into more stark relief.

As the first questionable aspect of the three tiers, he identifies social science methodologies and practices as "technical/analytical" intelligence in tier 1. He defines two forms of tier 1 intelligence, the first being the "technical knowledge and information required to be an IR professional on any given campus." As the second form, "Tier 1 intelligence is analytical and includes familiarity with and skill in using the tools of social science research." In effect, he levels the distinctive features of social science to produce generalizable knowledge into the same tier as the technical peculiarities of the institution. In essence, the mastery of scientific research design is of the same order of intelligence as understanding how an institution codes first-time, full-time students in a student information system. Herein, to use Nagel's formulation, Terenzini fails to distinguish between the "special excellence" of the social sciences and the "exclusive preoccupation" of common sense with the particularity of its immediate environs.

Secondarily, perhaps more importantly, Terenzini suggests that institutional researchers merely "be familiar with" social science methodology, not the mastery of a social scientific discipline. As he implies in his citation of Fincher regarding the scientific underpinnings of institutional research, he forwards little more than a superficial interest in the social scientific study of higher education. The summary relegation of social science as a subject of passing fancy for institutional researchers in the "technical/analytical" tier hobbles the potential for an institutionalized system of inquiry to scale with technical, issue, and contextual problems confronting a college or university. More detrimentally, Terenzini's schema precludes the formation of a community of researchers engaged in systematic investigation of descriptives, causes, and processes beyond what may be accomplished on "any given campus."

In a third respect, Terenzini repeatedly counseled against the deliberate development and adoption of technological solutions. In a publication regarding the preparation of institutional research "for the informational needs of the twenty-first century" in 1995, he warned institutional researchers to resist the diversion and potential of new technologies. He lectured practitioners, "The danger of being preoccupied with technology is that institutional researchers may increasingly be seen as technicians, good at what they do but with a limited perspective and understanding of important academic and administrative issues." Almost two decades later, his revisions for tier 1 intelligence reiterated his blanket suspicion of technology, "I fear the same outcome, perhaps more keenly now than 20 years ago." Notably, in contrast to the National Research Council's favor for technological advances as the potent source of scientific research in education, Terenzini's suspicion of technology extended to one of the most significant innovations in the first two decades of the twenty-first century:

> [I]t is vital to IR's utility, credibility, and respect in the eyes of faculty members and administrators that we avoid capitalizing on what's in a database just because it's there and just because we now have the capacity for doing 'big data' and 'data analytics' (and basking in the reflected glory of that and other analytical capacities). The danger, in my view, is that whatever we might turn up is likely to underspecify the complexity of most important problems.

He conjured Dressel to define the threat of big data and data analytics, warning of the potential for institutional researchers to self-direct studies and delve into database analysis guided only by their own research interests: "The new-and-cool technologies can be insidiously seductive." He declared that the most important question for an institutional researcher is who wants to know what so that the priorities of studies are set by the key players in each separate institution—or, the "partisan management needs" of deans and unit leaders, as Keller recommended.[16]

The one form of intelligence that comes closest to forming the basis for a disciplinary approach, tier 2, in that institutional research may draw upon a generalized knowledge about organizational behavior and higher education. Substantively, however, issue intelligence is not native to the institutional research profession but to the knowledge necessary for the faculty and administrators in functional units. The one capacity that tier 2 institutional researchers must possess is the ability to gain "knowledge of the kinds of issues and decisions that middle- and upper-level administrators in functional units face." Consequently, Terenzini understands institutional research expertise as wholly derivative of others' administrative expertise. As derivative information, Terenzini's conceptual framework seems to deliberately use the term "intelligence" as the keyword to describe the aptitudes of institutional research in distinction to the "knowledge" of administrators and faculty with decision-making capacities.

Alluding to the "adversarial model" of higher education administration, the discipline for institutional research is to know "the enemy," by which Terenzini meant the other persons and functional units in the entire college or university system. "Although [institutional research] work should not be a war-like activity, and one's colleagues should never be considered 'enemies,'" in the formal sense, Terenzini hedged, institutional researchers "must understand the roles, responsibilities, values, ways of thinking, formal and personal self-interests, and matters likely to be considered in decision-making by the administrators, faculty members, students, staff members, trustees, legislative staffers, and others." Institutional researchers add value by parsing what his or her partisan needs (issue) and wants (technical/analytical) from the tiers of organizational intelligence. In other words, institutional researchers had to become willing participants in the "ideology of institutional research...[to] serve as a means of implementing courses of action already decided upon" (Rourke and Brooks) by the functional units of the college or university.

For this reason, in the revisited definition from 2012, Terenzini reclaims the intellectual responsibilities of institutional research to a fact-finding role akin to Coleman Griffith's limited vision: "Beyond knowing the organization chart and the functional responsibilities and areas of decision-making in each of the major divisions, [institutional research] professionals today and in the future must know something about the contents of the literature in at least a couple of those substantive and functional areas." Despite this new demand for specialization within his tiers of intelligence, he understands issue intelligence only in terms of practical purposes and application as "helping administrators and faculty members avoid bad (and perhaps costly) decisions...[and] jumping on practice and policy bandwagons headed for nowhere." Institutional research remains an indirect agency in institutional leadership and decision-making (context) and specializes for reasons unrelated to the accumulation of knowledge about higher education in general (scholarship).

Terenzini's review of tier 3, context intelligence, then exposes the complications in the definition of applied research that chains each level of organizational intelligence to the inner workings of a single institution or institutional system. The premise implies that each institution is a discrete, unique, and incommensurate unit to a degree that mitigates the potential for institutional research to contribute to generalizable knowledge in its practice. In his original definition, context intelligence is information regarding the *this*-ness (his italics) of a particular college or university. In this regard, Terenzini's conceptual framework is devoid of any regard for colleges and universities as a confluence of common social forces in a typical educational setting, as Tyrrell theorized. In his tiers of intelligence, the prioritization of each institution, in effect, proves tantamount to examining a single row of data in a data set and marveling at its unique qualities.

Finally, Terenzini's attempt to enlarge what he called the "parochial and naive" scope of his original definition for the contextual tier demonstrates his inability to break with a key priority of the consensus paradigm. Although he extends context to include national and international climates, he fails to make a connection that firmly roots institutional research knowledge in a global context or discipline. His original scope overshadows the revision, declaring: "At the very least, campus-based [institutional research] professionals should be aware of these broader national and international issues and their potential impacts for their campuses." An institutional researcher needs only to "be aware of" (not study or research) larger contexts to the extent that these issues impact the particular institution served.

Moreover, Terenzini designates the externalities as "challenging, even threatening," in an effort to orient contextual intelligence against the "aggressiveness" of forces outside the college or university. Recalling the intervention of Rourke and Brooks nearly fifty years earlier, he proposed that "[institutional researchers] occupy the middle ground between, on the one hand, administrators and faculty members with limited awareness of the research on institutions and students, and, on the other hand, scholars who may have the theoretical and analytical skills but often lack the experience, tolerance for ambiguity, or understanding of higher education 'on the ground.'" To that end, Terenzini extends the responsibilities of institutional researchers to bolster the point of view of the faculty in their capacity both as members of an institution and as scholars of higher education.

In all three tiers, Terenzini features the particularity of a single institution as the foundational consideration for institutional research functions and knowledge production. Grounding institutional research "intelligence" in this fashion tacitly upholds the scholarship that renders the field incapable of becoming a discipline or a profession, in an academic sense, due to its nature as applied research for a single institution. Knowledge acquired from institutional research does not derive from professionally defined standards of investigation, but from the cultural particularity of the institution or the priorities defined by academic and functional unit administrators. Institutional research is entirely a derivative practice that tacitly positions other administrative and academic functions as the primary domains for leadership and decision-making. In a larger context, institutional research may be a conduit to protect the autonomy of the institution from "hostile challenges" and "simple solutions for complex problems," as defined by the scholars of higher education. In all these respects, institutional researchers gain intelligence by assimilating the primary knowledge of others and only after many years of service to one particular institution: the chronic self-deceit of institutional research that one may become a jack or jill of all trades, and gain legitimacy as the master of none.

The Unpleasant Surprise of a Loss of Legitimacy

McKinney and Hindera reasoned that a discipline may not take shape from the servicing of requests placed by others or prioritized according to the immediate psychological dispositions ("needs") of others. In the consensus paradigm, exemplified by the 1991 Annual Forum presenters, the key difference between institutional research and scholarly research in higher education is the distinction and practice of institutional research as an applied research rather than basic research. Contemporary scholars of higher education who contributed to the consensus defined the nature and role of institutional research in similar terms. Collectively, they imposed an order and vocabulary on the purview of institutional research that renders its practice as applied research in a pejorative sense and as a derivative function directed by the expertise and knowledge of other stakeholders. Offices of institutional research perform most effectively when they surrender their statistical findings as "facts" for the functional units and decision-makers to ply into their partisan courses of action.

The 2002 National Research Council (NRC) publication, *Scientific Research in Education*, rejected the simplicity and naïveté of assumptions circulating in the consensus literature on institutional research. Among the statements that deem the field of education as suitable for scientific research, the NRC acknowledges that education is an "applied field"— rendering moot the traditional distinction between applied and basic research used to distinguish research on higher education from its inferior cousin. "Like other applied fields," the NRC asserted, "education research serves two related purposes: to add to fundamental understanding of education-related phenomena and events, and to inform practical decision making." Contrary to the prejudice that science "only attempts to contribute to knowledge," as McKinney and Hindera claimed, the NRC advanced a number of guiding principles for scientific research that may serve scholars interested in organizing a community dedicated to applied research for the systematic investigation of higher education administration.

Despite the intervention of the NRC over fifteen years ago, the consensus literature on the nature of institutional research has not been critically revisited. The flawed assumptions and dubious conclusions of the scholarship presented to institutional researchers from the 1970s to 1990s still stands as the unimpeachable consensus. Institutional research remains, in theory, an applied research approximating "more an art than a science," at the margins of what defines professional activity, and subject to the whimsies of "decision-making on one's own campus."

After the release of the NRC report in 2002, both Volkswein and Terenzini in their capacities as editors and scholars had ample opportunity to reconsider the conceptual framework for institutional research that they

134

offered to practitioners during the 1990s. Their revisions at the 2008 and 2012 AIR forums entertained no such reservations about their prejudice for the separation of institutional research and research on higher education. Both affirmed the pejorative characterization of institutional research as dangerously technological and applied research largely performed by immature administrative offices at small colleges around the nation, more often than not, with insufficient contextual knowledge of higher education in general or the local history of the institution in which it was practiced.

When Van Vught attended the 1990 Annual Forum to challenge the direction of institutional research, he spoke against a future holding "the unpleasant surprise of a loss of legitimacy." What the European scholar failed to recognize was that prominent American scholars of higher education who presented themselves as specialists in institutional research, and the leadership of the Association for Institutional Research, solidly rejected the idea of "scientific underpinnings" for institutional research. The delegitimization of institutional research as a profession struck many of these scholars as neither unpleasant nor a surprise but rather warranted by its role and function as an applied research at one particular institution. The legitimacy and effectiveness of institutional research naturally was "relative to institutional culture and expectations and leaders' personalities and orientation toward decision-making," as one mid-1990s study to test the validity of Terenzini's framework for organizational intelligence discovered.[17] To highlight this ineluctable constraint on the legitimacy of institutional research, Terenzini concluded his 2012 presentation to the AIR forum by quoting T.S. Eliot's *Little Gidding*: "the end of all our exploring will be to arrive where we started and know the place for the first time."[18] In the consensus paradigm, each college or university served as the alpha and the omega for institutional research.

8 | GREAT VARIANCE IN ASSIGNMENTS AND RESPONSIBILITIES

A Field That Is at Best Unevenly Positioned to Support Change

With near unanimity, American scholars of higher education as a field of study redefined the profession of institutional research as applied research to support decision-making at one particular institution and as a rule did not contribute to generalizable knowledge about higher education or higher education administration. For presidents and provosts in higher education, the fundamental propositions regarding institutional research presented important implications that reinforced the sense that the "research" was a misnomer attached to the burdens of external reporting. In the first respect, the knowledge and understanding of institutional researchers were highly localized and did not contribute to chief executives' broader understanding of higher education or leadership qualities for administration. In the second respect, institutional researchers' basic "intelligence" was technical and analytical for the production of "facts and figures" about a single institution. In other words, institutional research offered little of pervasive and lasting significance to college presidencies.

Leaders of small to medium colleges, the most numerous by far, learned that their institutional research offices are immature—infantile or adolescent—likely incapable of carrying out "the most sophisticated research projects" as at doctoral and Research I universities. Moreover, the technical and immature institutional research offices sometimes threaten to become "information authorities" in their own right at the institution. Facing this prospect, executive leaders at small and midsized colleges may not be faulted for concluding that their institutions were best served by elaborate profusions of institutional research or an office with a single person capable of no more than the coordination of "data."[1] Presidents and provosts at doctoral-granting or Research I universities, on the other hand, found solace in the proposition that their adult or mature institutional research functions had the contextual intelligence and sophistication to deliver the best level of support for decision-making and institutional effectiveness—or so they assumed until recently.

In 2015, the National Association of System Heads (NASH) released its findings from a two-year study of the forty-four public college and university systems in the United States and Puerto Rico. "Faced with an imperative to increase student access and success without diluting quality and in the face of real financial constraints," the project surveyed the institutional research capacities of local and system offices in order to gauge their abilities "to respond to growing demands." The report found that institutional research offices within public systems varied considerably in their roles. Simple questions of facts, like data definitions, differed among campuses, limiting "capacity for either system or campus decision makers to compare performance across campuses or systems, to understand the reasons for differences and to use data to drive improvements."[2]

Contrary to the consensus scholarship that suggested the professional bureaucracies and elaborate profusions of institutional research functions offered the most effective capacities, NASH reached a more regrettable conclusion about the maturity of the profession. Its judgment on the state of institutional research in the nation's major public colleges and universities is worth quoting extensively:

> Against this backdrop of demand for IR [institutional research], the picture that emerges from this study is of a field that is at best unevenly positioned to support change. IR offices are running hard and yet many are still falling behind, deluged by demands for data collection and report writing that blot out time and attention for deeper research, analysis and communication. Many do not have the information they need to get at the performance questions of most interest to them, their boards or public officials, either because it doesn't exist or because it's not collected in a way that admits of analysis. The analytic functions in most systems and campuses remain topically stove-piped, with the named "IR" office focused primarily on student and student related research, with reporting and any research in other topical areas (resource use, efficiency and effectiveness, and personnel) handled by the budget and human relations offices. The overall ability of IR offices to use data to look at issues affecting many of the cross-cutting issues of the day—such as the connections between resource use and student success—is nascent at best.[3]

The NASH research, directed independently of prior studies about the nature and function of institutional research, affirmed the worst-case scenario foreseen by Van Vught twenty-five years earlier.

Following Saupe and Dressel's statement on the nature and role of institutional research, scholarship since the 1970s characterized the "elaborate profusion" or "virtual office" of institutional research functions as the most advanced form of organization. The discovery of "topically stove-piped" functions, however, told a very different story from the one Volkswein constructed with a theoretical trope taken from "organizational life cycles." In addition, corresponding to Terenzini's counsel to institutional researchers to forego scientific underpinnings and be wary of technological sophistication (Tier 1) in order to focus on local legitimacy gained from issue (Tier 2) and contextual (Tier 3) intelligence at a particular institution, the NASH report uncovers a field lacking in analytical and technical skills to the point that it has become unable "to use data to look at issues affecting many of the cross-cutting issues of the day." The primacy of derivative intelligences regarding the needs of unit leaders at a particular institution has resulted in the illegitimacy and loss of stature for institutional research at the highest levels of higher education administration.

For fifty years, scholars of higher education arrogated to themselves the responsibility to produce and disseminate generalizable knowledge about higher education and a "well-defined body of knowledge that is rigorously taught" regarding higher education administration. In the words of the authors of the 1992 code of ethics for the Association for Institutional Research, "that kind of [basic] research…properly belongs to the domain of the scholar."[4] NASH's independent study exposed academic scholars' hubris and their failure to fulfill that responsibility for practitioners of institutional research and the higher education executives who rely on centralized offices for their decision-making. The findings have raised troubling questions about the consensus paradigm that scholars have deployed to construct and disseminate knowledge about institutional research and higher education administration in general.

A Fairly Minimal Effort toward a Virtual Office

In 1990, Alton L. Taylor recommended, in a contribution to the *New Directions for Institutional Research* volume titled *Organizing Effective Institutional Research Offices*, that the offices in large universities "serve as a support-service unit located directly under the vice-president for academic affairs (a middle-line position)." The large universities tended to decentralize functions like institutional research as the executive leadership became more absorbed with "external relations and financial problems." In order to maintain a focus on the core business of faculty teaching, research, and service, he argued, institutional research offices should be under the direction of academic affairs and institutions should "consider whether or not other suitable units could examine" the external environment for long-range planning. In short, Taylor renewed the proposal first forwarded by Rourke and Brooks while providing a contemporaneous rationale for large universities to decentralize institutional research functions in an elaborate profusion, the most mature stage of development according to J. Frederick Volkswein in the same volume.[5]

At the 1993 Annual Forum of the Association for Institutional Research, Ronald P. Matross reported on his efforts to put the conceptual framework of "elaborate profusion" into practice at the University of Minnesota. In a presentation titled "The Virtual Office: An Organizational Paradigm for Institutional Research in the 90's," Matross described the decentralization of the university's institutional research functions in "a group of organizationally distinct units acting as if they were a single unit." Selected by the AIR's Publications Committee as "of high quality and of interest to others concerned with the research of higher education," the article notably reveals the unfortunate fate of the Office of Institutional Research at the University of Minnesota, providing a bookend to the era of centralization initiated with the report written by Ruth E. Eckert and Robert J. Keller from the mid-1950s.[6]

Breathlessly praising George Keller's 1990 presentation to the Annual Forum, Matross emphasizes the influence of decreasing budgets and the increasing pervasiveness of computing technology as factors driving decentralization at the university. Department and unit-level computer networks led to "individual information fiefdoms," which presented the institutional research office two options: seek to become a centralizing office that "sets standards and subdues" other offices or become one of the fiefdoms. As a third option, Matross presents the contours of a virtual office: "a set of disparate units and individuals working together in an area as if they were part of the same centralized organization." In essence, he provided an account of how the University of Minnesota redeployed institutional research functions in an elaborate profusion by design.

Matross states that virtual offices of institutional research organize "by project...and rely on cross-functional teams of peers to do much of their work." The project teams do not normally share a physical space or a place in the organizational structure of the college or university. He claims, without attribution or evidence, that institutions "which have successfully implemented the approach have dramatically improved their response to fast-changing market conditions." As Matross noted, the University of Minnesota approach targeted the units serving and recording student data and not the operational data stored in human resources, finance, and advancement offices.

The virtual office of institutional research had four key elements to foster coherence among the parts and the whole. First, "soft control through database design" was exercised via precoded variables according to central standards, an official census file for registration headcounts and enrollments, and an electronic fact book for summary statistics regarding the university. Second, a "favor bank" entailed a ledger recording the favors performed by and favors requested by team members as well as tacit agreement to the "de facto division of turf" at the university so that each separate office "stay out of another office's areas of responsibility unless asked by that office." Third, the "loose consortium of central office and collegiate unit institutional researchers" at the university contributed executive summaries of their reports for prior review by all members of the consortium so "that each author is aware of unforeseen unit sensibilities" before inclusion in a common circular, "Research on University of Minnesota Students." The fourth element, only in proposal form at the time of Matross's presentation, was "a shared master plan of ongoing projects" to encourage systematic repetition of the same study to yield trend data and "to anticipate the new questions that ever-expanding accountability demands will bring."

In some respects, Matross's discussion of the "virtual office" reflects an effort to organize institutional research along scientific principles at the scale of a single institution. Database design exercises its soft control by predetermining what the nature of key concepts like race and ethnicity is and also the class of facts from the student records that express that nature. The favor bank supplements the self-actuating objectives of basic research with a record of institutional debts for the accumulation of knowledge about university students. The university publication expressly attempts to accelerate institutional research dissemination through the process of peer review. The proposed master plan then fabricates the program of research that organically develops from a paradigm and practice of scientific investigation in order to resolve unknowns, ambiguities, or irreconcilable findings from prior studies.

On the other hand, the nature and role of the virtual office entirely fold into the purview of the politics and budgets of the separate, "adversarial" administrative and academic units of the university. The virtual office created "more checks and balances on central office analyses" and enabled departments and units to "use data to defend against budget cuts." The favor bank ossified the functional divisions of the university and relegated the centralized office of institutional research to fact-reporting duties: the units "supply the brains, and we supply the brawn...in terms of student record data and programmers who can analyze it." In its editorial process, the university-wide publication on research activities empowered every unit in the college to air its "sensibilities" about student-related studies. Even the master plan bent to the interests of the "culture of unit autonomy" at the university and Matross characterized the plan as "a shared series of studies, not a series of shared studies."

In nearly every organizational aspect of the virtual office, unit control of institutional research outweighs university or executive control. Matross makes this outcome evident when he attempted to generalize the virtual office concept despite the fact that he regarded the University of Minnesota as "one of the largest and most decentralized campuses in the country." Given the environment at his particular institution, he first hedged on the applicability of his organization: "Our four-part approach represents a fairly minimal effort toward a virtual office. Our campus culture demands that we go out of our way to respect individual unit autonomy. Our minimalist approach is probably most applicable to similar large campuses and to systems made up of several campuses. In both these situations there are likely to be competent unit analysts with a strong desire to maintain their autonomy." Nevertheless, he again cited Keller, who by his own admission did not know the profession of institutional research prior to his presentation three years earlier, and suggested that "[n]early all schools, large and small, provide low-cost access to powerful microcomputers and easy-to-use software." As a consequence, Matross supported the implementation of virtual offices at colleges and universities of all sizes: "Regardless of one's setting, it is now clear that the technological revolution in higher education is well underway, and institutional research must adapt its methods and organizations to the new circumstances." In other words, it was time for institutional research to grow up—and, in effect, decentralize.

Following the incorporation of the Association for Institutional Research, many of the foundational documents for the profession advocated for elaborate profusion or virtual offices without offering detail on how to do so and to what purpose. For the most part, the official white papers and presentations considered it sufficient to represent the diffusion of institutional research in a single college or university as its natural state in the early history of higher education (Saupe, 1970) or its most mature form at the largest research universities in the nation (Volkswein, 1990). Matross provided a rare window into an effort to organize a virtual office of institutional research for the express purpose of bending to decentralizing forces and empowering the various units across an institution to operate with "individual unit autonomy."

In deference to Rourke and Brooks, higher education scholars designated institutional research as an art and a function while also maintaining that institutional researchers as staff should refrain from active policy making and decision-making in the spirit of scientific research. The paradoxical cherry picking of what constituted the "nature of things" for institutional research as art and science severely compromised the ability of practitioners to participate directly in college and university administration. The consensus premise that institutional research is as an applied research for a particular institution or system, generally incapable of contributing generalizable knowledge through basic research on higher education, also precluded the development of the field into a full-fledged profession. These two complementary facets of the consensus paradigm for institutional research curtailed the influence of the office directors most closely identified with the administrative function at colleges and universities. At the same time, the consensus paradigm empowered faculty as scholars to devise a conceptual framework for institutional research that placed its power "to implement courses of action already decided upon" at the disposal of local units in each college and university. The primary concern for scholars of higher education was not how to make institutional research less ideological or more scientific but how to wrest the "ideology of institutional research" from the hands of central administration in order to bolster "the point of view of the faculty."

Criteria for What Makes a Solid Higher Education Doctoral Program

In 2013, an edited collection, *Advancing Higher Education as a Field of Study*, reassessed the qualifications for higher education as a field of study under the criteria set by Paul L. Dressel and Louis B. Mayhew in 1974. Despite progress over four decades, the authors addressed shortcomings in the advancement of the field and endeavored to offer "guidelines and some clearer criteria for what makes a solid higher education doctoral program." While most contributors to the volume emphasized the need for more growth, Robert M. Hendrickson considered whether higher education as a field of study had developed the core knowledge apropos of a discipline, the key criterion for measuring advancement. After a cursory review of the attributes of the field, Hendrickson concluded, "The discussion of the core knowledge that is the foundation for the study of higher education demonstrates clearly that the study of higher education is close to or has met the criteria of a legitimate field of study in education."[7] The self-congratulatory fortunes of research on higher education as a field of study contrast strongly with the circumstances in which the institutional research profession finds itself today.

Both fields of research trace the modern iteration of their practices to decisive interventions by Paul L. Dressel and Joe L. Saupe. The theoretical framework for scholarship introduced by these two scholars framed institutional research as unfit for research on higher education. In his 1979 article on professional development of the field, Dressel went further than he had in previous writings, strongly discouraging the training of institutional researchers in any discipline. "Dismayed" by the idea of "higher education programs as effective training programs," he advocated the position that institutional research have no disciplinary program whatsoever: "It would be tragic if institutional research become narrowly defined as a profession related to a particular doctoral program in any one department or college of a university."[8] As the subtitle of Dressel's article intimated, institutional researchers are created, not educated, by the functions and activities determined by the needs of unit leaders at a particular institution.

Dressel's close colleague Joe L. Saupe already said as much in 1964 at the fourth meeting of the National Institutional Research Forum and in three documents endorsed by the Association for Institutional Research in 1970, 1981, and 1990. With their associates Mayhew and Montgomery, they cast off the phenomena and methodologies of institutional research as categorically unsuited for the advancement of generalizable knowledge about higher education. The solution for institutional researchers interested in scholarly acknowledgment or scientific practices presumably would be as simple as applying Dressel and Saupe's criteria for higher education as a field of study to institutional research as a field of study. That position, however, fails to comprehend that the foundational precept of the consensus paradigm—for both research in higher education as a field of study and institutional research as a function—calls for a radical segregation between the two institutionalized systems of inquiry.

The recent laudatory volume on the development of research on higher education as a field of study and the uneven capacity of institutional research to perform crosscutting studies on the issues of the day, per NASH, exemplify the outcomes affected by adherents to the consensus paradigm. When scholars turn their attention to institutional research, the literature unsubtly reminds the reader why it differs from research on higher education. As Dressel and Mayhew suggested in 1971, the practice of institutional research is foreign to research on higher education: whereas one takes doctoral level education to explore the unfettered personal interests of basic research, the other may be learned on the job under the auspices of one particular institution. The consensus paradigm deeply ingrains a chasm between the two systems of inquiry.

The publication *Higher Education: Handbook of Theory and Research* offers a silent testament to the ironic distance between institutional research and the scholarship on higher education. The Association for the Study of Higher Education (ASHE), the successor to the Association of Professors of Higher Education organized by Dressel and his associates, has published over thirty volumes of the handbook since 1985. Each volume comprises "a compendium of thorough and integrative literature reviews on a diverse array of topics of interest to the higher education scholarly and policy communities." The association and publisher tout the series as "[a]n indispensable resource for administrators, researchers and policymakers in higher education."[9] Select any volume from the series, however, and the reader is hard pressed to find any discussion of institutional research and its relevance to administrators, let alone scholarly or policy communities.

The twenty-first volume of *Higher Education*, published in 2006, as a random example, offers sage analysis and insights of general interest to institutional researchers and college executives but provides little in regards to how to put the methods or findings into practice. A review of the index reveals, like the 2015 volume on the development of higher education as a field of study, that the phrase "institutional research" is not indexed or substantively mentioned in any formal sense. While only a single volume in the series, the absence of the practice of institutional research in a work on "theory and research" on higher education arguably would strike the founding members of the field of institutional research as an unintelligible oversight.[10]

On the whole, a review of abstracts from the past thirty years of the ASHE *Higher Education* series yields just three abstracts directly referencing "institutional research." Only the first reference, from 1989, substantively discusses institutional research on higher education. Examining "the institutional memory of higher education organizations by examining campus archives and offices of institutional research," the piece offers little detail other than to affirm the importance of the function in the memory of a particular institution. In 2000, an article on undergraduate persistence concluded that its "tentative findings suggest investments in institutional research and student success initiatives" revealed no clear correlation between the two. The most recent reference, in 2007, analyzes "the methods and goals of contemporary academic and institutional research investigating the effectiveness of collegiate educational practices" and concludes unfavorably that "the search for 'best practices' in its current form will be ineffectual."[11] Institutional research, the "heart" of the managerial revolution in administration, is almost entirely absent from consideration in a handbook on theory and research in higher education during its thirty years of publication.

In short, the premier publication on theory and research in higher education from the Association for the Study of Higher Education provides no substantive direction or clear description on how to organize or practice institutional research at a college or university. Although institutional researchers clearly advance the academic careers of the scholars who use IPEDS data or any of the myriad resources collected from student preparedness and engagement surveys that college and university administrators are compelled to conduct for accreditation, the academicians featured in the handbooks offer no concrete or comprehensive set of principles for the practice of institutional research as a discipline dedicated to the study of higher education. Ultimately, the edited collection for the advancement of higher education as a field of study evinces Dressel's perspective that no formal role may be afforded to institutional research for the advancement of higher education as a field of study. By dint of its omission, as well, institutional research drifts "in a pre-paradigm stage" by design, a priority of the consensus paradigm for higher education as a field of study.

Extraordinarily, *Research in Higher Education*, the premier journal associated with the Association for Institutional Research, exhibits the same indifference for its putative subscribers. Since the end of Volkswein's tenure as editor-in-chief in 2005, the phrase "institutional research," is cited only twenty times, including only six times in the past five years (2011–16)—or once per year—in its abstracts. Recently, the reference occurs more often than not with respect to student survey research such as the National Survey of Student Engagement or by the Cooperative Institutional Research Program rather than the effective organization and practices for institutional research on campuses. Terenzini's article on the revised "intelligences" of institutional research offers the most substantive, if flawed, discussion in the journal during the past five years.

In the final analysis, scholars of higher education fail to provide defined criteria for the effective organization and practice of institutional research, either in relation to the study of higher education or in terms of administering a single college or university. Through doctoral programs and the extent literature, presidents and provosts routinely learn the importance of enrollment management, finance, IT, student life, and so on, to institutional leadership and management. Given that no substantial body of literature informs higher education executives' understanding and value for effective organization of institutional research, the practice of institutional research unimaginatively depends on "institutional culture and expectations and leaders' personalities and orientation toward decision-making."[12]

In sum, the consensus paradigm advocates institutional research as an elaborate profusion or virtual office in higher education while also encouraging doctoral programs to neglect training future unit leaders and presidents how to effectively direct or engage institutional research. Whereas executives, midlevel administrators, and deans supposedly provide the "brains" to utilize institutional research in the consensus paradigm, scholars of higher education have been willfully remiss in their responsibility to provide generalizable knowledge that advances the efficiency and effectiveness of virtual offices. In so doing, scholars demonstrate their continuing prejudice against the "ideology of institutional research" and sustain the "adversarial" environment of personal politics in departmental or budgetary decisions. As a consequence, higher education doctoral programs not only deny institutional researchers a proper education and body of knowledge to form a discipline for a profession but also withhold sufficient training on data-driven decision-making for higher education administrators in general. Similar to the incongruities in its concept of art and science, the consensus paradigm deploys the twin pulls of centralization and decentralization as structural barriers to the advancement of institutional research as a function and profession in higher education.

The More Formal Characterization by Dressel and Associates

Thomas Kuhn's work on scientific inquiry suggests that a paradigm adheres to a concrete community and "the choice…between competing paradigms proves to be a choice between incompatible modes of community life." A paradigm for the study of higher education that unquestionably distinguishes institutional research from scholarship cannot be reconciled to a paradigm that explicitly includes institutional research in the fold of research on higher education. The community of scholars that formed around the paradigm that regards institutional research as an antithesis to research on higher education has been socialized, via educational requirements and professional associations, to see and uphold the distinction against signs to the contrary. In this respect, if evidence or logic suggests that the distinction is unwarranted or refuted by evidence, then scholars working within the consensus paradigm will seek solutions to reaffirm the "class of facts" or "nature of things" in their ideology and conserve the mode of community life, and scholarship, to which they are accustomed. In other words, scholarship on higher education provides a published record of the community that "uses its own paradigm to argue in that paradigm's defense" and for members' ideological honorifics.[13]

The National Research Council's 2002 monograph, *Scientific Research in Education*, provides the prism through which to understand the foundational priority of the consensus paradigm for institutional research. The NRC acknowledges that education is an "applied field," effectively rendering moot the traditional distinction between institutional research and research on higher education as the difference between applied and basic research. Confronted with this dilemma, higher education scholars likely had several options, but two, in particular were: 1) to rethink institutional research as research on higher education, or 2) redefine the distinction between institutional research and research in higher education on new grounds. The

146

former, as suggested in Kuhn's work, would require an entirely new paradigm for research on higher education that greatly expands the community of higher education "scholars" by welcoming institutional researchers into the fold. The latter option merely requires a new "class of facts" to uphold the "nature of things" according to the existing paradigm and an affirmation of the rarefied sphere of research on higher education for the existing community of scholars. To the former possibility, the edited collection on the advancement of higher education and the NASH study on institutional research provide evidence that the first option has not occurred during the past fifteen years. Evidence of the second possibility, therefore, may be found in other scholarship on higher education administration and institutional research.

In the 2015 volume entitled *Institutional Research and Planning in Higher Education: Global Contexts and Themes*, Karen L. Webber (editor) and Victor M. H. Borden dedicate an entire chapter to "compare and contrast" institutional research and research in higher education in an effort to buttress the consensus paradigm.[14] Borden, a former president of the Association for Institutional Research who has received the distinguished service award, had proposed ten years earlier an "action research paradigm" for institutional research due to the "onslaught of technological innovations"[15] Webber, a former president of a regional affiliate of the association and former chair of national association's Professional Development Services Committee, in 2003 joined the Institute of Higher Education at University of Georgia that Cameron Fincher directed for thirty years. Together, the two scholars picked up the mantle passed down from Rourke and Brooks to Dressel and Saupe to Terenzini and Volkswein.

The NRC monograph undermined the pejorative black-and-white distinction between applied and basic research. Webber and Borden had to distinguish institutional research from research on higher education using a different logic. To compare and contrast the two forms of research, a new "class of facts" was necessary in order to supplement the simple distinction between applied and basic research. In response to the challenge, Webber and Borden cite the definition of research and development defined by the Organization of Economic Cooperation and Development (OECD) in order to add a third mode of research: experimental development, "systematic work...which is directed to producing new materials, products or devices, to installing new processes, systems, and services, or to improving substantially those already produced or installed."[16]

Notably, this third mode of research, experimental development, closely aligned with Borden's concept of the "action research model" that he touted as an option for organization the year following the NRC's 2002 publication. At that time, he described action research as a "cyclical and participatory process" through which institutional researchers and unit leaders collaborated to conduct assessments and evaluations in order to identify mechanisms for continuous improvement in the "higher education setting." Borden positioned the action research model "as an alternative to the traditional applied research model," conceding that the latter was the dominant paradigm for the organization and direction of institutional research.[17]

With this tripartite division of research activities—basic research, applied research, and experimental development—the authors then proposed a revision to the standard distinction between institutional research and research on higher education:

> [Research on higher education] is perhaps best placed on the cusp between basic and applied research. As an applied field of study, [research on higher education] is necessarily geared toward applied research but its standards and practices require theoretical underpinnings and so theory development is part of the realm. [Institutional research] is better positioned on this spectrum between applied research and experimental development, with a focus on developing new systems and services as opposed to products.

The OECD manual and its guidance for measuring research and development, of course, provides no guidance to distinguish research on higher education from institutional research. Similarly, whereas ten years earlier Borden presented action research as a model that institutional researchers may or may not choose to adopt, he and Webber together argued that action research, *qua* experimental development, is the very nature of institutional research that sets it apart from research on higher education.

The introduction of the third mode of inquiry with which to triangulate institutional research and research on higher education serves therefore to bolster "the priority of the paradigm," to use Kuhn's terms. The authors, ceding that research on higher education is "an applied field," now claim a new "class of facts" that blocked a recursive consideration for institutional research as basic or "pure" research, and thus no different from their own scholarship on higher education. Instead, they invite readers to consider a third order of inquiry that explains how institutional research once again differs from research on higher education by the nature of its questions and purposes.

More surprising, however, the two unabashedly described the process of socialization through which students learn the priorities of the consensus paradigm for institutional research and research on higher education in doctoral programs. The chapter begins with the narration of a classroom exercise: "In a seminar on institutional research taught by one of the co-authors, doctoral students were asked what they thought most distinguishes" institutional research from research on higher education. As described, the exercise presupposes that institutional research differs from research on higher education from the outset. The doctoral students are not asked to consider whether the preknowledge—from prior socialization in other courses or preliminary hints from their instructors—that they have brought to the discussion should be challenged or refuted. Instead, as if relating a Socratic dialogue on inborn knowledge, the priority of the paradigm guides the authors' account of the differences cited by the "students," apparently without prior class preparation or any effort to conform to the expectations of their professors.

To summarize the class exercise, the authors cited Dressel's "formal case" for the distinction from the *Institutional Research in the University: A Handbook* from 1971, as if to show that no further scholarly progress to define institutional research has occurred or was necessary. They concluded, "The informed views of the doctoral students, and the more formal characterization by Dressel and associates, capture well the theoretical distinctions" between institutional research and research on higher education. As with other scholarship on the nature and role of institutional research, the authors assumed uncritically the need to distinguish institutional research from their own scholarship[18] and, in a work directed to international professionals of higher education, exported worldwide a process of socialization to the consensus paradigm.

Thomas Kuhn notes that one necessity for scientific revolutions is the ability of paradigms to exercise a powerful normative function that informs researchers understanding "about the entities that nature does and does not contain." Despite evidence to the contrary and problems in its explanatory power, a paradigm will persist for many years or decades due to sociological factors. The scholarship of higher education over the past forty years is characterized by the normativity and influence of its consensus paradigm in exactly this manner.

As Dressel argued for many years, the omission of institutional research from the advancement of higher education as a field of study tacitly positioned the profession as inessential to knowledge accumulation and effectiveness in higher education in general. Subsequent scholarship has routinely deployed simple binaries to differentiate institutional research from research on higher education in order to delegitimize the former as a profession and as a source of knowledge about higher education in general. Resulting from this base distinction, institutional research as a field of study continues to exhibit many shortcomings and only has "nascent" capabilities to address the crosscutting issues of the day according to state executives of higher education. Despite the mounting number of unresolved problems attributable to this priority in the paradigm, higher education scholars reinvent the nature of higher education research to maintain the consensus rather than address the critical flaw in their thinking, deterring both institutional research and research on higher education from developing into a social science. In this respect, scholars' distinctions between institutional research and scholarship serves to protect their vested interest in the scholarship that passes as generalizable knowledge about higher education but also to bolster the faculty point of view regarding the appropriate role of institutional research in higher education administration.

There Are as Many Different Roles Such Offices Can Play as There Are Universities

Possibly the most ironic difference between institutional research and scholarship on higher education is the standard of expertise imposed on the two fields of study. According to the literature, an institutional researcher must spend many years immersed in the contextual setting of a single institution to understand its historical and cultural inner workings in order to gain legitimacy and respect for his or her knowledge from peers and practitioners. In contrast, a scholar, whether in the discipline of higher education or an unrelated field such as political science, may administer a generic survey for descriptive statistics or extrapolate from abstract principles of applied and basic research to uncover a refined system of categorizations about the nature, role, function, maturity, intelligence, and effectiveness of institutional research in higher education. While institutional research may not generalize its findings beyond the one particular institution in which it is practiced, scholars at Research I universities may routinely generalize their concept of institutional research to promote the adoption of elaborate profusions or virtual offices at every college and university.

As J. Frederick Volkswein, Ying (Jessie) Liu, and James Woodell note in the 2012 handbook for institutional research, "Most of what we know about the profession of institutional research comes from several multistate and national surveys of AIR and regional members."[19] The National Association of System Heads (NASH) administered its study of institutional research along these traditional lines. As one would expect, the NASH findings are consistent with prior survey research: "There is a good deal of variability in the way the IR function is configured between systems and campuses." Designated institutional research offices focused on "reporting about student and enrollment patterns," while the budget office and human resource offices performed "analytics" about resources and personnel.[20] The NASH survey on institutional research offices, to be clear, did not discover anything that prior survey studies had not already reported. As

Rourke and Brooks wrote in 1966, "This review of the various activities which institutional research offices undertake on university campuses might well suggest that there are as many different roles such offices can play as there are universities." In 2008, Volkswein cautioned readers not to generalize "about the practice of institutional research, because we know that organizational arrangements are highly variable from campus to campus and state to state."[21]

The consensus paradigm elevated decentralization, virtual offices, and institutional particularity over standard practices to permanently secure the "unsystematic variegation" of institutional research functions. Scholarship on the organization of institutional research also emphasized institutional research as a staff function, wholly unrelated to the study of higher education to produce generalizable knowledge, bound to the political and historical context of a single institution, and legitimately under the direction of unit decision-makers who needed to protect departmental autonomy and budgeting from centralized control. For the past fifty years, to the extent they have showed any consideration for institutional research, scholars who considered the field one of their domains of specialization—and the doctoral programs in higher education that educate current and future executives of higher education—have advocated for the organization of institutional research functions in exactly this manner.

Consequently, the NASH survey of institutional research in the state systems and institutional offices offers an indictment of the organization of institutional research as defined by the consensus paradigm in higher education scholarship, the official documents of the Association for Institutional Research from the past fifty years, and the high regard for "elaborate profusions" as the most advanced development of institutional research (Volkswein's schema). The variability in the quality of institutional research functions reflects the long-held recommendations that institutional research root itself in particular institutions and pursue its practice without regard for contributions to generalizable knowledge. In the priorities of the paradigm, every innovation in computing technology gave cause to the decentralization of institutional research functions.

The NASH study differs only in its assessment of the effectiveness of institutional research as organized in this fashion. The NASH survey serves to illuminate how virtual offices or elaborate profusions of institutional research simply squandered the wealth of institutions—both in terms of revenue and knowledge production. What is surprising about the NASH survey, then, is that more than forty years passed before an organization representing executive officers of colleges and universities conducted any independent research to determine whether the literature on institutional research offered sound advice to executive leaders and board members at higher education institutions.

No doubt the scholastic niceties distinguishing scholarly research and institutional research as a difference between basic research and applied research have informed the "nature" and "role" of institutional research in higher education. The current paradigm for higher education as a field of study in this respect must be regarded as fatally flawed: research on higher education has been critically misguided in its rejection of administrative institutional research as an essential source of generalizable knowledge about higher education settings. The balkanization of institutional research, according to the NASH report, has led to "frequent disconnections between system and campus [institutional research] offices, caused by different IT systems and data definitions, even inside a single campus as well as within systems. This limits capacity for either system or campus decision makers to compare performance across campuses or systems, to understand the reasons for differences and to use data to drive improvements."[22]

The system heads suspected that institutional research would prove incapable of timely reform. Eager to study the crosscutting issues of the day, they require the assistance of a profession committed to generalizable knowledge about student success and its connections to resource allocations. In order for institutional research to rise to this challenge, proponents of institutional research need to debunk and replace the consensus paradigm for research on higher education—no small task, given that, as Kuhn declared, "When paradigms change, the world itself changes with them. Led by a new paradigm, scientists adopt new instruments and look in new places."[23] Nonetheless, this raises one last question: what world-transforming project to revitalize the practice and professionalization of institutional research has the Association for Institutional Research embarked on?

9 | ~~A NEW~~ AN OLD VISION FOR
INSTITUTIONAL RESEARCH

The Current Function of Institutional Research Is Not Clearly Defined

Aided by the largess of the Bill & Melinda Gates Foundation, the Association for Institutional Research launched an initiative in 2014, "Improving & Transforming Institutional Research in Postsecondary Education." Addressing the critical assessment of the profession in the NASH report, the association weakly acknowledged "a concern that current IR [institutional research] practices are not adequate for the challenges that face decision makers today." Ironically, the association summarized its fifty-year stewardship of the profession in the statement of purpose for the initiative: "the current function of IR is not clearly defined, and the future path of IR is unknown." To rectify the plight of the profession for its four thousand members, the association launched yet another survey of offices of institutional research at colleges and universities across the nation in its effort to draft statements of aspirational practices for the future of institutional research.[1]

By the time the association released the first draft of its aspirations, the sense of urgency to improve the offices of institutional research to meet the demands of the nation's public university systems had subsided.[2] Instead, the "Brief Summary" signaled a return to the priorities of the consensus paradigm for institutional research. The opening section recommits to the "50-year collaborative nature of the institutional research field…a hybrid model that includes professionals, some of whom work in dedicated offices of institutional research, and others who work in various units across the institution and share in efforts to collect, interpret, and use data to achieve an institution's mission." The summary statement praises the ability of units and virtual offices overseeing the functions of institutional research and then laments that "dedicated staff in 'traditional' offices of institutional research" no longer fulfill its designated role in the elaborate profusion of institutional research. Professionalization of the staff function in administrative offices of institutional research retarded the effectiveness and academic excellence of "decision makers—from managers to deans and vice presidents" who knew best "their unit's [sic] capacity to conduct data studies that align with their own information needs."

Shifting to the outlines of a solution, the summary statement intimates institutional research suffers from too much centralization or insufficient decentralization. A more elaborate profusion of institutional research functions must be secured, and units must hold precedence over the centralized office of institutional research. In order to remove "obstacles for institutional studies," the summary posits, functional directors and vice presidents must take greater responsibility for the organization of institutional research, echoing Victor Borden's claim for the benefits of action research. The office of institutional research must curtail its aspirations and leave institutional research functions to the units. The role of central offices of institutional research is to ferret out information from the data silos as a coordinator of the efforts and investments in functions distributed around the institution.

Moreover, the brief suggests that the concept of "decision-makers" also must become more generalized to include nearly any person with the potential to consume institutional data. The decision-making by unit leaders also tends toward too much centralization, and steps must be taken to make institutional research functions more responsive to "the thousands of decisions made by students themselves about their higher education experiences, by faculty about their own teaching and interactions with students, and by professional staff who work directly with students." In short, institutional research functions fail to achieve the goals of academic excellence because they are overly beholden to the administrative "structure" created for executive and managerial decision-making at colleges and universities.

To counterbalance overcentralization, a "student-focused paradigm" that places the interpretative frame in the student perspective must be adopted. For instance, the brief argues, "a study of faculty salaries can, and should, be placed in the context of putting students first by assuring the retention of outstanding faculty because of their critical importance in the student experience." More importantly, a student-focused paradigm elevates the nonadministrative rhythms of learning, which the AIR "Brief" portrays as the most impactful decisions on student success: those occurring on the "student and faculty calendars...not always align[ed] with administrative cycles." Institutional research functions must be timed to suit the decision-making of "students, faculty, and other stakeholders" rather than the decision-making of institutional unit leaders and executives, the AIR suggests.

As a whole, the brief summary of aspirational statements subsequently released by the Association for Institutional Research amplifies the perception of institutional research as a function unsuited for professionalization. As the AIR policy brief claims, the aspirational statements intend to be an "active re-envisioning of the institutional research function," not an active re-envisioning of the profession as the NASH report advised. The generalized concept of decision-makers that includes every faculty member and each student far removed from the executives of higher education administration solidifies institutional research as a nondisciplinary practice or a nonspecialized derivative research activity among lay consumers of institutional data. In other words, the data "stove-pipes" discovered by the NASH study did not signify a neglect for adequately centralized institutional research in one office but the failure to adequately decentralize the functions of institutional research for every decision-maker on campus.

When previous events exposed the unresolved problems in the concept of institutional research advanced by the Association for Institutional Research during its fifty-year history, the association's leadership dutifully doubled down on its commitment to institutional research as a nonprofessional function best left to the decision-making prowess of anyone but the professional institutional researchers in colleges or universities. As the association worked through its response to the challenges presented by the NASH report, the priorities of the consensus paradigm again reasserted control over the future of institutional research functions as an elaborate profusion in higher education. Despite ample evidence that higher education policy makers and decision-makers long for more rigorous, reliable, and valid research about the performance of students and institutions, the Association for Institutional Research once again counseled institutional researchers to plan for and accept an increasingly deprofessionalized role due to the disruption of technological innovations.

A Culture of Openness to Inquiry and Willingness to Use Data to Document and Improve Performance

Effective organization of offices of institutional research has been discussed since the 1950s, and yet the nation's state university system heads studied the need to "creat[e] a culture of openness to inquiry and willingness to use data to document and improve performance" for these offices only recently.[3] Institutional and system leaders directly determine the organization of institutional research functions, according to the consensus paradigm. The neglect to develop institutional research offices and professionals falls in part on the shoulders of the college executives and system heads of higher education who permitted the field to languish in this condition for the past fifty years. An indictment of institutional research professionals and their ability to adapt to the demands of the future is more generally an indictment of executive leadership in higher education and the doctoral programs that prepare them for leadership. Ultimately, to judge otherwise allows higher education executives, like higher education scholars before them, to absolve themselves of responsibility for the scientific study of higher education and for evidence-based improvements to higher education administration.

The reliance on virtual offices and elaborate profusions of institutional research in the state university systems has been well documented by survey research regarding the roles and functions of institutional research since the origins of the profession. Whatever deficiencies exist in the institutional research profession in the present day reflect the lapse of leadership in the institutions and the systems that rejected or abandoned the promise of institutional research during the past fifty years. Since the 1970s, higher education leaders at large public universities entertained the rude state of institutional research in which no specialization forms and every unit or department poses questions of planning and effectiveness for its own "partisan" interests. The lack of regard for the accumulation of knowledge and the lack of purpose other than carrying on the business of the institution reflect the pervasiveness and power of the consensus paradigm. The organization of institutional research functions in the nation's colleges and universities reflects the effort to protect departmental autonomy over institutional mission and institutional autonomy over the public's welfare from democratization and social justice in higher education.

The introduction to the AIR's National Survey of Institutional Research Offices conceded, "Not surprisingly, this work confirmed much of what was already believed about institutional research; there are vast differences in IR capacity and organizational arrangements that are idiosyncratic to individual colleges and universities." The research also revealed that "structure and resources" did not correspond to the "scale or scope" of the research portfolio under the direction offices.[4] Whether a one-person office at a small liberal arts college or an elaborate profusion at a large public university, institutional research rarely scales to the complexity of the problems facing higher education institutions. Most colleges and universities do not scale operations across the discrete spectra of the "golden triangle" from reporting to effectiveness and the types of scientific research questions on education from description to mechanism. The virtual office or elaborate profusion of institutional research at a particular institution and under the direction of unit leaders ensures that institutional research functions rarely progress from the first order of inquiry, descriptive statistics, and impede efforts in the second and third orders by virtue of the complexity and/or costs entailed. The preponderance of questions posed by institutions is thus directed to the compilation of descriptive statistics and correlations, while studies of causal factors or mechanism for academic improvements usually amount to nothing more than a passing fancy or a deferred hope.

In the introduction to his 1955 work *Problems of College Administration*, A. J. Brumbaugh laid out the fundamental challenges to effective higher education administration by decentralized institutional research functions:

> Problems of administration in higher education may be defined as perplexing situations, the solution to which is not immediately apparent. To find a solution to an administrative problem or perplexing situation of this type requires first of all a clear conception of what the problem is. Defining the problem is not always as easy as it sounds, because we are frequently inclined to confuse symptoms with the situation. It requires in the second place the marshaling of pertinent facts related to the problem; in the third place, there is required the formulation of a hypothesis or tentative solution to the problem; and then the verification of this tentative solution by trying it out or by getting a judgment of others concerning it.[5]

Consider, as an example, how institutional research on retention undertaken by decentralized functions or a virtual office more or less encounters problems at some point along the way in a manner consistent with the following anecdote about a college or university:[6]

The president asks for an enrollment projection for the upcoming year based on anticipated student retention. Retention reporting is a well-established institutional research function, and there will be a low-level registrar or programmer responsible for reporting retained student headcounts to the federal government. The responsible employee, however, may not have organized the institutional submissions into a fact book or compiled tables recording longitudinal retention rates. Even if so, an employee whose main role in retention is to count and report the number of students will likely not have the background or skills to build an enrollment projection model from the recruitment and retention trends of college students.

The research objective then falls to another person, likely an accountant, who seeks out the retention rates for the first time. Having rarely worked with student records, he or she soon discovers that the retention rates reported to the federal government apply only to first-time, full-time freshmen. Retention rates for entering transfer students and students at the sophomore level and up (including all graduate programs) are not reported. The admissions office has the data for students at the time of admission, so the accountant now needs records from the registrar and admissions. In a series of e-mail exchanges and meetings with the information technology (IT), registrar, and admissions offices, the accountant type secures the information necessary to trend and project enrollments. He or she discovers a disturbing decline in the retention rates of students during the past ten years.

After the enrollment projections reach the president, he or she then asks if the institution's peers have also experienced enrollment declines due to falling retention rates. No one in the room can answer the question because no one at the college has an official list of peer institutions. In addition, no one is aware that the federal government organizes and publishes colleges' submitted data into its IPEDS Data Center for institutional comparisons. Either by dint of an expensive consultant or e-mail exchanges with colleagues at other colleges, someone learns how to make peer comparisons and compiles tables for enrollments, first-time first-year retention rates, and the six-year graduation rates.

The results show that the freshman retention rates at the research-deficient institution have declined more rapidly than local peers selected from a list used by the admissions office. The president reasonably asks which types of students are leaving the institution before graduation. The members of the President's Cabinet turn to the provost as the head of academics and academic support. The provost is already saddled with too many responsibilities, so the head of academic support assumes the lead in the project. Sooner or later, this person learns that the institution's data reporter runs an SQL query each year to get a basic count and does not store an electronic file recording which students are retained.

A new, and even more extensive, series of e-mails and meetings with IT ensues in order to understand the census "freeze table" or to secure a data set to produce more trend tables with students sorted by gender, race and ethnicity, standardized test scores, HS GPA, and so forth. Once completed, the subsequent tables show that the institution is doing a poor job retaining non-traditional students who earned average or subaverage standardized test scores and/or high school GPAs. After reviewing the tables, the president then asks how the institution can improve the retention rate of the students who are "at risk" of withdrawing from the institution.

The education of students is the provost's responsibility, and an executive must now take the lead on this new project directly. The provost organizes a team of faculty and administrators from academic support into a committee to study ways to improve retention, and/or a consultant is hired—either way, the costs to the institution begin to increase exponentially. The head of the committee is an esteemed member of the college or department of education, who like many in the discipline prefers qualitative research over quantitative methods. The committee members engage in extensive readings on "best" or "high-impact" practices and then conduct a handful of focus groups with students retained from prior years to determine which practices to prioritize for implementation.[7]

The president eventually receives the provost's report recommending that the institution organize (more) learning communities, service learning and study abroad opportunities, first-year seminars, integrated curriculum, undergraduate research, service learning, internships, and other one-off solutions recommended in the literature. All will require faculty stipends and remissions to create and teach the new curriculum since the "best" practices require more extensive classroom preparation. Either that, the report intimates, or the Admissions Office must stop admitting so many unprepared college students.

Upon completing the report, the president forwards it to the human resources director to estimate costs to implement the committee's recommendations. The HR department manages its own submissions, so employee records are more or less available, but the HR director has no understanding of average class sizes or the course catalog. Another series of meetings and e-mails with IT and the registrar ensues, along with many signed forms recording why HR needs student enrollment records (in order to comply with IT audit standards). Eventually, the HR director receives the information necessary to project costs. The president reviews the report and sets it aside, astonished by the astronomical cost estimates for implementation of "best" practices to improve college student retention.

The provost is called for a special meeting regarding the committee's report. If the board is asked to invest that sum of money in faculty development for "best" practices, the president will have to project how much retention rates and revenue will improve.

Herein, the research becomes dicey for most institutions. Everyone involved in the research to this point has performed research with the native intelligence to count, to request SQL queries from IT, to perform routine calculations for planning on a calculator or MS Excel, and to read the literature on student retention in higher education. An effectiveness study to predict student success at the institution requires specialized skills and professional training in data analytics. If lucky, the college will have a business or computer science department with a specialist in data mining or a social scientist with notable experience in regression analysis, but someone unlikely to be an expert in higher education or student learning. If no such person is available, the institution will require a consultant. In any case, somebody is about to receive a chunk of the institution's resources in the form of a contract or remissions (plus the adjunct costs corresponding to the remission).

The request goes forward with the requisite number of meetings and e-mail exchanges between the consultant, IT, registrar, and admissions office. After the president receives the predictive analysis, the results will show that the improvements should go in one of three directions: 1) no implementation because costs are not recovered, 2) full implementation because costs are certain to be recovered, or 3) the most likely, a pilot implementation to see if the improvements work as designed. If the first, the research process returns to the provost to form a new committee to make new recommendations for improving student retention. If the second or third direction, the new program and interventions will require program evaluations to determine if the interventions are performing as designed and predicted—again, an effectiveness study requiring more institutional resources to be plowed into consultants or remissions.

At about this point, five to ten years have passed since the initial request for enrollment projections and the president announces to the campus community that he or she has taken a new presidential appointment at another college or university—in part, frustrated by the inability to get answers to the simple questions about student attrition and improving retention. Over the years, the pace of the work on improving retention waxed and waned as the budget targets for enrollments were missed or met. Work during the summers often grounded to a halt when faculty, committee members, or key personnel went on leave or vacation.

The new president on campus will soon learn, while seeking leadership synergies with key constituents,[8] that many in faculty and academic support were equally frustrated with the former president because of all the unusual pressure to improve student retention. The problems the institution faces, they say, are caused by an admissions office that admits too many students ill-prepared for college. Soon after, the chief enrollment officer leaves voluntarily or per the request of the new president.

The next strategic plan, largely crafted by key constituents of the institution who want to keep the new president in check, will state the goal of doubling the number of honors students, those who earn average scores for Critical Reading / Math SAT at 1300 and above. The strategic initiative is undertaken without the realization that around 11 percent of the high school population earns 1300 or higher SAT scores[9] and that the only such students who attend this particular institution receive 75 percent to 100 percent unfunded tuition discount rates. Five to ten years later, the new president departs, having not met general freshman recruitment targets but also having produced a million-dollar budget shortfall due to the success of the college's flagship, largely-subsidized honors program.

While not every college or university with a virtual office or elaborate profusion of institutional research experiences the above problems in an effort to improve retention, every institution proves incapable of researching some basic questions about its performance or effectiveness. The federal submissions by colleges and universities record thousands of facets of the operations: admissions, first-year students, total student body, twelve-month enrollment, degree completions, graduation rates, academic libraries, human resources, and finance. Each submission records anywhere from dozens to hundreds of variables. A question by the president about any one aspect of those submissions will engender the elaborate confusion described above if a trend table inadvertently shows some type of distress or decline at the college. As each problem is discovered or prioritized by the needs of the day, the entire institutional research enterprise of the college or university careens from one crisis to the next with no comprehensive plan for institutional effectiveness.

In each crisis, a half dozen or more individuals become responsible in turn for a project at some point because their expertise performing an operative function somehow makes them the most qualified to conduct reliable and valid research. The fragmented and byzantine systems of institutional reporting fail to facilitate the investigation of basic research questions regarding planning and each new question must be met with an extensive new project involving ad hoc "requests for data" to information technology specialists. When planning and projections call for action and the measurements of an effectiveness study, the institutional research functions hits a wall or requires the aid of external consultants.

The Growth of Capacity That Occurs Outside of the Office of Institutional Research

The description of retention research initiated by a president at a small college with a virtual office or at a university with an elaborate profusion of institutional research illustrates how another question immediately presents itself each time the president receives an answer to the research question at hand. At each stage in the process, a different leader from one of the functional units takes on the responsibility without prior knowledge or input into the previous stage of the research. The information technology department, equipped only to respond to requests for data, fields each stage in the process as if it is a wholly unrelated project driven by the needs of the functional units' decision makers. And yet the entire research process organically grows out of the questions of the president regarding how to improve retention and assure the viability of the institution. In other words, as Coleman Griffith understood in the first major article published about institutional research offices in 1938, institutional research itself begets the need for more institutional research along a spectrum of scientific types of questions and the golden triangle.

The portfolio of institutional research self-actualizes under the direction of the president, forming an "organization and classification of knowledge on the basis of explanatory principles." At the same time, according to the consensus paradigm for institutional research, the research process must begin as if for the first time with each new question and according to the discrete functions of the different units in the institution. The research process comes to a halt or an interruption when a key manager or executive departs for a new position, or the institution encounters a new crisis to address. What the findings from the NASH study truly reveal, contrary to the conclusions of the report, is that deficiencies for institutional research do not reside in the offices or profession of institutional research, but in "the stove-pipes"—the virtual offices and elaborate profusions—of institutional research functions in the public systems of higher education. In short, the decentralization of institutional research functions by the systems and colleges in a manner consistent with the consensus paradigm has erected barriers to "holistic analytics about overall performance" of public higher education.

The National Association of System Heads (NASH) faulted the unequal capacities of institutional research offices within a single state system as well as the "stove-piping" of institutional research throughout an institution. The profuse or networked arrangement of institutional research functions constrained the offices to the reporting of student statistics and distributed "other topical areas to…the budget and human resource officers." The distribution of institutional research functions throughout the institutions in a single system further led to both redundancy and undermined comparisons on basic institutional statistics: "While gaps exist in data governance and infrastructure among systems and their campuses, there is also a redundancy in reporting between system and campus, perhaps necessitated by different audiences for the different levels of work. This contributes to confusion about basic measures and metrics, and also gets in the way of potential efforts for greater sharing of work between campuses and systems in order to free up staff to do other things." The current condition of institutional research offices in the nation's public systems of higher education, per NASH, are arguably the direct outcome of a field defined as a function, not a profession, ill-prepared by higher education doctoral programs, inextricably beholden to decision-making at a single institution, and most effectively performed by "any component" of the university.[10]

Unfortunately, the Association for Institutional Research chose not to engage with the NASH findings substantively. Rather, the AIR ignores its own fifty-year history of advocating for elaborate profusions and virtual offices of institutional research functions. As signaled by the "Brief Summary," the association's immediate response evaded thoughtful responsibility for the current state of the practitioners it serves and renewed its commitment to the consensus paradigm long supported by scholars of higher education. In an unsubtle manner, the AIR's initiative to rethink the future of institutional research culminates in a series of statements on the great risk of "overprofessionalization," to quote Paul L. Dressel, for institutional research functions.

When the association released its "new vision for institutional research," the aspirational statements served to perpetuate the same four tenets for the practice of institutional research that the association has espoused since its earliest years. The severity of the unresolved problems for the consensus paradigm for institutional research, however, forced the association into new rationalizations. The statements rely on the fabrication of a usable past, a closer alignment of the field with common sense over applied research, and willful ignorance for the lack of preparation for institutional research provided by doctoral programs of higher education. Paradoxically, then, in its unwillingness to break with its own history, the Association for Institutional Research validates the conclusion reached by NASH: institutional research is "a field that is at best unevenly positioned to support change."

While the association's board provided oversight for the Gates Foundation initiative, the leadership ceded the responsibility to craft the reports and aspirational statements to Randy Swing, a former executive director of the Association for Institutional Research, supported by a freelance writer with no significant institutional research background. Prior to his leadership position with the AIR, Swing's career in higher education entailed many assessment posts, a narrow area of study in the portfolio of institutional research, primarily in units outside of the local office of institutional research. He trained at the University of Georgia for his PhD program, and cites as one of his mentors, Cameron Fincher, the scholar who argued that institutional research is an art not a science in the 1985 publication on professional development for persons in the field. He left his post with AIR in January 2016, after initiating the project during his tenure, and the association retained him under contract specifically to complete the aspirational statements for the future of institutional research functions.

Swing's report on behalf of the AIR, "A New Vision for Institutional Research," effectively reverses the findings and conclusions of the NASH study from two years earlier and repackages the association's fifty-year old, failed vision for institutional research as new aspirations for the future.[11] As evidenced above, the AIR's official position for most of its existence has been that institutional research is 1) a staff function, 2) divorced from scholarship on higher education, 3) circumscribed in a particular institution, and 4) effectively decentralized in an "elaborate profusion" of local units and decision-makers. In Swing's "new" vision, the AIR once again recapitulates the same four tenets at the heart of its stewardship of the profession, with few semantic differences.

In two paragraphs from the lead section on "a new vision for the institutional research function," he recites the old vision:

> The move to an institutional research function—via a federated network model or matrix network model—is needed to assure that informed decisions routinely occur across an organization with the speed and flexibility required for real-world management of modern postsecondary education... [I]nstitutional researchers should be counted on to know and use the discoveries of others in forming a blended view of higher education relevant to real-world, locally-centered problems and opportunities. It is unlikely that basic research or traditional scholarly research will account for more than a minor advisory role in the future function of institutional research.

Notably, the statement feigns that the "move to an institutional research function" is a new development for the field or the association, whereas the semantic revision simply substitutes "federated networks or matrix network model" for the previous phrases: "any component of the university," "elaborate profusion," and "virtual office." The statement explicitly discourages connection to "basic research or traditional scholarly research" for the field. It reaffirms the limits of the institutional research domain to a single institution, "real-world, locally-centered problems and opportunities," subject to the authority of "informed decisions...across an organization." In just a few lines, the aspirational statement succinctly rephrases the four facets of the consensus paradigm for institutional research originally crafted by Rourke, Brooks, Dressel, and Saupe—the priorities of the paradigm, to be sure.

In order to maintain the status quo, however, the "new vision" required a different set of facts about institutional research in order to recast the old vision as a fresh outlook. Instead of critical self-reflection on the elaborate profusion of institutional research functions advocated by the AIR in the prior literature, the new vision ignores the historical record and grossly oversimplifies the practice of institutional research in the past. Against the overwhelming evidence that decentralization has been the official position of the AIR and the dominant trajectory for institutional research since 1965, the new vision claims that institutional researchers long exercised centralized powers over such functions: "Offices of institutional research once held the uncontested right as the 'one source of the truth' because of the special skills needed to access institutional data and use sophisticated analytic tools."[12]

With this assertion, the AIR's "New Vision" blithely dismisses the long trail of scholarship in its own annals and rewrites the history of institutional research offices. For instance, J. Frederick Volkswein must wonder what has happened to his lifelong scholarly contributions on the diversity of institutional research offices. Despite its flaws, Volkswein's scholarship never suggested the offices once held "the uncontested right as the 'one source of the truth.'" Likewise, the hyperbolic claim contradicts the forum presentations by Keller, McKinney and Hindera, and Matross, to name just a few who the AIR Publications Committee selected for honors in the prior twenty-five years.

In lieu of more sophisticated scholarship, Swing's historical reading serves up little more than a straw man. An unsubstantiated revision to scholarship on institutional research, the myth of the "uncontested" centralized office facilitates his questionable advocacy for a new era of elaborate profusions: "The prominent shift in [a federated network model] is the growth of capacity that occurs outside of the office of institutional research." In terminology reminiscent of Joe L. Saupe's statements on the functions of institutional research forty years earlier, Swing describes the federated network model "as an organization-wide resource…[in which] additional value is developed by the array of independent and linked components *operating as a function*" (emphasis in the original). Reversing the first of many findings from the independent NASH study, then, the AIR claims that centralization of functions under the direction of institutional research professionals—the individuals who form the vast majority of its dues-paying membership—is the real culprit in the low quality of institutional research capacities.

New Wild, Wild West of Independent Data and Information Brokers

Another significant step to shore up the consensus paradigm may be found in Swing's disregard for the characterization of institutional research as applied research, action research, or as experimental development, to cite Webber and Borden. As the "Brief Summary" hinted, the AIR's new vision also regards centralization in "the components" or units of the institution as an added problem for the effective organization of institutional research functions. To this end, the definition of decision-maker broadens to include the everyday decisions of student, faculty, and staff members. To use Ernst Nagel's distinction between science and common sense, to wit, the new vision implicitly strips institutional research of any pretension to science— the research misnomer—and anchors the functions in the commonsense decisions that take place on a campus in any given moment. Consequently, rather than targeted professional development for office personnel, the AIR's new vision calls for an investment in broad staff training: "The task is not to create a thousand skilled staff members who could work in an office of institutional research, but rather to develop an appropriate level of data literacy for decision-support roles that exist already."[13]

The AIR's new vision turns on its head the call by NASH to create better systems of collaborative research to facilitate shared workloads among campuses and within systems. Acknowledging that federated networks of institutional research functions risk leading to "silos of efforts that are wasteful and complicated by turf battles," the AIR suggests that institutions and institutional researchers must resign themselves to the conditions as an outcome of technological determinism: "Whether individuals welcome this new Wild, Wild West of independent data and information brokers, or fear the Tower of Babel that might result, the movement toward a federated network is already well-established and rapidly growing." In short, "institutional research has (already) left the office," and, as its metaphor of the "new Wild, Wild West" evokes, a new era of lawlessness and rugged individuality (decentralization) will further erode data standards and redistribute institutional research functions into the manifold stovepipes of college operations.

The modifications to "the class of facts" to support the consensus paradigm for institutional research, at the same time, betray the ideological commitments readily apparent from prior statements on the nature and role of "the function." Foremost, reviving "the common propensity of academic man [sic] to look with alarm upon any apparent extension in the power of university administration" (Rourke and Brooks), the aspirational statement and new vision for institutional research openly question the effectiveness of executive administration in general. Characterizing the ineffectiveness of centralized institutional research as a misalignment of decision timing, Swing calls into question the usefulness of administrative planning: "student and faculty calendars and decision cycles do not always align with administrative cycles." In this manner, the "Brief Summary" explicitly moves the locus of decision-making from "senior campus leaders" to students and faculty.

The final report, "Statement of Aspirational Practice for Institutional Research," picks up on the theme in its rationale for the expanded definition of decision-makers: "Top-down policies and structures alone do not ensure informed choices and commitments to successful pathways." The *New Vision* article published for a general readership evidences the old animosity for institutional research offices under the direction of executive leadership. As explanation for the NASH conclusions, the AIR's "New Vision" expands on the idea that institutional research offices, not the elaborate profusion of functions, are at the heart of the field's dim future: "the dominant structure of institutional research is based on service relationships with a small set of key decision makers." Again, despite decades of scholarship documenting the elaborate profusions of functions and official documents advocating for decentralization with each new computing innovation, the AIR managed to turn the independent findings of the NASH study into an indictment of the limited control over institutional research functions that practitioners and executives currently exercise on many college and university campuses.

The new vision for institutional research reveals a second commitment to the consensus paradigm in the designation of students, faculty, and staff support as decision-makers. In this sense, institutional research remains a field dedicated to "decision support" without direct responsibility for decision-making. Moreover, the expanded definition of decision-makers who consume the output of institutional research functions also endorses the distance between institutional research and research on higher education. Institutional research functions and the decisions they support are not professional competencies associated with expertise in a discipline. Students, as much as faculty and staff, have the native faculties for "data literacy" and the natural competency for reaching decisions with these faculties. Though these "key consumers and clients of institutional research" may require "coaching" and "training" to become "data-informed" decision-makers, workshops and on-the-job experience clearly provide the best education for the new breed of institutional researchers.

To be clear, rather than standardizing and improving the quality of analytic capabilities to bring institutional research functions out of the stovepipes of decision-making and address the issue of institutional comparability as the NASH study proposed, the AIR's new vision as crafted by its former executive director recommends that colleges and universities distribute the functions of institutional research in each institution as "data studies," with little to no formal controls for rigorous practices, further eroding their ability to conduct research and to make comparisons within systems. The federated network, like the elaborate profusion and virtual office before it, favors the allocation of institutional research resources and budgets in the functional units of higher education administration. This conceptual framework of institutional research discourages the creation and evolution of technology specifically designed for institutional researchers. Technological innovation comes from outside the field and seemingly drives practitioners to the adoption of tactics and strategies that erect barriers to quality performance in their own offices and accelerate the diffusion of functions to the "decision-makers" of institutional research at the college or university.

The overt lack of professional standards for practitioners underlies another consistency in Swing's ideological commitment to the consensus paradigm for institutional research. In a policy paper delivered to the Institute for Higher Education Policy as part of its series "Envisioning the National Postsecondary Data Infrastructure in the 21st Century," Swing suggested that institutional research offices should take their "lessons from prior disruptive innovations" in higher education: "the printing field changed quickly when desktop publishing turned personal computers into personal printing presses." Presenting on behalf of AIR, he likened the future of the institutional researcher to the "savvy print ship manager...[who] understood that some decline in professionalism was overcome by the quantity of communications that institutions were able to create." Likewise, mainframe computing gave way to network computing, reducing "top-down control." From both of these examples, he implied, institutional research as a network of functions and decentralized processes offered quantity over quality: "far more production and greater distribution of data for decision support will far exceed the negative reactions to some data studies that do not represent best practices."[14] In consonance with the prior literature on the nature and role of institutional research functions, the new vision skirts consideration for professional standards in institutional research and even discourages such pretensions.

While the new vision contemplates the establishment of a new cabinet-level role, the Chief Institutional Research Officer, the AIR in no way links the new cabinet officer to the specialized practice of institutional research. "The individuals who become chief institutional research officers (CIROs), a new position for many colleges and universities, will have varied professional backgrounds," the AIR's new vision advises. The CIROs may be found in many locations, "including current directors of institutional research who are poised to transition to the role, and other professionals whose paths may not include traditional institutional research experience." In short, the chief officer of institutional research at an institution does not necessarily require any technical training or expertise with institutional research as much as charisma: "Communications and strategic relationship skills rise in importance. Technical and statistical skills diminish in importance." Paraphrasing Saupe, one might say, Swing suggests that any individual at the college or university may have chief responsibility for institutional research.

Use of Data for Institutional Research Cannot Be Restricted to One Office

The official statements by the AIR about the nature and function of institutional research, in the past and present, bolster the faculty point of view (Rourke and Brooks) on two levels. First, the emphasis on nonprofessional, decentralized institutional research functions endorses the concept of institutional research originating in the scholarship on higher education. The line of scholarship running through Dressel, Saupe, Fincher, Terenzini, Volkswein, Matross, and Swing perpetuates "a pre-paradigm stage" for institutional research as an artful function with no relation to the discipline of higher education. Swing wrote in 2016, in the tradition of Dressel since the early 1970s, "It is unlikely that basic research or traditional scholarly research will account for more than a minor advisory role in the future function of institutional research." The two fields of research activity on higher education are worlds apart. Whether defined as a distinction between basic research versus applied research, applied research versus experimental development, and, now, science versus common sense, the priority of the consensus paradigm demands that "never the twain shall meet."

Second, the AIR's official statements on the organization and role of institutional research as an artful function distributed in federated networks, formerly known as elaborate profusions or virtual offices, at a single institution bolsters the faculty point of view at the local institutions. As the Matross description of the virtual office demonstrates, the elaborate profusion of institutional research functions serves to anchor the direction of institutional studies to the partisan departmental and budgetary politics at the local institution. The new vision upholds the primacy of decentralized functional units over the centralized institutional research office and then takes the further step of elevating the decision-making of faculty and staff support, who supposedly operate on a different calendar than administrative executives and managers. With each new articulation, the priority of the paradigm pushes the control of institutional research functions out of the structured institutional research office organized under professionals and into unstructured decision-making among nonadministrators who exercise their innate faculty for common sense.

As the Keller, Matross, and Swing documents illustrate, the Association for Institutional Research defaults to the position that institutional research offices must deprofessionalize with each new advance in computing technology. Mainframes, personal computers, network computing, and "big data" have in turn, during the past fifty years, been identified as the driver of decentralization and deprofessionalization of institutional research functions in order to establish a new era of control over institutional data by faculty and unit leaders. Presumably, in this version of technological determinism, the data literate end-users eagerly seize the opportunity to exercise their new control over institution research functions and decision-making. In practice, however, the end-users often enough find that their departmental partisan interests are served simply by deferring the centralization of institutional research standards. As the NASH study of the public system offices discovered, the concept of institutional research encouraged by the AIR creates stovepipes, leads to data ambiguities, engenders vastly disparate functional capacities within the same system, and frustrates collaborative comparative research on "the cross-cutting issues of the day."

The AIR characteristically suggests that the solution for policy makers is to train faculty, staff, and nonresearch administrators to utilize existing technologies rather than develop new technologies or skills for institutional research professionals: "Many of the enhancements to [institutional research] capacity are not highly dependent on new or expanded technologies. Still, technology can provide opportunities to increase efficiencies and allow maximum use of the existing investment in postsecondary education. More efficient use of existing technologies depends on advancing the technical knowledge and skills of the faculty, staff, and administrators who work at institutions as producers or consumers of postsecondary data."[15] Thus, rather than question its assumptions about decentralization, data literacy, and expansive decision-making, the AIR recommends more decentralization and more general training for the entire campus community. Despite the opening to demonstrate the relevance of institutional research offices to the state public university systems, the AIR repackaged its same four tenets on the organization of institutional research functions under the guise of a "new vision" that shepherds a renewed commitment to decentralization.

An unresolved problem with the consensus paradigm, from the beginning, is that the AIR endorses the premise that scholars and doctoral programs of higher education have no responsibility to train institutional researchers—whether understood as a profession or a function—except perhaps in a "minor advisory role." For their own reasons, scholars who design higher education doctoral programs exclude the development of institutional research from consideration in the criteria to advance the field of study in general. Consequently, the theory and parameters for professional training do not exist in the literature provided by scholars or the AIR. In the final analysis, institutional research, the new vision as in the old vision, will perdure in "a pre-paradigm stage" conducted in fits and starts as determined by the episodic crises at an institution, incapable of more complex research questions "such as the connections between resource use and student success." Concurrently, the unresolved problems of the consensus paradigm will continue to mount and force its defenders to make more and more tenuous claims about the history, nature, and future of institutional research—and, of course, the need for (more) decentralization and deprofessionalization of its functions.

The ongoing neglect for the field by the Association for Institutional Research since its earliest years rests in its refusal to provide a scientific paradigm and program for institutional research to advance its status as a profession through the acquisition of generalizable knowledge about what works in higher education administration. What is most alarming, however, is that disruptive innovations clearly have increased, not decreased, the demand for the professionalization of institutional research and its capacity for multi-institutional comparisons and analytics—yet the AIR continues to run in the opposite direction. In short, the AIR's long-held official vision for institutional research will continue to retard institutional capacities, to vex higher education leadership, and to deter national and statewide efforts to improve student success. The question is: when will a new paradigm for the study of higher education emerge and displace the half-century-old ideology at the heart of the current scholarship?

EPILOGUE | FROM INSTITUTIONAL RESEARCH TO DATA SCIENCE

In the era of "big data" and data science, recent studies of institutional research offices and functions raise significant concerns about the future of the profession. Executive leaders in higher education question the potential for institutional research to substantively improve student success today. In essence, the dismal state of institutional research as a viable source of knowledge about what works for student success represents a wholesale rejection of the "nature and role" of institutional research as advanced during the past fifty years. By extension, then, higher education institutions now recognize their inability to manage operations without the insights of multi-institutional research and machine learning coordinated by suppliers of data science.

Nonetheless, data science for student success will encounter many of the important policy questions regarding students, faculty, and administrators that sidelined institutional research. As data science develops the capabilities to provide optimal solutions for student and institutional success at a granular level, who will exercise the power of data-driven decision-making? For instance, when a trusted predictive model shows the optimal path to student success, should the institution allow an individual student to pursue a nonoptimal choice of paths? To what extent should faculty or institutions be held accountable for the nonoptimal outcomes of students in a course? Should state and federal government fund students making nonoptimal choices or institutions providing non-optimal courses of study for student success?

In the 1960s, institutional research portended a transformation of higher education administration that could have shifted responsibilities from the individual institutions to a coordinating agency and scientific program across multiple institutions. The vendors and practitioners of data science will inevitably run into the buzz saw of anti-intellectualism that some higher education stakeholders have deployed to frustrate institutional research efforts and to preserve local institutional control. The conclusion therefore recaps the keywords and conceptual framework that impeded the development of institutional research as a scientific enterprise, while

172

offering data scientists specializing in the study of college student success insight into the resistance to scientific research on higher education administration that they will likely face.

To Guide Students through the Maze of Decision-Making about Their Future Careers

In defense of his assertion that institutional research is "a practicing art, not a science," Cameron Fincher considered the reason for the lack of theoretical bases in the knowledge produced by institutional research:

> Colleges and universities are remarkably diverse institutions, and despite many similarities in structure and functions, there are few useful generalizations that would apply to all. Although occasional attempts are made at theory building in higher education, most institutions have a justifiable claim to the *uniqueness* [my emphasis] that they profess in the presence of evaluation committees, prospective students, and newspaper reporters. Given the premise that institutional research should be the systematic, objective study of internal operations and processes, it follow that neither institutional research nor its object of study is best described by its nomothetic or lawlike characteristics.[1]

The first or foundational priority of the consensus paradigm for research on higher education may well be the premise that each higher education institution is unique. The premise is not itself offered as a testable hypothesis in a theory of higher education. There is no effort to define institutional uniqueness, or any prior experiment or scholarship cited, that reveals the uniqueness of each higher education institution.

To the contrary, each institution's uniqueness derives entirely from stakeholders' "justifiable claim" about the "nature of things" in higher education—or what common sense can tell anyone about higher education as an "object of study." What Fincher seeks to make clear, then, is that institutional uniqueness precludes the scientific study of higher education because institution A is not institution B is not institution C and so on and so on. Of course, the same could be said of the planets: Venus is not Earth is not Mars…The study of the solar system is not subject to useful generalizations that would apply to all planets. The planets "wander" where they will, according to their unique terrestrial qualities, without "nomothetic or lawlike characteristics." As Ernst Nagel observed about social theories in general, Fincher's assertion about the nature of higher education is better understood as "a social or moral philosophy rather than social science…made up in large measure of general reflections on

173

the…justifications or critiques of various social institutions."[2] Fincher's proscription for what institutional research "should be" figures into the larger moral philosophy to justify the uniqueness of higher education institutions and, more specifically, academic programs—what Paul L. Dressel understood as the priority when faced by the prospect of "overprofessionalization" in institutional research.

"Who controls academe" is closely related to institutional uniqueness in the priorities of the consensus paradigm: "If a college or university is effectively to define its purposes and select or invent the means of attaining them, it must have a high degree of autonomy."[3] Thus, efforts to compare external characteristics and coordinate institutions as exemplified by California in the 1950s contradict the underlying uniqueness and autonomy of institutions. Likewise, the study of inherent qualities for academic excellence in higher education institutions belies the commonsense notion that no two institutions share the same "nature of things:" effectiveness, purposes, means, and the like, determined by the local institution. *Qua* unique, the most that one can say is, metaphorically, "Institution A is like institution B," a reason for the widespread use of case studies in the literature on higher education. Further generalizations often result in ironic statements designed to uphold a priority of the consensus paradigm. For example, Ronald Matross began with the premise that the virtual office best suited large universities like the University of Minnesota but then concluded that all colleges and universities should decentralize institutional research functions due to a "technological revolution in higher education." In this respect, the uniqueness and autonomy of institutions as a conceptual framework defy scientific studies of higher education but solicit generalizations that advance rules stemming from these two priorities in the consensus paradigm.

There are of course lawlike universals, derived from general reflections, that scholars who contributed to the consensus paradigm for the study of higher education agree on: "the common propensity of academic man to look with alarm upon any apparent extension in the power of university administration" (Rourke and Brooks); "the ideology of institutional research…serves as a means of implementing courses of action already decided upon" (Rourke and Brooks); "Institutional research is different from the research of faculty members in a number of ways" (Dressel and Mayhew); "institutional research should not be expected to produce knowledge of pervasive and lasting significance" (Saupe and Montgomery); "typical institutional research…is not collaborative at all" (Spitzberg); "others set the agenda for institutional research…There is little incentive for this [to] change" (McKinney and Hindera); and, "It is unlikely that basic research or traditional scholarly research will account for more than a minor advisory role in the future function of institutional research" (Swing).

Briefly, institutional research is not scholarship on higher education.

The distinction between institutional research and scholarship on higher education, however, is more than just a professional grudge: it is the question of who controls academe. Scholars of higher education distinguish between "administrative and professional authority" in the colleges and universities. "The primary expertise in higher education is possessed by the faculty," whereas administrative authority in higher education erroneously apes business firms in which "central leadership typically possess the primary knowledge."[4] If institutional research had developed as a scholarly discipline and profession as A. J. Brumbaugh and Philip Tyrrell envisioned in the early 1960s, the distinction between administrative and professional authority would have dissolved. Administrative research on higher education would be no less the basis for professional authority than faculty research on higher education.

Instead, as I have argued, Paul L. Dressel and his colleagues formed a consensus paradigm for the study of higher education that prevented the "overprofessionalization" of institutional research as a form of scholarship. Moreover, when scholars of higher education advocate for institutional uniqueness and autonomy, it is not in the interest of institutional administration—it is "bolstering the point of view of the faculty" at particular institutions who best know how to exercise professional authority in higher education. Thus, the shifting grounds on which scholars have erected the division between institutional research and scholarship have never been as important to the consensus paradigm as the unquestioned perpetuation of some distinction by doctoral programs for higher education.

In the consensus paradigm, as Fincher and Swing implied thirty years apart, scholars of higher education have no interest in or intention to offer a falsifiable theory of uniqueness among higher education institutions. Institutional research simply studies "internal operations and processes" at one and only one given college or university—a college or university unlike any other. Articles about institutional research focus on techniques and processes, not the accumulation of knowledge or tests of theory about a common "object of study." The handbook, designed to be held by an individual who works in isolation from his or her peers, provides guides for the piecemeal application of research methods—as directed by deans and unit heads responsible for partisan decision-making at the local institution.[5]

In the final analysis, the scholars who "properly" own the domain of basic research need not propose an underlying theory, a school of thought, and a focused or balanced portfolio of research for a scientific community for the study of higher education. In turn, institutional research professionals, as practical artists, need only create disparate reporting and analytic systems as if each institution is a canvass on which to record their contextual knowledge. Thus, while a substantial body of literature on tools and case studies to support "applied research" on higher education exists, most studies must be regarded as codicils to the handbooks of institutional research or personal testaments of longevity at a single institution. Neither, however, contributes to the accumulation of knowledge and theoretical explorations about "what works" in higher education.

In the fifty years since the founding of the Association for Institutional Research, higher education institutions have witnessed a manifold increase in the phenomena of their educational settings now accessible to institutional researchers. Student information systems record tens of thousands of transactions and records regarding the normal educational practices of postsecondary students: academic preparedness, institutional fit, socioeconomic background, registration patterns, grade outcomes, behavior issues, group affiliations, absenteeism, counseling, residential life, and so forth—all of which are supplemented by i) student survey research on intentions, attitudes, engagement, and outcomes; ii) assessment of student learning outcomes; iii) student tracker outcomes from the National Student Clearinghouse; and iv) other collectible data at the institution.

The educational settings of colleges and universities, moreover, are far more complex confluences of social forces than in the past: global investments in higher education systems as drivers of national wealth, national rationalization of democratic systems of higher education, state and local service to occupational markets, and small communities loosely united by mission, vision, and values. Despite the prolific array of new phenomena for the study of higher education, the portfolio of institutional research studies has failed to evolve much beyond the portfolio devised by those who first collaborated to apply scientific methods to the study of higher education prior to 1965.

Since 1965, institutional research has oscillated between the artfulness of the consensus paradigm for the study of higher education and the field's historical underpinnings in the scientific study of higher education. Data science for student success augurs the most recent momentum in the swing of the pendulum toward scientific studies. Whichever technology industry partners earn the trust of institutional executives, data science for student success nevertheless must recognize its fundamental differences with the commonsense moral philosophy of institutional uniqueness and autonomy in higher education. The point of introducing data science will be to eliminate nonoptimal choices by the faculty and staff that perpetuate ineffective counseling and intervention practices for student success. The NASH survey of institutional research offices notwithstanding, the primary shortcoming in institutional research with regards to student success solutions always has been the reluctant mobilization of faculty and staff to consider or adopt new management techniques that encroach on the traditional practices "justifiably claimed" as the pith of an institution's uniqueness and autonomy. Arguably, then, integration of data science for student success in the normal operations of a college or university will entail the modification of behaviors among administrators, faculty, and staff that produce nonoptimal outcomes for students—or, the professional authority to "reengineer the university," to echo William F. Massy.

The Success of Data Science Types in Institutional Research

At the origins of institutional research, the conditions to form a scientific community dedicated to professional research on higher education in a manner that would lead to the advancement of institutional research and education research together existed. Instead, scholars of higher education, who arrogated to themselves the responsibilities to define generalizable knowledge and produce a well-defined body of knowledge about institutional research, failed to deliver on the promise of the profession for over fifty years. Within five years of the organization of the Association for Institutional Research, higher education researchers introduced their predilection for a distinction between institutional research and their own scholarly research into its official documents. Following the organization of the Association for the Study of Higher Education, the consensus paradigm for higher education set as its paramount priority a system of classification regarding the differences between the knowledge generated by institutional research and by tenured scholars. To this day, the distinction has circumscribed the domain and findings of institutional research to the particularity of the institutions studied and frustrated the formation of a healthy scientific community for the study of higher education effectiveness as defined by the National Research Council in its publication *Scientific Research in Education.*

College presidencies often succeed and fail based on the quality of institutional research, planning, and continuous improvement at their institutions.[6] Yet the history of institutional research since the 1960s shows that chief executives of higher education largely disengaged from the profession about the same time that scholars of higher education, many active in the Association for Institutional Research, redefined the field as a decentralized staff function to generate transient facts in support of decision-making at a particular institution. Institutional researchers in general proved reluctant to take it upon themselves to reexamine "concepts, assumptions, and strategy" for higher education, as Philip Tyrrell advocated, when confronted by this resistance to a scientific community on higher education with qualities similar to other social science disciplines. Either out of deference or a lack of understanding for the paradigm offered by higher education scholars, college presidents and institutional researchers alike adopted the consensus paradigm.

The resulting stagnation in higher education research created a favorable environment for the externally driven regiment of institutional reporting to both governmental agencies and print media. In particular, for-profit publications devised their own systems for generalizing knowledge about higher education in the absence of leadership and serious scholarship about higher education administration for a democratic American society.[7] In an ironic twist, the grotesque national agenda to commodify knowledge about American higher education as "rankings," "ratings," "scorecards," and "dashboards" for publications and ad-supported websites for the families of college-goers forced the industry of higher education into a partnership with private industry that now allocates, annually, millions in operational dollars for questionable measurements of educational effectiveness and academic excellence at American colleges and universities. Whatever its value to the college students and their families, the annual rhythm of submissions and rankings became inextricably conflated with the practice of institutional research.

Independent survey research by the heads of the nation's public university systems exposed the inefficacy of the fifty-year-old consensus paradigm for institutional research functions as "a field that is at best unevenly positioned to support change." The system heads call for a transformation of the institutional research profession such that each office is better able to operate as "the interpreter and analyst of data." Nonetheless, skepticism for the capacity of their institutional research offices to effect timely reform resulted in an opening for the data science of student success as an effective external partnership for the administration of higher education. The heads of the public systems and institutions of higher education in America, eager to study the crosscutting issues of the day, increasingly turn to the private sector for partnerships capable of providing generalizable knowledge about student success and its connections to resource allocations.

In recent years, institutional researchers have recognized vaguely that their diminished role in the production of both generalizable knowledge about higher education and local knowledge about academic excellence has undermined their development as professionals. Most institutional researchers care deeply about the profession and the students affected by the quality of academic excellence at their institutions. Many, per the scholarship of a former AIR president, William Knight, agonize over the possibility that their personal lack of emotional intelligence accounts for the ineffectiveness of their offices.[8] Despite Randy Swing's efforts to renew the old aspirations of institutional research defined by the consensus paradigm, the membership recently compelled its board to form an ad hoc committee, the "IR Future Committee…to think deeply about the future of our profession."[9] Lastly, as the *Chronicle of Higher Education* reported after the 2017 AIR forum, "Institutional-research professionals have expressed concern that they are often disconnected from key decision makers."[10] Whatever else institutional researchers may lack, the professional ambition to advance the fortunes of executive leadership and the personal willingness to develop leadership skills for the benefit of their institutions is not at issue.

At least one-third of institutional research office executives now have earned a doctoral degree according to the recent survey conducted by the Association for Institutional Research. For many educated in the social science disciplines, the application of data science methodologies offers an approach to institutional research that may redeem the promise of the profession. In 2015, Jesse Lawson self-published *Data Science in Higher Education*, in which he considered "the success of data scientist types in institutional research" and the "practical application" of the emerging field for "science-minded educational researchers and scholar-practitioners."[11] Anecdotally, more and more institutional researchers list the skill "data science" on their professional résumés, while the larger offices increasingly claim "data science" positions or capacities among their staff.[12] The move away from institutional research and to data science in higher education has gained momentum as practitioners in the "traditional research office in higher education" recognize the limitations of the consensus paradigm or respond to the current favor accorded to data science.[13]

The institutional researchers' turn to data science nonetheless will face complications due to the customary practices of the field under the conceptual framework advanced by the Association for Institutional Research for the past fifty years. The association leadership has consistently counseled its membership to regard the practice of institutional research as an art or craft, not a science or a profession. The appeal of data science, then, lies not in its scientific potential but the perceived need to add yet another area of skill focus for the jack or jill of all trades. In this respect, data science for student success may amount to nothing more than an additional chapter in a future handbook of institutional research—one of many possible office capacities adopted and modified by institutions according to their own particular designs. Data science, adopted in this fashion, will become integrated into the consensus paradigm as one of the many complex analytical or institutional studies falling under the umbrella of institutional research as "a practicing art," as Cameron Fincher argued— another color on the palette of the artists.

The institutions and institutional executives introduced to data science through the prism of institutional research will soon conclude that its methods and results share the same flaws as institutional research. If the implementation of data science for student success fails to challenge and displace the consensus paradigm for research on higher education, the new field as applied to the industry of higher education will stall in the "pre-paradigm stage" in which institutional research finds itself. If the institutional research profession is unable to turn back the clock and return to its scientific underpinnings, the application of data science for student success has the potential to displace its antithesis—the practice of institutional research as art. This is no small task, however; as Kuhn declared, "When paradigms change, the world itself changes with them. Led by a new paradigm, scientists adopt new instruments and look in new places."[14] Whatever the future holds for the administration of higher education, the proponents of data science for student success must understand that the real challenge before them is the work to replace the consensus paradigm for research on higher education and its moral philosophy of institutional uniqueness and autonomy.

With Unique Expertise and Experience at the Forefront of Behavioral Science

Disruptive innovation in higher education portends greater centralization, not greater decentralization, for institutional studies. The system heads of NASH exposed the need for more rigorous and valid research studies regarding student success and resource allocations than the silos and elaborate profusions of institutional research functions are able to provide. In addition, recent trends among for-profit student success vendors, behavioral science NGOs, and association leadership at large point to the need for greater professionalization and standardization in the deployment of institutional research. Undeniably, thought leaders in disruptive innovation in student success and higher education leadership look to the professional standards of social scientific scholarship as the preferred model for both the rigor and ethical use of research. Thus, at a time when stakeholders inside and outside of higher education demand greater validity and reliability from institutional studies, new forms of industry-academe partnership for the scientific study of academic excellence and student success potentially exist.

The competition among data science vendors to build multi-institutional databases of student records to "probe deeply" into student success across higher education in general, rather than a single institution, marks an important break with the consensus paradigm. An organization like the PAR Framework, prior to its acquisition by Hobson's, was "a student success collaborative with more than two dozen member institutions." Likewise, Civitas Learning has attracted "advocates for higher education transformation" and acquired other ed-tech startups in order to leverage its network of "more than 880 campuses reaching more than 3.2 million students worldwide." Institutional research often is limited to the study of student decision-making at a single college or university attended by its students. Relying on data in the student information system at a single institution, such studies are unable to analyze student success between institutions at the student-record level. The databases compiled by the vendors of data science for student success potentially provide an unprecedented opportunity to study the differential probabilities of student success at many institutions. In other words, higher education institutions are no longer unique but a variable in a complex equation to optimize student success broadly conceived—that is, as the democratic principle that the Truman Commission first proposed.[15]

Beyond for-profit ventures to deliver the quality analytics that college leaders seek, non-profit organizations aim to provide better guidance on how to effectuate student success mechanisms through the lens of established social scientific practices. ideas42, a nonprofit "with unique expertise and experience at the forefront of behavioral science," released a comprehensive report on sixteen different projects to improve student success at a number of partner institutions, *Nudging for Success: Using Behavioral Science to Improve the Postsecondary Student Journey*. While not quite as groundbreaking as the press release suggests, ideas42 served as a coordinating agent to direct the study of student success initiatives and to report independently the results of the interventions. Notably, the nonprofit did not report results on one intervention because it was "unable to run randomized controlled trial for this intervention." In addition to the seemingly rigorous standards for results testing, the report includes precise baseline results that can be referenced if the group replicates its studies on other campuses.[16] Implicit to the studies and report, ideas42 elevated scientific replication as principle of responsible institutional research and scholarship on student success.

Lastly, Stanford University and Ithaka S+R, a provider of "research and strategic guidance to help the academic community navigate economic and technological change," convened the conference Asilomar II: Student Data and Records in the Digital Era to discuss the ethical use of student data in the new era of prescriptive analytics and the application of behavioral science to student success. The resources posted on the conference site record the trend toward the development of more professional standards for research using the vast amounts of data available through learning environments as well as the ethical use of student data to advance student success. As one organizer states, "There is a value to having a sectorwide conversation and coming up with a set of standards." Although the attendees did not reach consensus, *Inside Higher Ed* reports that the participants "made progress on articulating a handful of ideas that participants said should guide the responsible use of student data."[17] As opposed to an intractable Wild, Wild West of data studies forecast by the Association for Institutional Research, the Asilomar II conference organizers clearly articulate the need for standards to guide studies of student success and academic excellence when student records are involved—and students' futures are at stake.

Thus, while the AIR insists that disruptive innovation and technological innovation in higher education (again) portend more deprofessionalization for institutional research functions and a diminished need for rigorous research studies, for-profit vendors of data science, nonprofit organizations for the study of behavioral sciences, and the industry-academic partnerships such as the Stanford-Ithaca S+R collaboration trend toward greater professionalization and standardization with regard to the deployment of what has traditionally been regarded as institutional research on student success. Moreover, the leaders in disruptive innovation and student success look to the professional standards of social scientific scholarship as the preferred model for both the rigor and ethical use of student success research. In this new climate in which higher education leadership both inside and outside the academy recognizes the demand for greater validity and reliability from institutional research on academic excellence and student success, the Association for Institutional Research effectively sidelines its membership from the discussion: "It is unlikely that basic research or traditional scholarly research will account for more than a minor advisory role in the future function of institutional research."

Institutional researchers sit atop a mountain of recorded phenomena in the educational setting of colleges and universities—to which academic researchers and functional unit leaders do not have the same access. In the United States, the policies for human subjects research have further endowed higher education institutions with the power and responsibility to conduct research to determine how best to educate students in "established or commonly accepted educational settings." And yet the typical structure and operation of institutional research functions in higher education are designed to respond to informal questions ("needs," "requests," and similar) from administrators with no scientific background, no defined agenda, no discernible standards, purposefully decentralized to empower political interference, and without focused intention beyond the immediate concerns of impromptu decisions. Institutional research, in this respect, has been too closely bound to self-study and too long burdened by the partisan decision-making at particular institutions.

Rather than lowering the bar on data studies and student success, the vendor of data science, Civitas Learning, raises expectations that the standards of analytics will evolve from current practices for descriptive and diagnostic analytics (such as fact books and correlation testing) to predictive and prescriptive analytics (what it labels, "What is the best that can happen and how can we make it so?"). In an effort to warn institutional leaders about the rising bar for student success, Civitas Learning makes clear that "most institutions now lag behind the rising standards of analytics best practices." While these prognostications for data science may seem far-fetched in practice at this time, these claims already exist in the marketing materials of leading student success vendors like Civitas Learning and its "team's vision of dramatically improving student outcomes by developing an education analytics system."[18]

The vision for a singular "system" with which to study higher education and student outcomes far outstrips the insular, inconsequential decentralized profusions at particular institutions that the Association for Institutional Research and higher education scholars defined as the nature and role of institutional research for the past fifty years. The renewed vision for a scientific, centralized, professional, and instrumental technology (a "total information system" per Henle) for the study of student success augurs an opportunity to replace the consensus paradigm in research on higher education with an industry-academe partnership based in the study of what works for student success. The future of American higher education in the twenty-first century will hinge on the successful formation of a partnership between college administrators and data scientists for the study of higher education and its administration in general. As Clark Kerr described the conditions in California in 1960, the future of higher education turns on "whether to rely on a plan, or on 'guidance,' or on atomistic competition."

To be certain, one future is the continued hegemony arising from the commonsense moral philosophy of institutional uniqueness and autonomy that favors atomistic competition. If stakeholders in an institution or scholars of higher education come to see data science for student success as "another unnecessary appendage to administrative bureaucracy," the effort to reengineer college and university management will founder. For instance, when data science for student success discovers an optimal course of intervention within the normal operations and processes of an institution, the moral philosophy of institutional uniqueness and autonomy can empower administrators, faculty, and staff to continue taking the nonoptimal course of action due to tradition or mission. Having deflected the perils of institutional research for fifty years, American colleges and universities are well-versed in the use and abuse of the commonsense moral philosophy of institutional uniqueness and autonomy.

A second future for industry-academe partnerships for college student success is broad systems of planning or, in the case of data science, autonomous systems for optimizing internal operations at institutions or for student choices generally. This is to say the analytics systems may assume control of optimization without regard for academic freedom or professional autonomy of college and university personnel. As the data science for student recommendations and academic progress proliferate, the responsibility for college education will shift gradually from higher education institutions to the technology vendors for college student success. For example, IBM proposes that its Watson Engagement Advisor will "guide students through the maze of decision-making about their future careers to enhance their employment opportunities." IBM creates no illusions about what (or who?) will be advising students: IBM's Watson. Deakin University's news release suggests, "Watson will revolutionise and simplify student problem-solving: the more questions it is asked, the more informative its answers will become." IBM Watson is the agent in student problem-solving. As Watson learns to answer questions better, students problem-solving becomes easier—provided students listen to IBM Watson more readily than they listen to faculty or staff. One assumes, as IBM Watson learns, its Engagement Advisor will be able to provide students with recommendations for programs of study, course schedules, which courses or faculty to avoid, how much financial aid loans to accept, so on and so forth—and eventually which college to attend without ever asking the student to consult with an admissions staff member.

The third future, then, is an industry-academe partnership founded in guidance and "a mutually supportive community." The third option envisions scholars of higher education in general as well as faculty and staff at institutions embracing the study of higher education as a scientific discipline. The administrative authority informed by the data science of college student success will be recognized as on par with the professional authority of faculty. Administration and staff will accept retraining and welcome guidance on how best to optimize each and every student's success at a college or university. Rather than recede into comfortable unaccountability of institutional uniqueness and autonomy, colleges and universities will open themselves to greater scrutiny made possible by the aggregation of student-record level studies conducted on a regional or national scale.

No doubt the third future is the least likely, but the advent of data science for student success in some sense has renewed Philip H. Tyrrell's vision for the study of higher education, and his enthusiasm for the future may once again be within reach:

The opportunity for honest inquiry, humbly pursued, may never have been greater for education; it certainly has never had the resources which exist or have been promised and which must be nurtured, paradoxically, with boldness and with care.

If [the data scientists for student success] achieve effective programming, they will facilitate immeasurably the activities of the assembly of scholars whom they serve and of whom they are apart. Concurrently, the total institution as a creative enterprise will be enabled to contemplate without despair a future.[19]

As with promise of institutional research seventy-five years ago, the direction of higher education once again depends on the formation of a healthy scientific community for the study of higher education.

The future of higher education then is a choice among commonsense notions derived from a moral philosophy of institutional uniqueness and autonomy, the Delphic counsel provided to college students by a self-determining artificial intelligence, or an institutionalized system of inquiry with the "special excellence" of a social science that guides the community of scholars and practitioners in higher education—what more to say: dare to know.

NOTES

PROLOGUE I THE CROSS-CUTTING ISSUES OF THE DAY

1. Blumenstyk, Goldie. "A Top Proponent of Higher-Ed Disruption Moves to Put His Theories into Practice," *The Chronicle of Higher Education*, October 12, 2015, http://www.chronicle.com/blogs/wiredcampus/a-top-proponent-of-higher-ed-disruption-moves-to-put-his-theories-into-practice/57485; Michael B. Horn, "Stepping aside to dig deeper: My next career move," accessed on March 23, 2017, http://www.christenseninstitute.org/blog/stepping-aside-to-dig-deeper-my-next-career-move/.
2. "Student Success," Ellucian, accessed March 23, 2017, http://www.ellucian.com/Student-Success/; "Solution: Student Success Model," Blackboard, accessed March 23, 2017, http://www.blackboard.com/sites/deved/solutions/student-success-model.asp.
3. Civitas Learning, "Warburg Pincus Leads an Investment of up to $60 Million in Higher Education Data Pioneer," *MarketWatch*, September 28, 2015, http://www.marketwatch.com/story/warburg-pincus-leads-an-investment-of-up-to-60-million-in-higher-education-data-pioneer-2015-09-28; "Home (Page)," Civitas Learning, accessed March 23, 2017, https://www.civitaslearning.com/; Civitas Learning, "Civitas Learning Acquires College Scheduler, Leader in Schedule Planning Solutions," *Yahoo! Finance*, January 20, 2016, http://finance.yahoo.com/news/civitas-learning-r-acquires-college-143000707.html.
4. "IBM Forms New Watson Group to Meet Growing Demand for Cognitive Innovations," IBM, January 9, 2014, https://www-03.ibm.com/press/us/en/pressrelease/42867.wss; "Deakin and IBM unite to revolutionise the student experience," Deakin University, October 8, 2014, http://www.deakin.edu.au/about-deakin/media-releases/articles/deakin-and-ibm-unite-to-revolutionise-the-student-experience; Carl Straumsheim, "'Augmented Intelligence' for Higher Ed," November 16, 2016, https://www.insidehighered.com/news/2016/11/16/blackboard-pearson-join-ibms-ecosystem-bring-watson-technology-higher-ed.
5. Laura Ascione, "Hobsons acquisition targets retention, educational outcomes," *eCampus News*, January 12, 2016, http://www.ecampusnews.com/top-news/hobsons-retention-outcomes-892/; "PAR Framework: Overview," PAR Framework, accessed March 23, 2017, http://www.parframework.org/about-par/overview/.
6. Thomas H. Davenport and D. J. Patil, "Data Scientist: The Sexiest Job of the 21st Century," *Harvard Business Review*, October 2012, https://hbr.org/2012/10/data-scientist-the-sexiest-job-of-the-21st-century.

7. Robert Birnbaum, *Management Fads in Higher Education: Where They Come From, What They Do, Why They Fail* (2000).

8. William F. Massey, *Reengineering the University: How to Be Mission Centered, Market Smart, and Margin Conscious* (2016).

9. National Association of System Heads (NASH), "Meeting Demand for Improvements in Public System Institutional Research: Progress Report on the NASH Project in IR," March 2014, http://nashonline.org/wp-content/uploads/2017/08/Assessing-and-Improving-the-IR-Function-in-Public-University-Systems.pdf, 2–6. NASH released a final report echoing the same conclusions in the next year: "Meeting Demand for Improvements in Public System Institutional Research: Assessing and Improving the Institutional Research [IR] Function in Public University Systems," February 2015, http://nashonline.org/wp-content/uploads/2017/08/Assessing-and-Improving-the-IR-Function-in-Public-University-Systems.pdf. The original location of these two reports changed in August, 2017. Both accessed on October 13, 2017. Earlier versions of the e-documents were accessed on March 23, 2017.

10. Francis E. Rourke and Glenn E. Brooks, *The Managerial Revolution in Higher Education* (1966), 44.

11. Ibid., 66.

12. Paul L. Dressel, ed., *Institutional Research in the University: A Handbook* (1971), 38.

13. Joe L. Saupe, and James R. Montgomery, "The Nature and Role of Institutional Research…Memo to a College or University," November 1970, p. 8, accessed March 23, 2017, http://files.eric.ed.gov/fulltext/ED049672.pdf.

14. E. Bernadette McKinney and John J. Hindera, "Science and Institutional Research: The Links," *Research in Higher Education* 33, no. 1 (February 1992), 19–29.

15. American Council on Education (ACE), "Moving the Needle on Predictive Analytics," May 2015, http://www.acenet.edu/news-room/Documents/Quick-Hits-Predictive-Analytics.pdf, n.p.

16. "Institutional Research," Wikipedia, accessed March 24, 2017, https://en.wikipedia.org/wiki/Institutional_research.

17. Rodney M. Ito II, Brian Gratton, and Joseph Wycoff, "Using the 1940 and 1950 Public Use Microdata Samples: A Cautionary Tale," *Historical Methods* 30, no. 3 (1997), 137–47.

18. I refer to David Szatmary, Vice Provost of Educational Outreach at the University of Washington from 1999 to 2014.

19. Darlena Jones, *Impact of Business Intelligence on Institutional Research* (2013), 8.

20. William E. Knight, *Leadership and Management in Institutional Research* (2014), iii.

21. ACE, "Moving the Needle," 1.

22. The most comprehensive publication is Gary Rice (Project Coordinator), *Association for Institutional Research: The First Fifty Years*. The Association for Institutional Research (2011).

23. R. J. Shavelson and L. Towne, eds., *Scientific Research in Education*, Committee on Scientific Principles for Education Research, Center for Education, Division of Behavioral and Social Sciences and Education, National Research Council [NRC], (2002). Electronic text available at http://www.nap.edu/catalog/10236/scientific-research-in-education.

24. Rourke and Brooks, *Managerial Revolution*, 66.

25. Randy L. Swing, "Institutional Research Capacity: Foundations of Federal Data Quality," Association for Institutional Research (2016), accessed May 2, 2017, https://www.airweb.org/Resources/IRStudies/Documents/institutional_research_capacity.pdf.

1 | THE SCIENTIFIC COMMUNITY THAT ENABLES SCIENTIFIC PROGRESS

1. Donald N. Dedmon, "Institutional Research: An Evolving Misnomer," *Vital Speeches of the Day* XLIV, no. 16 (June 1, 1978), 482–83. Dedmon, president of Radford College, cited a report by Walter Kronkite suggesting that "government paper work" of all types cost the nation $100 billion per year and a case study that indicated federal mandated programs cost higher education institutions between 1 percent and 4 percent of their operating budgets at that time (1977).

2. Dawn Geronimo Terkla, ed., *Institutional Research: More than Just Data*, New Directions for Higher Education no. 141 (2008), 1.

3. Shavelson and Towne, *Scientific Research*, passim.

4. Ernst Nagel, *The Structure of Science: Problems in the Logic of Scientific Explanation* (1979), 1–4.

5. Ibid., 5–12.

6. "Improving & Transforming Institutional Research in Postsecondary Education," Association for Institutional Research, accessed June 29, 2015, http://www.airweb.org/Resources/ImprovingAndTransformingPostsecondaryEducation/P ages/default.aspx; "A Brief Summary of Statements of Aspirational Practice for Institutional Research," Association for Institutional Research, n.p., accessed March 26, 2017, http://admin.airweb.org/Resources/ImprovingAndTransformingPostsecondaryEducation/ Documents/AIR%20Statements%20of%20Aspirational%20Practice%20for%20IR%20- %20Summary.pdf.

7. "Data studies" is a colloquialism for uncoordinated, distributed institutional research functions under the control of departmental "decision-makers" as advocated by the Association for Institutional Research.

8. Immanuel Kant, "What Is Enlightenment?" in *The Portable Enlightenment Reader*, ed. Isaac Kramnick (1995), 1–2.

9. "45 CFR Part 690: Federal Policy for the Protection of Human Subjects, Subpart A: The Common Rule for the Protection of Human Subjects," National Science Foundation, accessed March 28, 2017, https://www.nsf.gov/bfa/dias/policy/docs/45cfr690.pdf.

10. "Human Subject Regulations Decision Charts," US Department of Health and Human Services, accessed March 28, 2017, https://www.hhs.gov/ohrp/regulations-and-policy/decision-charts/index.html.

11. US Department of Health and Human Services, "The Belmont Report," accessed March 28, 2017, https://www.hhs.gov/ohrp/regulations-and-policy/belmont-report/index.html.

12. John William Ridge, "Organizing for Institutional Research," Association for Institutional Research, *The AIR Professional File* no. 1 (fall 1978), 1; Mark D. Johnson, "Career Development in Institutional Research," Association for Institutional Research, *The AIR Professional File* no. 12 (spring 1982), 1.

13. Johnson, "Career Development," 2; William P. Fenstemacher, "The Institutional Research Director: Professional Development and Career Path," Association for Institutional Research, *The AIR Professional File* no. 13 (summer 1982), 5.

14. Shavelson and Towne, *Scientific Research*, ix.

15. Ibid., 13, 19. Perhaps here as well a reason for the peculiar absence of institutional research functions in the literature on higher education and higher education administration examined in chapter 7.

16. Ibid., 20, 99.

17. Integrated Postsecondary Education Data System (IPEDS) provides the data sets compiling the institutional submissions. The data sets are available through https://nces.ed.gov/ipeds/Home/UseTheData (accessed March 29, 2017).

18. Stéphan Vincent-Lancrin, "What Is Changing in Academic Research? Trends and Future Scenarios," The Organisation for Economic Co-operation and Development (OECD), accessed June 23, 2017, http://www.oecd.org/edu/ceri/37481256.pdf.

19. The US government has already acted on the initiative to make education a more evidence-based field by the establishment of the Institute of Education Sciences (http://www2.ed.gov/about/offices/list/ies/index.html) and its What Works Clearinghouse (http://ies.ed.gov/ncee/wwc/).

20. Shavelson and Towne, *Scientific Research*, 132.

21. Ibid., 3–5.

22. William H. Bergquist and Kenneth Pawlak, *Engaging the Six Cultures of the Academy* (2008). They define the six cultures as: collegial, managerial, developmental, advocacy, virtual, and tangible.

23. Shavelson and Towne, *Scientific Research*, 2.

24. Ibid., 20, 106.

25. Ibid., 19, 57.

2 | A FACT-FINDING AGENCY DIRECTLY RESPONSIBLE TO THE PRESIDENT

1. Shavelson and Towne, *Scientific Research*, 2.

2. Ibid., 3.

3. William F. Lasher, "The History of Institutional Research and its Role in American Higher Education over the Past 50 Years (Chapter 2)," in "AIR, The First Fifty Years," ed. Rice, 10–15; https://www.airweb.org/AboutUs/History/Pages/Books-Papers-Manuscripts.aspx (requires membership). Donald J. Reichard was also tasked with presenting a history of institutional research for *The Handbook of Institutional Research*, eds. Richard D. Howard et al., 2012, "The History of Institutional Research," 3–21. Lasher indicates the two coordinated to provide very similar historical accounts for the AIR.

4. Lasher, "History of Institutional Research," 14.

5. Walter C. Eells, *Surveys of American Higher Education* (1937); W. H. Cowley, "Two and a Half Centuries of Institutional Research," in R. G. Axt and Hall T. Sprague, eds., *College Self Studies: Lectures on Institutional Research* (1960), 1–16; W. L. Tetlow, "Institutional Research: The Emergence of a Staff Function in Higher Education," (Cornell University, unpublished doctoral dissertation, 1973); and J. L. Doi, "The Beginnings of a Profession: A Retrospective View," in *Professional Development for Institutional Research*, ed. Robert G. Cope, New Directions for Institutional Research no. 23 (1979), 33–41.

6. Reichard, passim.

7. Walter Crosby Eells, "Bigger and Better Surveys," *American Journal of Education* 41, no. 8 (October 1933), 628; Eells, *Surveys*, 54.

8. W. W. C., "Editorial Comment: Institutional Research," *The Journal of Higher Education* 6, no. 5 (May 1935): 281.

9. Christopher Green, "Psychology Strikes Out: Coleman R. Griffith and the Chicago Cubs," *History of Psychology* 6, no. 3 (2003): 267–283.

10. Lasher notes, "Many agree that this was probably the first administrative unit created for the purpose of ongoing institutional research." He does not mention Griffith or his original publication from the mid-1930s. "History of Institutional Research," 13.

11. Coleman R. Griffith, "Functions of a Bureau of Institutional Research," *The Journal of Higher Education* 9, no. 5 (May 1938): 248–255. Cited in passim in subsequent paragraphs. While Griffith does not provide the date the office was organized, Lasher fixes the year as 1918 in *AIR, The First Fifty Years*, 13.

12. Doi, "The Beginnings," 38.

13. Ruth E. Eckert and Robert J. Keller, eds., *A University Looks at Its Program: The Report of the University of Minnesota Bureau of Institutional Research, 1942–1952* (1954). The origins of the bureau are described on pages 3–5. Cited in passim in subsequent paragraphs.

14. Ruth E. Eckert, "A Journey toward Understanding," *The Journal of Higher Education* 50, no. 3 (May–June, 1979), 233–255.

15. Minnesota Commission on Higher Education, *Higher Education in Minnesota* (1950). See also, as a precursor to this statewide work, Ruth E. Eckert, *Minnesota's Needs for Post-High School Education: Reports 1–7* (1946).

16. Eckert and Keller, *A University*, 10. Cited in passim in subsequent paragraphs.

17. L. J. Lins, ed., *Basis for Decision: A Composite of Current Institutional Research Methods and Reports for Colleges and Universities*, published as *The Journal of Experimental Education* 31, no. 2 (December 1962).

18. The Fordham contributor to *Basis for Decision*, ed. Lins, was Francis J. Donohue, "A New Re-Accreditation Pattern Based on Institutional Research: The Self-Study at Fordham University," 101–105.

19. Loring M. Thompson, "Institutional Research, Planning, and Politics," in *Basis for Decision*, ed. Lins, 89.

20. Thompson, "Institutional Research," 89, 91; Edward M. Stout and Irma Halfter, "Institutional Research and Automation," in *Basis for Decision*, ed. Lins, 95.

21. Nagel, *The Structure*, 4; Shavelson and Towne, *Scientific Research*, 30.

22. Ibid., 99–100.

23. Griffith, "Functions," 248.

24. Ruth E. Eckert, "Graduate Students in Education," in *A University*, eds. Eckert and Keller, 175.

25. Thompson, "Institutional Research," 91.

26. James I. Doi, "The Role of Institutional Research in the Administrative Process," in *A Conceptual Framework for Institutional Research, The Proceedings of the 4th Annual National Institutional Research Forum (Minneapolis, Minnesota, 1964)*, ed. Clarence H Bagley (1964), 52. Membership records show that women held 10 percent of the positions in the AIR at its formation. See Rice, *AIR, The First Fifty Years*, 117.

27. Doi, "The Role of Institutional Research," 52.

3 | ESSENTIAL FOR EFFICIENT AND ECONOMICAL EDUCATIONAL PROCEDURES

1. Doi, "The Beginnings," 38; Paul E. Lingenfelter in collaboration with James R. Mingle, "Public Policy for Higher Education in the United States: A Brief History of State Leadership," State Higher Education Executive Officers, 61st Annual Meeting, July 2014, http://www.sheeo.org/sites/default/files/publications/Public_Policy_Higher_Ed_Lingenfelter_Mingle_062014.pdf.

2. T. C. Holy, H. H. Semans, and T. R. McConnell, *A Restudy of the Needs of California in Higher Education*, Prepared for the Liaison Committee of the Regents of the University of California and the California State Board of Education (1955); California Department of Education, *A Master Plan for Higher Education in California, 1960–1975*, prepared for the

Liaison Committee of the State Board of Education and the Regents of the University of California…by the Master Plan Survey Team (1960).

3. George F. Zook, *Higher Education for American Democracy: A Report* (1947), 1, 8.

4. Ibid., 101.

5. Ibid., 82, 29.

6. John Dale Russell, "Basic Conclusions and Recommendations of the President's Commission on Higher Education," *The Journal of Educational Sociology* 22, no. 8, Report of the President's Commission on Higher Education (April 1949), 493–508.

7. Lingenfelter, "State Policy Leadership For Higher Education: A Brief Summary of the Origins and Continuing Evolution of a Profession," State Higher Education Executive Officers Association (August 2012), http://www.sheeo.org/sites/default/files/publications/State_Policy_Leadership_History.pdf.

8. Holy et al., *A Restudy*, 1.

9. George D. Strayer and Edward L. Thorndike, *Educational Administration: Quantitative Studies* (1913), v.

10. T. R. McConnell, "A Reply to the Critics," *The Journal of Educational Sociology* 22, no. 8 (1949): 533–50.

11. Holy et al., *A Restudy*, 15–16. Cited in passim in subsequent paragraphs.

12. Thad L. Hungate, *Finance in Educational Management of Colleges and Universities* (1954), 94–105.

13. The section on institutional research is found at Holy et al., *A Restudy*, 239–240.

14. T. C. Holy and H. H. Semans, *A Study of the Need for Additional Centers of Public Higher Education in California*, Liaison Committee of the Regents of the University of California and the California State Board of Education (1957). Cited in passim in subsequent paragraphs.

15. To support the assumption, the 1957 report cites the input from a faculty conference: *Proceedings of the University of California Eleventh All-University Faculty Conference* (April 1956), 23–35.

16. Holy and Semans, *Need for Additional Centers*, chapter V.

17. John R. Thelin, *Essential Documents in the History of American Higher Education* (2014), 237; Simon Marginson, *The Dream Is Over: The Crisis of Clark Kerr's California Idea of Higher Education* (2016), 12.

18. Clark Kerr, *Higher Education Cannot Escape History* (1994), 123–24 (quote); see also, Paul H. Mattingly, "Clark Kerr: The Unapologetic Pragmatist," *Social Science History* 36, no. 4 (winter 2012), 481–97.

19. The Joint Staff completed a study on faculty demand and supply in 1958: California. Liaison Committee of the Regents of the University of California and the State Board of Education, *A Study of Faculty Demand and Supply in California Higher Education, 1957–70* (1958).

20. See Committee on Government and Higher Education, *The Efficiency of Freedom* (1959); Malcolm Moos and Francis E. Rourke. *The Campus and the State* (1959); Lyman A. Glenny, *Autonomy of Public Colleges: The Challenge of Coordination* (1959); and Frank C. Abbott, *Government Policy and Higher Education: A Study of the Regents of the State of New York, 1784–1949* (1958).

4 | A COMPREHENSIVE AND UNIFIED APPROACH

1. Doi, "The Beginnings," 38.
2. A. J. Brumbaugh, *Research Designed to Improve Institutions of Higher Learning* (1960), 2.
3. J. W. Hicks and F. L. Kidner, *California and Western Conference Cost and Statistical Study for the Year 1954–55* (1955). Cited in passim in subsequent paragraphs.
4. Ibid. See figure 1, page 17.
5. W. Hugh Stickler, *Institutional Research Concerning Land-Grant Institutions and State Universities, A Report Prepared for the Joint Office of Institutional Research of the American Association of Land-Grant Colleges and State Universities and the State Universities Association* (1959). Cited in passim in subsequent paragraphs.
6. Brumbaugh, *Research Designed to Improve*. Cited in passim in subsequent paragraphs.
7. A. J. Brumbaugh, *American Universities and Colleges*, American Council on Education (1948); A. J. Brumbaugh and Ralph F. Berdie, *Student Personnel Programs in Transition* (1952); A. J. Brumbaugh, *Problems in College Administration* (1956). A. J. Brumbaugh, *The Coordination of Higher Education in Illinois: A Report to the Committee on Governing Boards of the State of Illinois Higher Education Commission* (1956).
8. Brumbaugh, *Problems*, 7.
9. Rice, *AIR: The First Fifty Years*, 57.
10. Philip H. Tyrrell, "Programming the Unknown: Guidelines for the Conduct of Institutional Research," in *Basis for Decision*, ed. Lins, 94.

5 | THE CENTER OF CONFLUENCE FOR MANY SOCIAL FORCES

1. Eckert, "A Journey," 247.
2. Lins, "Foreword," in *Basis for Decision*, ed. Lins, 88.
3. Several of these clauses paraphrase statements from chapter 2, "Accumulation of Scientific Knowledge," in Shavelson and Towne, *Scientific Research*, 28–49.
4. Thomas S. Kuhn, *The Structure of Scientific Revolutions*, second edition, enlarged (1970), 22, 25, 43–49, 49 (final quote).
5. Edward M. Stout and Irma Halfter, "Institutional Research and Automation," in *Basis for Decision*, ed. Lins, 95–98.
6. Tyrrell, "Programming the Unknown," 92.
7. Tyrrell's themes parallel thoughts expressed by Clark Kerr on the historical situation and influence of universities in the late 1950s and early 1960s. See Ethan Schrum, "To 'Administer the Present': Clark Kerr and the Purpose of the Postwar American Research University," *Social Science History* 36, no. 4 (winter 2012), 499–523.
8. Tyrrell, "Programming the Unknown," 93–94.
9. Kuhn, *Structure*, 25–27, 25 (quote).
10. Christopher D. Green, "The Flaw at the Heart of Psychological Research," *The Chronicle of Higher Education*, June 26, 2016 , http://www.chronicle.com/article/The-Flaw-at-the-Heart-of/236916/. As recently affirmed in reports on the inability of scientists to replicate research studies in psychology. The problem is more severe in education research according to Matthew C. Makel and Jonathon A. Plucker, "Facts Are More Important Than Novelty: Replication in the Education Sciences," *Educational Researcher* XX no. X (2015), 1–13.
11. John Dale Russell and Floyd W. Reeves, *Finance* (1935); Lloyd Morey, "Assembling and Weighting Data (Review of *Finance*)," *Journal of Higher Education* 7 no. 5 (May 1936), 283.

12. Clarence H Bagley, ed., *A Conceptual Framework for Institutional Research, The Proceedings of the 4th Annual National Institutional Research Forum (Minneapolis, Minnesota, 1964)* (1964). Cited in passim in subsequent paragraphs.

13. Robert J. Henle, *Systems for Measuring and Reporting the Resources and Activities of Colleges and Universities*, National Science Foundation (1967). Henle went on to become the president of Georgetown University. The publication provides a concrete application of the abstract ideas Tyrrell expressed in 1962.

14. Ibid., 13, 3.

15. In 1990, Michael F. Middaugh reduced the portfolio of research subjects into a one-dimensional axis under the headings "input-process-output." See Michael F. Middaugh, "The Nature and Scope of Institutional Research," in *Organizing Effective Institutional Research Offices*, ed. Jennifer B. Presley, New Directions for Institutional Research no. 66 (1990), 36–43. In 2008, J. Frederick Volkswein organized the research subjects of institutional research in a simpler system defined by only "function-customer." See J. Fredericks Volkswein, "The Foundations and Evolution of Institutional Research," in *Institutional Research: More than Just Data*, ed. Dawn Geronimo Terkla, New Directions for Higher Education no. 141 (2008), 15–16.

16. In his original formulation, the triangle was formed by "(1) institutional research and analysis, (2) planning and budgeting, and (3) assessment, effectiveness, accreditation." See Volkswein, "Foundations and Evolution," 6–7. I prefer to reserve the phrase, "institutional research," for a broader designation than one corner of the golden triangle. I use his more recent restatement from J. Fredericks Volkswein, "Gaining Ground: The Role of Institutional Research in Assessing Student Outcomes and Demonstrating Institutional Effectiveness," National Institute of Learning Outcomes Assessment, *Occasional Paper* no. 11 (September 2011), 8 (see figure 2).

17. The use of automation at individual institutions and for state reporting systems remains highly variable. In the 2010s, Illinois and New York have vastly different systems for state reporting, one largely automated for information systems and the other largely reliant on static survey forms requiring hand or keystroke entry.

18. Quotes reflect the language of Shavelson and Towne, *Scientific Research*, 2.

6 | PRODUCTION OF KNOWLEDGE WITHOUT PERVASIVE AND LASTING SIGNIFICANCE

1. Lasher, "History," 18–19; Rice, *AIR, The First Fifty Years*, 57; Doi, "Beginnings," 34–36.

2. Doi, "Conceptual Framework," 53–55.

3. Rourke and Brooks, *Managerial Revolution*, 44; Saupe and Montgomery, "The Nature and Role of Institutional Research," 16; and Reichard, "History of Institutional Research," 7.

4. Francis E. Rourke and Glenn E. Brooks, "The 'Managerial Revolution' in Higher Education," *Administrative Science Quarterly* 9, no. 2 (September 1964), 166.

5. Rourke and Brooks, *Managerial Revolution*, chapter 3.

6. Ibid., 44, 66.

7. Carl E. Wedekind, Joe L. Saupe, and James Doi, in *A Conceptual Framework*, ed. Bagley, 34, 53, and 89.

8. John E. Stecklein, "The Birth of a Profession: President's Address," *Research on Academic Input, Proceedings of Association for Institutional Research Annual Forum (6th, Boston, Massachusetts, 1966)*, ed. Clarence H. Bagley (1966), 9–13.

9. L.E. Hull, "Fact, Doubt, and Myth," in *Institutional Research and Academic Outcomes, Proceedings of the Association for Institutional Research Annual Forum (8th, San Francisco, California, 1968)*, ed. Cameron Fincher (1968), 1–6.

10. Thomas R. Mason, "Communication in Institutional Research: The Purpose of the Association," in *Institutional Research and Communication in Higher Education. Proceedings of the Association for Institutional Research Annual Forum on Institutional Research (10th, New Orleans, Louisiana, 1970)*, ed. Patricia S. Wright (1970), 7–8.

11. Joe L. Saupe, "Assessing Program Quality," in *The Challenge and Response of Institutional Research, Proceedings of the Association for Institutional Research Annual Forum (9th, Chicago, Illinois, 1969)*, ed. Cameron Fincher (1969), 1–12.

12. Saupe and Montgomery, "The Nature and Role of Institutional Research." Cited in passim in subsequent paragraphs.

13. Ibid., see footnote 1, referencing Joe L. Saupe, "Some General Remarks on the Nature, Scope and Function of Institutional Research," Michigan State University, mimeographed, August 1968.

14. James R. Montgomery, "Institutional Research—A Future Unfolding," in *The Instructional Process and Institutional Research. Proceedings of the Association for Institutional Research Annual Forum (7th, Athens, Georgia, 1967)*, ed. Galen N. Drewry (1967), 1–10.; James R. Montgomery, "An Effective Role for Institutional Research," in *Institutional Research and Communication*, ed. Wright, 140–42.

15. Reichard, "History of Institutional Research," 12.

16. Dressel, *Institutional Research*, 23, 38, 310–11.

17. G. Lester Anderson and Fred F. Hacleroad, eds., *Higher Education: A Developing Field of Study, Proceedings of the Annual Meeting of the Association of Professors of Higher Education (3rd, Chicago, Illinois, 1974)* (1974). Quote from E. D. Duryea, "Some Thoughts on the Service Role of Departments of Higher Education," 92.

18. "Lewis Mayhew, outspoken critic of higher ed, dies at 75," Stanford University, October 6, 1992, https://web.stanford.edu/dept/news/pr/92/921006Arc2092.html.

19. Lewis B. Mayhew, "Imperatives for Institutional Research," in *Academic Input*, ed. Bagley, 1–8.

20. Paul L. Dressel and Lewis B. Mayhew, *Higher Education as a Field of Study* (1974), 82.

21. Ibid., 173, 124.

22. Joe L. Saupe, *The Functions of Institutional Research*, first edition, Association for Institutional Research (1981), https://www.airweb.org/AboutUs/History/Documents/Papers-Books-Manuscripts/Functions-of-IR-Saupe-1edition.pdf.

23. Lewis B. Mayhew studied at Michigan State University where he formed his partnership with Dressel.

24. Jack Testerman and others, "Institutional Research: A Review of Literature to 1972" (1972), accessed April 14, 2017, http://files.eric.ed.gov/fulltext/ED077476.pdf, 4–5.

25. Dedmon, "Institutional Research," 482–83.

26. Paul L. Dressel, "Institutional Researchers: Created or Educated?" 45, and Robert G. Cope, "A Young Profession: An Overview," 97, both in *Professional Development for Institutional Research*, ed. Robert G. Cope, New Directions for Institutional Research no. 23 (1979).

27. Irving J. Spitzberg, Jr., "Monitoring Social and Political Changes," 15, and Jack Lindquist, "Improving the Teaching-Learning Environment," 297–98, both in *Improving Academic Management: A Handbook of Planning and Institutional Research*, eds. Paul Jedamus, Marvin W. Peterson, and Associates (1980). Dressel contributed as an associate editor to the volume. In general, while less antagonistic, the edited volume advocates for decentralized responsibility for institutional research and planning as similarly outlined by Rourke and

Brooks. Typically, the underlying motivations or ideology came to the surface in the lines quoted.

7 | IN A PRE-PARADIGM STAGE IN PERPETUITY

1. Cameron L. Fincher, "On the Predictable Crises of Institutional Research," *Research in Higher Education* 8, no. 1 (1978), 93–96.
2. Cameron L. Fincher, "The Art and Science of Institutional Research," in *Institutional Research in Transition*, eds. M. Corcoran and M. W. Peterson, New Directions for Institutional Research no. 46 (1985), 17–37.
3. Frans Van Vught, "A Fundamental Challenge for the Institutional Research Profession," in *Institutional Research Coming of Age, General Session Presentations at Annual Forum of Association for Institutional Research (30, Louisville, Kentucky, 1990)*, ed. Jean Endo (1990), 23–32; membership estimate from Rice, *AIR, The First Fifty Years*, 116 (Figure 4.3).
4. George Keller, "What Does the Future Hold for Institutional Research," in *Institutional Research Coming of Age*, ed. Endo, 9–10.
5. Ibid., 11–12, 15–16.
6. Joe L. Saupe, *The Functions of Institutional Research*, second edition, Association for Institutional Research (1990). https://www.airweb.org/educationandevents/publications/pages/functionsofir.aspx, 6. Cited in passim in subsequent paragraphs.
7. E. Bernadette McKinney and John J. Hindera, "Science and Institutional Research: The Links," *Research in Higher Education* 33, no. 1 (February 1992), 28.
8. Ibid. The abstract asserts that "institutional research…is distinct from science."
9. Michael E. Schlitz, ed., *Ethics and Standards in Institutional Research*, New Directions for Institutional Research no. 73 (1992), 7–8, 18, 40. The rationalizations for the designation of institutional research as a craft raise impossible standards for any profession. In the *Structure of Scientific Revolutions*, Kuhn considers the different levels of expertise in quantum physics that physicists attain for their specializations. Between institutions, there is often little uniformity from one academic program to another in physics, history, or higher education.
10. J. Frederick Volkswein, "The Diversity of Institutional Research Structures and Tasks," in *Organizing Effective Institutional Research Offices*, ed. Jennifer B. Presley, New Directions for Institutional Research no. 66 (1990), 7–26.
11. Ibid., 23–25.
12. Volkswein, "Foundations and Evolution," 9.
13. P. T. Terenzini, "On the Nature of Institutional Research and the Knowledge and Skills It Requires," *Research in Higher Education* 34, no. 1 (February 1993), 1–10.
14. Patrick T. Terenzini, "'On the Nature of Institutional Research' Revisited: Plus Ça Change…?" *Research in Higher Education* 54, no. 2 (March 2013), 137–148. I attended the 2012 forum in New Orleans and I have attempted to apply Terenzini's categorizations in the creation of offices responsible for institutional research.
15. Fincher, "The Art," 17–37.
16. Patrick Terenzini, "From the Series Editor," *Preparing for the Information Needs of the Twenty-First Century*, New Directions for Institutional Research no. 85 (1995), 91: Terenzini, Plus Ça Change," 139.
17. William E. Knight, Michael E. Moore and Corby A. Coperthwaite, "Institutional Research: Knowledge, Skills, and Perceptions of Effectiveness," *Research in Higher Education* 38, no. 4 (August 1997), 419–433.

18. Terenzini, "Plus Ça Change," 148; quoting T.S. Eliot, "Little Gidding," in *Four Quartets* (1943), 49–59.

8 | GREAT VARIANCE IN ASSIGNMENTS AND RESPONSIBILITIES

1. The paragraph summarizes criticism of the scholarship on institutional research by higher education scholars, but also presents the implications by the order summarized in J. Fredericks Volkswein, "The Foundations and Evolution," 5–20.
2. NASH, "Assessing and Improving the IR Function," n.p. (page 4 of the pdf).
3. Ibid., n.p. (page 3 of the pdf).
4. Schlitz, *Ethics and Standards*, 40.
5. Alton L. Taylor, "Options for Location in the Organizational Structure," in *Organizing Effective Institutional Research Offices*, ed. Jennifer B. Presley, New Directions in Institutional Research no. 66 (1990), 30–31.
6. Ronald P. Matross, "The Virtual Office: An Organizational Paradigm for Institutional Research in the 90's. AIR 1993 Annual Forum Paper," paper presented at the Annual Forum of the Association for Institutional Research (1993), accessed April 27, 2017, http://eric.ed.gov/?id=ED360919. Cited in passim in subsequent paragraphs.
7. Robert M. Hendrickson, "The Core Knowledge of Higher Education," in *Advancing Higher Education as a Field of Study: In Quest of Doctoral Degree Guidelines, Commemorating 120 Years of Excellence*, eds. Sydney Freeman, Jr., et al. (2014), 231.
8. Dressel, "Institutional Researchers," 45.
9. Description taken from the Association for the Study of Higher Education web page, "Higher Education: Handbook of Theory and Research," accessed April 25, 2017, http://www.ashe.ws/ashe_handbook_tr.
10. J. C. Smart, ed., *Higher Education: Handbook of Theory and Research* XXI (2006).
11. From *Higher Education: Handbook of Theory and Research*: J. R. Thelin and M. V. Krotseng, "Higher Education's Odd Couple: Campus Archives and the Office of Institutional Research," V (1989); M. Bonous-Hammarth, "Value Congruence and Organizational Climates for Undergraduate Persistence," XV (2000); A. C. Dowd and V. P. Tong, "Accountability, Assessment, and the Scholarship of 'Best Practice,'" XXII (2007).
12. Knight et al., "Institutional Research," abstract.
13. Kuhn, *Structure*, 94.
14. Victor M. H. Borden and Karen L. Webber, "Institutional and Educational Research in Higher Education," in *Institutional Research and Planning in Higher Education: Global Contexts and Themes*, eds. Karen L. Webber and Angel J. Calderon (2015), 16–27. Cited in passim in subsequent paragraphs.
15. Michele J. Hansen and Victor M. H. Borden, "An Action Research Paradigm for Institutional Research," paper presented at the 2003 AIR Forum, accessed June 29, 2017, http://irds.iupui.edu/Portals/SDAE/Files/Documents/AIR%20Action%20Research%205.2.03.pdf.
16. The Organisation for Economic Co-operation and Development (OECD), *Proposed Standard Practice for Surveys on Research and Experimental Development* (2002).
17. Borden and Webber, "Institutional and Educational Research," 23.
18. Ibid., 16. The authors describe themselves as "(professors) in higher education academic programs."
19. J. Fredericks Volkswein, Ying (Jessie) Liu, and James Woodell, "The Structure and Functions of Institutional Research Offices," in *The Handbook of Institutional Research*, eds. Richard D. Howard et al. (2012), 22–39.

20. NASH, "Assessing and Improving the IR Function," n.p. (page 17 of the pdf).

21. Rourke and Brooks, *Managerial Revolution*, 53; Taylor, "Options," 31; Volkswein, "Foundations and Evolution," 9.

22. NASH, "Assessing and Improving the IR Function," n.p. (page 4 of the pdf).

23. Kuhn, *Structure*, 111.

9 | A NEW AN OLD VISION FOR INSTITUTIONAL RESEARCH

1. "Improving & Transforming Institutional Research in Postsecondary Education," Association for Institutional Research, accessed June 29, 2015, http://www.airweb.org/Resources/ImprovingAndTransformingPostsecondaryEducation/Pages/default.aspx; membership estimate from Rice, *AIR, The First Fifty Years*, 116 (Figure 4.3).

2. "A Brief Summary of Statements of Aspirational Practice for Institutional Research," Association for Institutional Research (2015), accessed May 2, 2017, http://admin.airweb.org/Resources/ImprovingAndTransformingPostsecondaryEducation/Documents/AIR%20Statements%20of%20Aspirational%20Practice%20for%20IR%20-%20Summary.pdf.

3. NASH, "Assessing and Improving the Institutional Research Function," n.p. (page 4 of the pdf).

4. R. L. Swing, D. Jones, and L. E. Ross, "The AIR National Survey of Institutional Research Offices," Association for Institutional Research (2016), accessed June 20 2017, http://www.airweb.org/nationalsurvey.

5. Brumbaugh, *Problems*, 1.

6. The following anecdote is a pastiche of personal experiences and stories shared by other professionals. The details do not recount actual events at a specific college or university.

7. This is to say that the research is conducted with students who have already been retained, revealing little to nothing directly about nonretained students.

8. A reference to the "shared leadership" model described by Peter D. Eckel and Adrianna Kezar, "Presidents Leading: The Dynamics and Complexities of Campus Leadership," in *American Higher Education in the Twenty-First Century*, eds. Philip G. Altbach, Patricia J. Gumport, and Robert O. Berdahl (2011), 304.

9. The College Board, "SAT® Percentile Ranks for Males, Females, and Total Group," accessed May 2, 2017, https://secure-media.collegeboard.org/digitalServices/pdf/sat/sat-percentile-ranks-composite-crit-reading-math-2014.pdf.

10. NASH, "Assessing and Improving the Institutional Research Function," n.p. (page 3 of the pdf).

11. Randy L. Swing and Leah Ewing Ross, "A New Vision for Institutional Research," *Change: The Magazine of Higher Learning*, 48 no. 2 (2016), 6–13, http://dx.doi.org/10.1080/00091383.2016.1163132. Cited in passim in subsequent paragraphs.

12. Ibid., 7.

13. The statement's unnecessary hyperbole—"a thousand skilled staff members"—deflects from the intent of the "new vision" to maintain IR as a function dispersed across the institution in an "elaborate profusion" (now, "federated network"). See page 8.

14. Swing, "Institutional Research Capacity,"3–4.

15. Ibid., 2.

EPILOGUE | FROM INSTITUTIONAL RESEARCH TO DATA SCIENCE

1. Fincher, "The Art," 21.

2. Nagel, *Structure*, 447.

3. Frank A. Schmidtlein and Robert O Berdahl, "Autonomy and Accountability: Who Controls Academe?" in *American Higher Education in the Twenty-First Century: Social, Political, and Economic Challenges*, eds. Philip G. Altbach, Patricia J. Gumport, and Robert O. Berdahl, Third Edition (2011), 69.

4. Ibid., 70.

5. From 2012, Reichard's review of the debate on whether institutional research is theoretical or operational research ends with the so-called "middle ground" proposed by Paul Dressel that "[t]he basic purposes of institutional research is to probe deeply into all aspects of an [i.e., a particular] institution." See "History of Institutional Research," 12.

6. Stephen Joel Trachtenberg, Gerald B. Kauvar, and E. Grady Bogue, *Presidencies Derailed: Why University Leaders Fail and How to Prevent* (2013). The authors emphasize the "failure to meet business objectives" as one of the six themes of presidential derailments at all levels and as the first theme of failure by presidents of private liberal arts colleges. See pages 22–23.

7. The list of higher education rankings is extensive, beginning with the *U.S. News and World Report*, *Forbes*, *Washington Monthly*, *Times Higher Education*, and many more.

8. Knight, *Leadership and Management*, passim.

9. Ellen Peters, "The Future Awaits," *e-AIR Newsletter* (June 2017), accessed July 3, 2017, http://www.airweb.org/eAIR/Pages/eAIRNewsletterJune2017.aspx.

10. Audrey Williams June , "In Improving Outcomes, Institutional Researchers Can Be an Untapped Resource," *The Chronicle of Higher Education,* June 20, 2017, http://www.chronicle.com/article/In-Improving-Outcomes/240394.

11. Jesse Lawson, *Data Science in Higher Education: A Step-by-Step Introduction to Machine Learning for Institutional Researchers* (2015), 9, 149.

12. Harvard Office of Institutional Research, "Data, Data Science, and the Research University," Harvard University, presentation, September 7, 2016, https://projects.iq.harvard.edu/applied.stats.workshop-gov3009/presentations/972016-victoria-liublinski.

13. Richard Kent Plott, "The Transition from Institutional Research to Data Science in Higher Education," LinkedIn, June 12, 2017, https://www.linkedin.com/pulse/transition-from-institutional-research-data-science-kent-plott.

14. Kuhn, *Structure*, 111.

15. American Council on Education, "ACE Blog Series on Data Offers Campus Leaders Ideas to Spur Institutional Change," July 25, 2016, http://www.acenet.edu/news-room/Pages/ACE-Blog-Series-on-Data-Offers-Campus-Leaders-Ideas-to-Spur-Institutional-Change.aspx; Ascione, "Hobsons Acquisition;" Civitas Learning, "Longtime Advocates for Education Innovation Join Civitas Learning," *Market Wired*, March 21, 2016, http://www.marketwired.com/press-release/longtime-advocates-for-education-innovation-join-civitas-learning-2107678.htm; and Civitas Learning, "Civitas Learning Acquires." Some states such as Illinois have worked to build student-record level databases for K-20 education. These are more comprehensive records of a student's educational history but lack the ability to track students across state lines.

16. ideas42, *Nudging for Success: Using Behavioral Science to Improve the Postsecondary Student Journey,* white paper, June 2016, http://www.ideas42.org/wp-

content/uploads/2016/09/Nudging-For-Success-FINAL.pdf; ideas42, "ideas42 Tackles America's College Completion Crisis," *Market Wired*, June 22, 2016, http://www.marketwired.com/press-release/ideas42-tackles-americas-college-completion-crisis-2136676.htm. ideas42 is not, strictly speaking, a vendor of data science for student success. The example is cited as evidence of the renewed value of scientific methods in the study of higher education.

17. "Home (Page)," Asilomar II, accessed July 5, 2017, https://sites.stanford.edu/asilomar/; Carl Straumsheim, "Preparing for 'Era of Data Ubiquity,'" *Inside Higher Ed*, June 28, 2016, https://www.insidehighered.com/news/2016/06/28/researchers-outline-guidelines-ethical-use-student-data.

18. Jennifer Rees, "What Every Leader Needs to Know about Student Success Analytics," Civitas Learning, October 23, 2015, https://www.civitaslearningspace.com/what-every-leader-needs-to-know-about-student-success-analytics/.

19. Tyrrell, 94. The quote substitutes "data science for student success" in lieu of "institutional research."

ACKNOWLEDGMENTS

I am the first to acknowledge that this work would have benefited from more opportunities to present at professional associations or more time to publish selections in peer-reviewed journals.

The work is intended to be the product of historical analysis and not journalism. With only one exception, I did not reach out directly to scholars whose work I cited in the text. I am certain an oral history or journalistic investigation may have provided additional context, but my object of study was the published discourse regarding the nature, role, and function of institutional research. I must leave it to others to refute or revise the details of my narrative with their personal insights or memories.

My original interest in the subject arose from a 2015 forum session presenting the then-unpublished aspirational statement for institutional research. At the time, I had already turned a critical eye to the content of the annual forums and the literature published through the national association. Soon after the annual forum concluded, I posted my initial reflections on the sessions. Over the next year, I found myself deeply engaged by research and writings about the history of institutional research.

As I discovered evidence of the disparity in the literature before and after the formation of the national association, it became clear to me that the "new vision" for institutional research looked too much like the old vision of the association. I posted my findings for my colleagues to read. Despite efforts in 2015–16 to get its leadership to reconsider, the national association released its "aspirational statement" with no discernible reflection on its similarities with the past. Through that experience, I came to understand the consensus paradigm's hold on the profession and the vested interests in the national association.

The ideology of institutional uniqueness and autonomy—the basis for regarding institutional research as an art—is largely unassailable to the circle of scholars who specialize in the study of higher education administration, especially the subfield of institutional research. A critique of the leadership of the national association and higher education scholarship in general, as presented in this work, likely gives cause for concern among those who have gained much by adherence to the consensus paradigm for institutional research.

I never considered self-publishing previously, but the value to an open society is readily apparent to the casual observer. I am grateful to CreateSpace, an Amazon.com Company, for the tools and services they have provided. The errors in this text are my own, but they would have been far more unbearable without the editing services and informative resources provided to authors. Without the option of self-publication, the scholarly world would be a far less diverse place.

No independent scholar is successful without the access and resources provided by local libraries. I am deeply indebted to the Chicago Public Library system. I found many publications cited in this work at the Harold Washington Library or, when unavailable, through the interlibrary loan system. Chicago offers its citizens many social and intellectual advantages, but the ability to obtain free-of-charge almost any work of scholarship written at any time, in any place, and about an obscure subject matter like institutional research must be regarded as one of its most democratic treasures.

The Newberry Library, an independent research library in Chicago, also provides valuable resources to researchers as well as an aesthetic setting in which to sit and write for hours. I had a short research fellowship at the Newberry many years ago and the opportunity to use the library services again as a local patron helped to shore up my spirit for independent scholarship.

When the antiseptic silence of the libraries became unsettling, I discovered just the right mix of conversation and distractions at a historic tavern on Printers Row in Chicago. Nicole served up the week's selection of America's finest craft brews, allowing me to stretch out one or two more pages during a session. If any portion of this work has insight or proves amusing, it is likely attributable to the cheerful ambience of the people and patrons at Kasey's.

Lastly, nothing I have ever completed in my adult life has been possible without the support of my long-time partner, Donnell. She has patiently supported me for the past two years while my professional projects and interests have oscillated between consultancy and scholarship. This project would have ended in a series of web posts if not for her insistence that I collect my research into a book-length manuscript.

SELECTED BIBLIOGRAPHY

"45 CFR Part 690: Federal Policy for the Protection of Human Subjects, Subpart A: The Common Rule for the Protection of Human Subjects." National Science Foundation. Accessed March 28, 2017. https://www.nsf.gov/bfa/dias/policy/docs/45cfr690.pdf.

"A Brief Summary of Statements of Aspirational Practice for Institutional Research." Association for Institutional Research. Accessed March 26, 2017. http://admin.airweb.org/Resources/ImprovingAndTransformingPostsecondaryEducation/Documents/AIR%20Statements%20of%20Aspirational%20Practice%20for%20IR%20-%20Summary.pdf.

Abbott, Frank C. *Government Policy and Higher Education: A Study of the Regents of the State of New York, 1784–1949.* 1958.

"About (Page)." Institute of Education Sciences. Accessed March 30, 2017. http://www2.ed.gov/about/offices/list/ies/index.html.

"About (Page)." What Works Clearinghouse. Accessed March 30, 2017. http://ies.ed.gov/ncee/wwc/.

American Council on Education (ACE). "Moving the Needle on Predictive Analytics." May 2015. http://www.acenet.edu/news-room/Documents/Quick-Hits-Predictive-Analytics.pdf.

American Council on Education. "ACE Blog Series on Data Offers Campus Leaders Ideas to Spur Institutional Change." July 25, 2016. Accessed June 2, 2017. http://www.acenet.edu/news-room/Pages/ACE-Blog-Series-on-Data-Offers-Campus-Leaders-Ideas-to-Spur-Institutional-Change.aspx.

Ascione, Laura. "Hobsons acquisition targets retention, educational outcomes." *eCampus News,* January 12, 2016. https://www.ecampusnews.com/top-news/hobsons-retention-outcomes-892.

Association for Institutional Research. "A Brief Summary of Statements of

Aspirational Practice for Institutional Research." 2015. Accessed May 2, 2017. http://admin.airweb.org/Resources/ImprovingAndTransformingPostsecondar yEducation/Documents/AIR%20Statements%20of%20Aspirational%20Practi ce%20for%20IR%20-%20Summary.pdf.

Association for Institutional Research. "Improving & Transforming Institutional Research in Postsecondary Education." Accessed June 29, 2015. http://www.airweb.org/Resources/ImprovingAndTransformingPostsecondary Education/Pages/default.aspx.

Bagley, Clarence H., ed. *A Conceptual Framework for Institutional Research, The Proceedings of the 4th Annual National Institutional Research Forum (Minneapolis, Minnesota, 1964).* 1964.

Bergquist, William H., and Kenneth Pawlak. *Engaging the Six Cultures of the Academy.* 2008.

Birnbaum, Robert. *Management Fads in Higher Education: Where They Come From, What They Do, Why They Fail.* 2000.

Blumenstyk, Goldie. "A Top Proponent of Higher-Ed Disruption Moves to Put His Theories into Practice." *The Chronicle of Higher Education,* October 12, 2015. http://www.chronicle.com/blogs/wiredcampus/a-top-proponent-of-higher-ed-disruption-moves-to-put-his-theories-into-practice/57485.

Bonous-Hammarth, Marguerite. "Value Congruence and Organizational Climates for Undergraduate Persistence." *Higher Education: Handbook of Theory and Research XV,* edited by J. C. Smart, 339–370. 2000.

Borden, Victor M. H., and Karen L. Webber. "Institutional and Educational Research in Higher Education." In *Institutional Research and Planning in Higher Education: Global Contexts and Themes,* edited by Karen L. Webber and Angel J. Calderon, 16–27. 2015.

Brumbaugh, A. J. *American Universities and Colleges.* American Council on Education. 1948.

Brumbaugh, A. J. *Problems in College Administration.* 1956.

Brumbaugh, A. J. *Research Designed to Improve Institutions of Higher Learning.* 1960.

Brumbaugh, A. J. *The Coordination of Higher Education in Illinois: A Report to the Committee on Governing Boards of the State of Illinois Higher Education Commission.* 1956.

Brumbaugh, A. J., and Ralph F. Berdie. *Student Personnel Programs in Transition.* 1952.

C., W. W. "Editorial Comment: Institutional Research." *The Journal of Higher Education* 6, no. 5 (May 1935): 281–282.

California Department of Education. *A Master Plan for Higher Education in California, 1960–1975.* Prepared for the Liaison Committee of the State Board of Education and the Regents of the University of California...by the Master Plan Survey Team. 1960.

California State Board of Education. *Proceedings of the University of California Eleventh All-University Faculty Conference.* April 1956.

Civitas Learning. "Civitas Learning Acquires College Scheduler, Leader in Schedule Planning Solutions." *Yahoo! Finance,* January 20, 2016. http://finance.yahoo.com/news/civitas-learning-r-acquires-college-143000707.html.

Civitas Learning. "Longtime Advocates for Education Innovation Join Civitas

Learning." *Market Wired*, March 21, 2016. http://www.marketwired.com/press-release/longtime-advocates-for-education-innovation-join-civitas-learning-2107678.htm.

Civitas Learning. "Warburg Pincus Leads an Investment of up to $60 Million in Higher Education Data Pioneer." *MarketWatch*, September 28, 2015. http://www.marketwatch.com/story/warburg-pincus-leads-an-investment-of-up-to-60-million-in-higher-education-data-pioneer-2015-09-28.

Committee on Government and Higher Education. *The Efficiency of Freedom*. 1959.

Cope, Robert G. "A Young Profession: An Overview." In *Professional Development for Institutional Research*, edited by Robert G. Cope, 97–99. New Directions for Institutional Research no. 23, 1979.

Cowley, W.H. "Two and a Half Centuries of Institutional Research." In *College Self Studies: Lectures on Institutional Research*, edited by R. G. Axt and Hall T. Sprague, 1–16. 1960.

Davenport, Thomas H., and D. J. Patil. "Data Scientist: The Sexiest Job of the 21st Century." *Harvard Business Review*, October 2012. https://hbr.org/2012/10/data-scientist-the-sexiest-job-of-the-21st-century.

"Deakin and IBM unite to revolutionise the student experience." Deakin University, October 8, 2014. http://www.deakin.edu.au/about-deakin/media-releases/articles/deakin-and-ibm-unite-to-revolutionise-the-student-experience.

Dedmon, Donald N. "Institutional Research: An Evolving Misnomer." *Vital Speeches of the Day* XLIV, no. 16 (June 1, 1978): 482–85.

Doi, James I. "The Role of Institutional Research in the Administrative Process." In *A Conceptual Framework for Institutional Research, The Proceedings of the 4th Annual National Institutional Research Forum (Minneapolis, Minnesota, 1964)*, edited by Clarence H. Bagley, 51–58. 1964.

Doi, James L. "The Beginnings of a Profession: A Retrospective View." In *Professional Development for Institutional Research*, edited by Robert G. Cope, 33–41. New Directions for Institutional Research no. 23, 1979.

Donohue, Francis J. "A New Re-Accreditation Pattern Based on Institutional Research: The Self-Study at Fordham University." In *Basis for Decision: A Composite of Current Institutional Research Methods and Reports for Colleges and Universities*, edited by L. J. Lins, 101–105. Published as *The Journal of Experimental Education* 31, no. 2 (December 1962).

Dowd, A. C., and V. P. Tong. "Accountability, Assessment, and the Scholarship of 'Best Practice'." In *Higher Education: Handbook of Theory and Research XXII*, edited by John C. Smart, 57–119. 2007.

Dressel, Paul L. "Institutional Researchers: Created or Educated?" In *Professional Development for Institutional Research*, edited by Robert G. Cope, 43–48. New Directions for Institutional Research no. 23, 1979.

Dressel, Paul L., and Lewis B. Mayhew. *Higher Education as a Field of Study*. 1974.

Dressel, Paul L., ed. *Institutional Research in the University: A Handbook*. 1971.

Duryea, E.D. "Some Thoughts on the Service Role of Departments of Higher Education." In *Higher Education: A Developing Field of Study, Proceedings of the Annual Meeting of the Association of Professors of Higher Education (3rd, Chicago, Illinois, 1974)*, edited by Fred F. Harcleroad, 89–92. 1974.

Eckel, Peter D., and Adrianna Kezar. "Presidents Leading: The Dynamics and

Complexities of Campus Leadership." In *American Higher Education in the Twenty-First Century*, third edition, edited by Philip G. Altbach, Patricia J. Gumport, and Robert O. Berdahl, 279–314. 2011.

Eckert, Ruth E. "A Journey Toward Understanding." *The Journal of Higher Education* 50, no. 3 (May-June, 1979): 233–255.

Eckert, Ruth E. *Minnesota's Needs for Post-High School Education: Reports 1–7.* 1946.

Eckert, Ruth E., and Robert J. Keller, eds. *A University Looks at Its Program: The Report of the University of Minnesota Bureau of Institutional Research, 1942–1952.* 1954.

Eells, Walter C. *Surveys of American Higher Education.* 1937.

Eells, Walter Crosby. "Bigger and Better Surveys." *American Journal of Education* 41, no. 8 (October 1933): 628–631.

Fenstemacher, William P. "The Institutional Research Director: Professional Development and Career Path." Association for Institutional Research. *The AIR Professional File* no. 13 (summer 1982).

Fincher, Cameron L. "On the Predictable Crises of Institutional Research." *Research in Higher Education* 8, no. 1 (1978): 93–96.

Fincher, Cameron L. "The Art and Science of Institutional Research." In *Institutional Research in Transition*, edited by M. Corcoran and M. W. Peterson, 17–37. New Directions for Institutional Research no. 46, 1985.

Glenny, Lyman A. *Autonomy of Public Colleges: The Challenge of Coordination.* 1959.

Green, Christopher D. "The Flaw at the Heart of Psychological Research." *The Chronicle of Higher Education*, June 26, 2016. http://www.chronicle.com/article/The-Flaw-at-the-Heart-of/236916/.

Green, Christopher. "Psychology Strikes Out: Coleman R. Griffith and the Chicago Cubs." *History of Psychology* 6, no. 3 (2003): 267–283.

Griffith, Coleman R. "Functions of a Bureau of Institutional Research." *The Journal of Higher Education* 9, no. 5 (May 1938): 248–255.

Hacleroad, Fred F., ed. *Higher Education: A Developing Field of Study, Proceedings of the Annual Meeting of the Association of Professors of Higher Education (3rd, Chicago, Illinois, 1974).* 1974.

Hansen, Michele J., and Victor M. H. Borden. "An Action Research Paradigm for Institutional Research." Paper presented at the 2003 AIR Forum. Accessed June 29, 2017. http://irds.iupui.edu/Portals/SDAE/Files/Documents/AIR%20Action%20Research%205.2.03.pdf.

Harvard Office of Institutional Research. "Data, Data Science, and the Research University." Harvard University, presentation, September 7, 2016. Accessed June 21, 2017. https://projects.iq.harvard.edu/applied.stats.workshop-gov3009/presentations/972016-victoria-liublinski.

Hendrickson, Robert M. "The Core Knowledge of Higher Education." In *Advancing Higher Education as a Field of Study: In Quest of Doctoral Degree Guidelines, Commemorating 120 Years of Excellence*, edited by Sydney Freeman, Jr. et al., 229–240. 2014.

Henle, Robert J. *Systems for Measuring and Reporting the Resources and Activities of Colleges and Universities.* National Science Foundation. 1967.

Hicks, J. W., and F. L. Kidner. *California and Western Conference Cost and Statistical Study for the Year 1954–55.* 1955.

"Higher Education: Handbook of Theory and Research." The Association for the Study of Higher Education. Accessed April 25, 2017. http://www.ashe.ws/ashe_handbook_tr.

Holy, T. C., and H. H. Semans. *A Study of the Need for Additional Centers of Public Higher Education in California.* Liaison Committee of the Regents of the University of California and the California State Board of Education. 1957.

Holy, T. C., H. H. Semans, and T. R. McConnell. *A Restudy of the Needs of California in Higher Education.* Prepared for the Liaison Committee of the Regents of the University of California and the California State Board of Education. 1955.

Horn, Michael B. "Stepping aside to dig deeper: My next career move." Accessed March 23, 2017. http://www.christenseninstitute.org/blog/stepping-aside-to-dig-deeper-my-next-career-move/.

Hull, L. E. "Fact, Doubt, and Myth." In *Institutional Research and Academic Outcomes, Proceedings of the Association for Institutional Research Annual Forum (8th, San Francisco, California, 1968),* edited by Cameron Fincher, 1–6. 1968.

"Human Subject Regulations Decision Charts." U. S. Department of Health and Human Services. Accessed March 28, 2017. https://www.hhs.gov/ohrp/regulations-and-policy/decision-charts/index.html.

Hungate, Thad L. *Finance in Educational Management of Colleges and Universities.* 1954.

"IBM Forms New Watson Group to Meet Growing Demand for Cognitive Innovations." IBM. January 9, 2014. https://www-03.ibm.com/press/us/en/pressrelease/42867.wss.

ideas42. "ideas42 Tackles America's College Completion Crisis." *Market Wired,* June 22, 2016. http://www.marketwired.com/press-release/ideas42-tackles-americas-college-completion-crisis-2136676.htm.

ideas42. *Nudging for Success: Using Behavioral Science to Improve the Postsecondary Student Journey.* White paper, June 2016. http://www.ideas42.org/wp-content/uploads/2016/09/Nudging-For-Success-FINAL.pdf.

"Improving & Transforming Institutional Research in Postsecondary Education." Association for Institutional Research. Accessed June 29, 2015. http://www.airweb.org/Resources/ImprovingAndTransformingPostsecondary Education/Pages/default.aspx.

"Institutional Research." Wikipedia. Accessed March 24, 2017. https://en.wikipedia.org/wiki/Institutional_research.

"Integrated Postsecondary Education Data System (IPEDS)." Institute of Education Sciences. National Center for Education Statistics. Accessed March 29, 2017. https://nces.ed.gov/ipeds/Home/UseTheData.

Ito II, Rodney M., Brian Gratton, and Joseph Wycoff. "Using the 1940 and 1950 Public Use Microdata Samples: A Cautionary Tale." *Historical Methods* 30, no. 3 (1997): 137–47.

Jedamus, Paul, Marvin W. Peterson, and Associates, eds. *Improving Academic Management: A Handbook of Planning and Institutional Research.* 1980.

Johnson, Mark D. "Career Development in Institutional Research." Association for Institutional Research. *The AIR Professional File* no. 12 (spring 1982).

Jones, Darlena. *Impact of Business Intelligence on Institutional Research.* 2013.

June, Audrey Williams. "In Improving Outcomes, Institutional Researchers Can Be an Untapped Resource." *The Chronicle of Higher Education*, June 20, 2017. http://www.chronicle.com/article/In-Improving-Outcomes/240394.

Kant, Immanuel. "What Is Enlightenment?" In *The Portable Enlightenment Reader*, edited by Isaac Kramnick, 1–6. 1995.

Keller, George. "What Does the Future Hold for Institutional Research?" In *Institutional Research Coming of Age, General Session Presentations at Annual Forum of Association for Institutional Research (30, Louisville, Kentucky, 1990)*, edited by Jean Endo, 9–16. 1990.

Kerr, Clark. *Higher Education Cannot Escape History*. 1994.

Knight, William E. *Leadership and Management in Institutional Research*. 2014.

Knight, William E., Michael E. Moore, and Corby A. Coperthwaite. "Institutional Research: Knowledge, Skills, and Perceptions of Effectiveness." *Research in Higher Education* 38, no. 4 (August 1997): 419–433.

Kuhn, Thomas S. *The Structure of Scientific Revolutions*, second edition, enlarged. 1970.

Lasher, William F. "The History of Institutional Research and its Role in American Higher Education over the Past 50 Years (chapter 2)." In *Association for Institutional Research: The First Fifty Years*, edited Gary Rice (Project Coordinator), 10–15. The Association for Institutional Research. 2011. Available at https://www.airweb.org/AboutUs/History/Pages/Books-Papers-Manuscripts.aspx (requires membership).

Lawson, Jesse. *Data Science in Higher Education: A Step-by-Step Introduction to Machine Learning for Institutional Researchers*. 2015.

"Lewis Mayhew, outspoken critic of higher ed, dies at 75." Stanford University, news release first published on October 6, 1992. Accessed June 2, 2017. https://web.stanford.edu/dept/news/pr/92/921006Arc2092.html.

Liaison Committee of the Regents of the University of California and the State Board of Education. *A Study of Faculty Demand and Supply in California Higher Education, 1957–70*. 1958.

Lingenfelter, Paul E. "State Policy Leadership For Higher Education: A Brief Summary of the Origins and Continuing Evolution of a Profession." State Higher Education Executive Officers Association. August 2012. http://www.sheeo.org/sites/default/files/publications/State_Policy_Leadership_History.pdf.

Lingenfelter, Paul E., with James R. Mingle. "Public Policy for Higher Education in the United States: A Brief History of State Leadership." State Higher Education Executive Officers, 61st Annual Meeting, July 2014. http://www.sheeo.org/sites/default/files/publications/Public_Policy_Higher_Ed_Lingenfelter_Mingle_062014.pdf.

Lins, L. J., "Foreword." In *Basis for Decision: A Composite of Current Institutional Research Methods and Reports for Colleges and Universities*, edited by L. J. Lins, 88. Published as *The Journal of Experimental Education* 31, no. 2 (December 1962).

Lins, L. J., ed. *Basis for Decision: A Composite of Current Institutional Research Methods and Reports for Colleges and Universities*. Published as *The Journal of Experimental Education* 31, no. 2 (December 1962): 87–228.

Makel, Matthew C., and Jonathon A. Plucker. "Facts Are More Important Than Novelty: Replication in the Education Sciences." *Educational Researcher* XX no. X (2015): 1–13.

Marginson, Simon. *The Dream Is Over: The Crisis of Clark Kerr's California Idea of Higher Education.* 2016.

Mason, Thomas R. "Communication in Institutional Research: The Purpose of the Association." In *Institutional Research and Communication in Higher Education, Proceedings of the Association for Institutional Research Annual Forum on Institutional Research (10th, New Orleans, Louisiana, 1970),* edited by Patricia S. Wright, 7–8. 1970.

Massey, William F. *Reengineering the University: How to Be Mission Centered, Market Smart, and Margin Conscious.* 2016.

Matross, Ronald P. "The Virtual Office: An Organizational Paradigm for Institutional Research in the 90's. AIR 1993 Annual Forum Paper." 1993. Accessed April 27, 2017. http://eric.ed.gov/?id=ED360919.

Mattingly, Paul H. "Clark Kerr: The Unapologetic Pragmatist." *Social Science History* 36, no. 4 (winter 2012): 481–97.

Mayhew, Lewis B. "Imperatives for Institutional Research." In *Research on Academic Input, Proceedings of Association for Institutional Research Annual Forum (6th, Boston, Massachusetts, 1966),* edited by Clarence H. Bagley, 1–8. 1966.

McConnell, T. R. "A Reply to the Critics." *The Journal of Educational Sociology* 22, no. 8 (1949): 533–50.

McKinney, E. Bernadette, and John J. Hindera. "Science and Institutional Research: The Links." *Research in Higher Education* 33, no. 1 (February 1992): 19–29.

Middaugh, Michael F. "The Nature and Scope of Institutional Research." In *Organizing Effective Institutional Research Offices,* edited by Jennifer B. Presley, 36–43. New Directions for Institutional Research no. 66, 1990.

Minnesota Commission on Higher Education. *Higher Education in Minnesota.* (1950).

Montgomery, James R. "An Effective Role for Institutional Research." In *Institutional Research and Communication in Higher Education, Proceedings of the Association for Institutional Research Annual Forum on Institutional Research (10th, New Orleans, Louisiana, 1970),* edited by Patricia S. Wright, 140–42. 1970.

Montgomery, James R. "Institutional Research—A Future Unfolding." In *The Instructional Process and Institutional Research, Proceedings of the Association for Institutional Research Annual Forum (7th, Athens, Georgia, 1967),* edited by Galen N. Drewry, 1–10. 1967.

Moos, Malcolm, and Francis E. Rourke. *The Campus and the State.* 1959.

Morey, Lloyd. "Assembling and Weighting Data (Review of Finance)." *Journal of Higher Education* 7 no. 5 (May 1936): 283.

Nagel, Ernst. *The Structures of Science: Problems in the Logic of Scientific Explanation.* 1979.

National Association of System Heads (NASH). "Meeting Demand for Improvements in Public System Institutional Research: Progress Report on the NASH Project in IR." March 2014. http://nashonline.org/wp-content/uploads/2017/08/Progress-Report-on-NASH-IR-Project-March-2014.pdf.

National Association of System Heads (NASH). "Meeting Demand for Improvements in Public System Institutional Research: Assessing and Improving the Institutional Research [IR] Function in Public University Systems." February 2015. http://nashonline.org/wp-content/uploads/2017/08/Assessing-and-Improving-the-IR-Function-in-Public-University-Systems.pdf.

"PAR Framework: Overview." PAR Framework. Accessed March 23, 2017. http://www.parframework.org/about-par/overview/.

Peters, Ellen. "The Future Awaits." Association for Institutional Research. *e-AIR Newsletter*, June 2017. Accessed July 3, 2017. http://www.airweb.org/eAIR/Pages/eAIRNewsletterJune2017.aspx.

Plott, Richard Kent. "The Transition from Institutional Research to Data Science in Higher Education." LinkedIn, June 12, 2017. Accessed June 20, 2017. https://www.linkedin.com/pulse/transition-from-institutional-research-data-science-kent-plott.

Rees, Jennifer "What Every Leader Needs to Know about Student Success Analytics." Civitas Learning. October 23, 2015. Accessed May 27, 2017. https://www.civitaslearningspace.com/what-every-leader-needs-to-know-about-student-success-analytics/.

Reichard, Donald J. "The History of Institutional Research." In *The Handbook of Institutional Research*, edited by Richard D. Howard et al., 3–21. 2012.

Rice, Gary (Project Coordinator), ed. *Association for Institutional Research: The First Fifty Years*. The Association for Institutional Research. 2011.

Ridge, John William. "Organizing for Institutional Research." Association for Institutional Research. *The AIR Professional File* no. 1 (fall 1978).

Rourke, Francis E., and Glenn E. Brooks, "The 'Managerial Revolution' in Higher Education," *Administrative Science Quarterly* 9, no. 2 (September 1964): 154–181.

Rourke, Francis E., and Glenn E. Brooks. *The Managerial Revolution in Higher Education*. 1966.

Russell, John Dale, and Floyd W. Reeves. *Finance*. 1935.

Russell, John Dale. "Basic Conclusions and Recommendations of the President's Commission on Higher Education." *The Journal of Educational Sociology* 22, no. 8, Report of the President's Commission on Higher Education (April, 1949): 493–508.

Saupe, Joe L. "Assessing Program Quality." In *The Challenge and Response of Institutional Research, Proceedings of the Association for Institutional Research Annual Forum (9th, Chicago, Illinois, 1969)*, edited by Cameron Fincher, 1–12. 1969.

Saupe, Joe L. "Some General Remarks on the Nature, Scope and Function of Institutional Research." Michigan State University, mimeographed, August 1968.

Saupe, Joe L. *The Functions of Institutional Research*, first edition. Association for Institutional Research. 1981. https://www.airweb.org/AboutUs/History/Documents/Papers-Books-Manuscripts/Functions-of-IR-Saupe-1edition.pdf.

Saupe, Joe L. *The Functions of Institutional Research*, second edition. Association for Institutional Research. 1990. https://www.airweb.org/educationandevents/publications/pages/functionsofir.aspx.

Saupe, Joe L., and James R. Montgomery. "The Nature and Role of Institutional Research...Memo to a College or University." Association for Institutional Research. 1970. Accessed March 23, 2017.

http://files.eric.ed.gov/fulltext/ED049672.pdf.

Schlitz, Michael E., ed. *Ethics and Standards in Institutional Research.* New Directions for Institutional Research no. 73, 1992.

Schmidtlein, Frank A., and Robert O Berdahl. "Autonomy and Accountability: Who Controls Academe?" In *American Higher Education in the Twenty-First Century: Social, Political, and Economic Challenges,* third edition, edited by Philip G. Altbach, Patricia J. Gumport, and Robert O. Berdahl, 69–87. 2011.

Schrum, Ethan. "To 'Administer the Present': Clark Kerr and the Purpose of the Postwar American Research University." *Social Science History* 36, no. 4 (winter 2012): 499–523.

Shavelson, R. J., and L. Towne, eds. *Scientific Research in Education.* Committee on Scientific Principles for Education Research. Center for Education. Division of Behavioral and Social Sciences and Education. National Research Council. 2002. Electronic version of the text available at http://www.nap.edu/catalog/10236/scientific-research-in-education.

Smart, J. C., ed. *Higher Education: Handbook of Theory and Research XXI.* 2006.

"Solution: Student Success Model." Blackboard. Accessed March 23, 2017. http://www.blackboard.com/sites/deved/solutions/student-success-model.asp.

Stecklein, John E. "The Birth of a Profession: President's Address." In *Research on Academic Input, Proceedings of Association for Institutional Research Annual Forum (6th, Boston, Massachusetts, 1966),* edited by Clarence H. Bagley, 9–13. 1966.

Stickler, W. Hugh. *Institutional Research Concerning Land-Grant Institutions and State Universities, A Report Prepared for the Joint Office of Institutional Research of the American Association of Land-Grant Colleges and State Universities and the State Universities Association.* 1959.

Stout, Edward M., and Irma Halfter. "Institutional Research and Automation." In *Basis for Decision: A Composite of Current Institutional Research Methods and Reports for Colleges and Universities,* edited by L. J. Lins, 95–98. Published as *The Journal of Experimental Education* 31, no. 2 (December 1962).

Straumsheim, Carl. "'Augmented Intelligence' for Higher Ed." *Inside Higher Ed,* November 16, 2016. https://www.insidehighered.com/news/2016/11/16/blackboard-pearson-join-ibms-ecosystem-bring-watson-technology-higher-ed.

Straumsheim, Carl. "Preparing for 'Era of Data Ubiquity.'" *Inside Higher Ed,* June 28, 2016. https://www.insidehighered.com/news/2016/06/28/researchers-outline-guidelines-ethical-use-student-data.

Strayer, George D., and Edward L. Thorndike. *Educational Administration: Quantitative Studies.* 1913.

"Student Success." Ellucian. Accessed March 23, 2017. http://www.ellucian.com/Student-Success/.

Swing, Randy L. "Institutional Research Capacity: Foundations of Federal Data Quality." Association for Institutional Research. 2016. Accessed May 2, 2017. https://www.airweb.org/Resources/IRStudies/Documents/institutional_research_capacity.pdf.

Swing, Randy L., and Leah Ewing Ross. "A New Vision for Institutional Research." *Change: The Magazine of Higher Learning* 48 no. 2 (2016): 6–13.

http://dx.doi.org/10.1080/00091383.2016.1163132.

Swing, Randy L., D. Jones, and L. E. Ross. "The AIR National Survey of Institutional Research Offices." Association for Institutional Research. 2016. Accessed June 20, 2017. http://www.airweb.org/nationalsurvey.

Taylor, Alton L. "Options for Location in the Organizational Structure." In *Organizing Effective Institutional Research Offices*, edited by Jennifer B. Presley, 27–34. New Directions for Institutional Research no. 66, 1990.

Terenzini, Patrick T. "From the Series Editor." In *Preparing for the Information Needs of the Twenty-First Century*, edited by Timothy R. Sanford, 91. New Directions for Institutional Research no. 85, 1995.

Terenzini, Patrick T. "'On the Nature of Institutional Research' Revisited: Plus Ça Change…?" *Research in Higher Education* 54, no. 2 (March 2013): 137–148.

Terenzini, Patrick T. "On the Nature of Institutional Research and the Knowledge and Skills It Requires." *Research in Higher Education* 34, no. 1 (February 1993): 1–10.

Terkla, Dawn Geronimo, ed. *Institutional Research: More Than Just Data*. New Directions for Higher Education no. 141, spring 2008.

Testerman, Jack, et al. "Institutional Research: A Review of Literature to 1972." 1972. Accessed April 14, 2017. http://files.eric.ed.gov/fulltext/ED077476.pdf.

Tetlow, W. L. "Institutional Research: The Emergence of a Staff Function in Higher Education." Cornell University, unpublished doctoral dissertation. 1973.

The College Board. "SAT® Percentile Ranks for Males, Females, and Total Group." Accessed May 2, 2017. https://secure-media.collegeboard.org/digitalServices/pdf/sat/sat-percentile-ranks-composite-crit-reading-math-2014.pdf.

The Organisation for Economic Co-operation and Development (OECD). *Proposed Standard Practice for Surveys on Research and Experimental Development*. 2002.

Thelin, John R., ed. *Essential Documents in the History of American Higher Education*. 2014.

Thompson, Loring M. "Institutional Research, Planning, and Politics." In *Basis for Decision: A Composite of Current Institutional Research Methods and Reports for Colleges and Universities*, edited by L. J. Lins, 89–91. Published as *The Journal of Experimental Education* 31, no. 2 (December 1962).

Trachtenberg, Stephen Joel, Gerald B. Kauvar, and E. Grady Bogue. *Presidencies Derailed: Why University Leaders Fail and How to Prevent It*. 2013.

Tyrrell, Philip H. "Programming the Unknown: Guidelines for the Conduct of Institutional Research." In *Basis for Decision: A Composite of Current Institutional Research Methods and Reports for Colleges and Universities*, edited by L. J. Lins, 92–94. Published as *The Journal of Experimental Education* 31, no. 2 (December 1962).

US Department of Health and Human Services. *The Belmont Report*. 1979. Accessed March 28, 2017. https://www.hhs.gov/ohrp/regulations-and-policy/belmont-report/index.html.

Van Vught, Frans. "A Fundamental Challenge for the Institutional Research Profession." In *Institutional Research Coming of Age, General Session Presentations at Annual Forum of Association for Institutional Research (30, Louisville, Kentucky, 1990)*, edited by Jean Endo, 23–32. 1990.

Vincent-Lancrin, Stéphan. "What Is Changing in Academic Research? Trends and

Future Scenarios." The Organisation for Economic Co-operation and Development (OECD). Accessed June 23, 2017. http://www.oecd.org/edu/ceri/37481256.pdf.

Volkswein, J. Frederick, Ying (Jessie) Liu, and James Woodell. "The Structure and Functions of Institutional Research Offices." In *The Handbook of Institutional Research*, edited by Richard D. Howard et al., 22–39. 2012.

Volkswein, J. Frederick. "The Diversity of Institutional Research Structures and Tasks." In *Organizing Effective Institutional Research Offices*, edited by Jennifer B. Presley, 7–26. New Directions for Institutional Research no. 66, 1990.

Volkswein, J. Frederick. "The Foundations and Evolution of Institutional Research." In *Institutional Research: More Than Just Data*, edited by Dawn Geronimo Terkla, 5–20. New Directions for Higher Education no. 141, 2008.

Volkswein, J. Fredericks. "Gaining Ground: The Role of Institutional Research in Assessing Student Outcomes and Demonstrating Institutional Effectiveness." National Institute of Learning Outcomes Assessment. *Occasional Paper* no. 11 (September 2011).

Zook, George F. *Higher Education for American Democracy: A Report*. President's Commission on Higher Education (Truman Commission). 1947.

INDEX

accountability, institutional, 5, 11, 48, 52, 105, 116, 140

American Association of Land-Grant Colleges and State Universities and the State Universities Association, 65, 67, 195, 213

American Council on Education, 6–7, 10, 12, 30, 35, 47, 61, 68–74, 78, 96, 100

Association for Institutional Research, 5, 6, 9, 11, 13, 17, 21, 26, 29, 30, 61, 75, 84, 97, 99–106, 108, 110, 112, 116–124, 126, 128–129, 135, 138–139, 141, 143, 145, 147, 150–156, 162—171, 176–183

Association for the Study of Higher Education, 109, 143–144, 177

Borden, Victor M. H., 147–148, 154, 165

Brooks, Glenn E., 4–6, 12–13, 100–103, 106, 109, 112–113, 116, 120, 125, 133, 139, 141, 147, 151, 164, 166, 168, 174

Brumbaugh, A. J., 68–74, 77, 80, 92, 100, 157, 175

California and Western Conference Cost and Statistical Study, 62, 195, 208

common sense, 15, 17–18, 27, 29, 130, 163, 165, 169, 173

data science, 1–3, 10–11, 13, 94–95, 172, 176, 178–180, 182–184

democracy, 46–47, 54, 59, 74

Doi, James I., 34, 43–46, 48, 61, 97–100, 102, 114

Dressel, Paul L., 5–6, 106, 108–114, 118, 120, 123–124, 127–129, 131, 137, 142–143, 145–147, 149, 163–164, 169, 174, 175

Eckert, Ruth E., 35–36, 39, 65–66, 77–78, 90, 92, 139

education technology, 1–3, 10

Eells, Walter Crosby, 31

Fincher, Cameron, 116–118, 124–125, 129–130, 147, 163, 169, 173–175, 179

Keller, George, 118–120, 131, 139, 141, 165, 169

Griffith, Coleman R., 31–36, 39, 42, 77, 84, 89, 92, 102, 128, 132, 161

Halfter, Irma, 80, 84–87, 89, 92, 95

Henle, R. J., 86–88, 95, 116

Hindera, John J., 121–124, 134, 165, 174

Human Subjects Research, 19–21, 191, 205

Hungate, Thad L., 50, 194, 209

Hunter, G. Truman, 84, 85, 89
IBM (International Business Machines Corporation), 2, 84–85, 184
institutional research, and centralization, 30, 40, 45, 61, 66, 68, 93, 99, 101, 106, 118, 127, 139, 146, 154, 165, 169, 180; and decentralization, 6, 9, 99, 126–127, 138–141, 145, 150–151, 153–157, 160–164, 166–167, 169, 174; as an art, 6, 80, 84, 90, 116–124, 129, 134, 141, 146, 163, 173, 179, 180; as applied research, 22, 23, 26, 79–82, 90, 107, 109, 113, 119–124, 127–128, 132–136, 141, 148, 152, 163, 165, 169, 176; as craft, 122–123, 125, 127, 163, 179; as function, 4, 6, 11, 13, 17, 21, 30–31, 33, 44, 51, 56, 70–73, 75, 79, 98–99, 102, 105–107, 112–113, 120–126, 128, 134–135, 137, 141–146, 149–155, 157, 161–170, 174, 177, 182; golden triangle of, 89–90, 95, 156, 161, 196; offices, 4–6, 9–13, 16, 22–24, 28–42, 44–46, 56, 58, 61, 66–69, 72, 74–82, 89–94, 96, 98–99, 101–105, 108–109, 125–127, 129, 135–139, 141, 144–145, 150–156, 161–162, 164–170, 172, 176, 178–179; reporting, 16; statewide, 5, 36, 40, 45–50, 52, 55–56, 58–62, 65–68, 73, 77, 92, 171
Kant, Immanuel, 18, 21, 191, 210
Keller, Robert J., 35–36, 39, 65–66, 77
Kerr, Clark, 5, 54–55, 59–60, 183
Knight, William E., 9, 178

Kuhn, Thomas, 79, 83, 88, 122, 146–149, 152, 180
Lins, L. J., 37–40, 78, 80–81, 91–93, 100, 128
Mason, Thomas R., 103–105
Massey, William F., 4
Master Plan for Higher Education in California, 1960–1975, 5, 12, 46, 52, 54–60, 68
Matross, Ronald P., 139–141, 165, 169, 174
Mayhew, Lewis B., 109–113, 142–143, 174
McConnell, Thomas R., 46, 49
McKinney, E. Bernadette, 121–124, 134, 165, 174
Montgomery, James B., 5, 105–108, 110, 112, 120, 143, 174
Nagel, Ernest, 15, 17, 24, 41, 130, 165, 173
National Association of System Heads, 4, 6, 9, 96, 137–138, 143, 147, 150–153, 155, 162–167, 169, 176, 180
National Center for Educational Statistics, 20, 22
National Institutional Research Forum, 43, 81, 84, 97, 143
National Research Council, 11, 16, 22–29, 38, 41, 44, 59, 74, 80, 83, 87, 90–91, 95, 131, 134, 146, 147, 177
National Science Foundation, 19–20, 83, 86
New Directions for Higher Education, 15
New Directions for Institutional Research, 114, 117, 124, 138
New England Board of Higher Education, 61
North Central Association, 30, 35, 77, 84, 90

Organisation for Economic Co-operation and Development, 22, 23, 147–148
outsourcing, 1, 3, 7
policy making, 13, 33–34, 36, 45–46, 52, 60, 67, 70, 74, 77, 89, 91, 104–106, 108, 110, 129, 141
Reeves, Floyd W., 49, 78, 84
Reichard, Donald J., 30, 100, 108
Research in Higher Education, 6, 97, 122, 128, 129, 145
Restudy, California (1955), 46, 48–53, 55, 58–60, 62, 68
Rourke, Francis E., 4–6, 12–13, 100–103, 106, 109, 112–113, 116, 120, 125, 133, 139, 141, 147, 151, 164, 166, 168, 174
Russell, John Dale, 45–46, 48–49, 84, 106
Saupe, Joe L., 5–6, 102, 104–108, 110, 112–114, 118, 120–121, 123–124, 127, 129, 137, 141–143, 147, 164–165, 168–169, 174
self-study, 11, 21, 26, 28–30, 34–36, 38–40, 43–46, 59, 62, 66, 68, 71, 76, 81–84, 106, 113, 183
social science, 10–12, 15–18, 20–22, 24–27, 29, 34, 40, 42–45, 59, 68, 78, 80, 83, 87–88, 95, 118–119, 130, 150, 173, 178–179, 185; six guiding principles, 24, 38, 47, 134; types of questions, 41, 161
Southern Regional Education Board, 61, 69
State Higher Education Executive Officers Association, 48
Stickler, W. Hugh, 65–68, 72, 94, 113

Stout, Edward M., 80, 84–86, 89, 92, 95
Strayer, George D., 48–51
student success, 1–4, 6–8, 10–14, 25–26, 94–95, 137, 144, 152, 154, 159, 170–173, 176, 178–185
Survey Era, 30, 45, 49, 76, 78, 83
Swing, Randy, 163–169, 174–175, 179
Taylor, Alton L., 138–139, 199–200, 214
Terenzini, Patrick T., 124, 126, 128–135, 138, 145, 147, 169
Thompson, Loring M., 38, 42
Truman Commission, 11, 46–49, 51, 54, 59, 74, 75, 82, 181
Tyrrell, Philip, 75, 81–83, 86–88, 93, 95, 98–99, 132, 175, 177, 184
U.S. Department of Health and Human Services, 20
University of California, 37, 48, 51–58, 60, 62, 105
University of Georgia, 116, 147, 163
University of Illinois, 29, 31–35, 39, 69, 89, 91
University of Minnesota, 34–37, 39, 42, 46, 49, 65–66, 69, 77, 81, 89, 91–93, 103, 128, 139–141, 174
Van Vught, Frans, 117–124, 128, 135, 137
Volkswein, J. Frederick, 89–91, 124–127, 129, 134, 138–139, 141, 145, 147, 150–151, 164, 169
Webber, Karen L., 147–148, 165
Wedekind, Carl E., 102–103
Western Interstate Commission for Higher Education, 61, 104
Zook, George F., 47, 49, 74

ABOUT THE AUTHOR

Joseph H. Wycoff, PhD, is a higher education researcher and consultant who has worked in academic, market, and institutional research during the past twenty-five years. He holds a doctorate in US history with an emphasis on business and consumer history from the University of Washington. His professional and institutional research experience includes posts in three sectors of higher education: a community college in Illinois, a private nonprofit institution in New York, and the University of Washington in Seattle. He currently is an institutional effectiveness consultant and an independent scholar in Chicago, Illinois.

Made in the USA
Middletown, DE
27 June 2021